MEXICO

BY

RAIL

Gary A. Poole

HUNTER
PUBLISHING INC.

Hunter Publishing, Inc.
300 Raritan Center Parkway
Edison NJ 08818
(908) 225 1900

ISBN 1-55650-605-8

Available in the UK from:
Bradt Publications
41 Nortoft Road
Chalfont St. Peter, Bucks. SL9 0LA

Photo Credits:
Pages 95, 99, 100, 116, 160, 291, 297 by Dottie Kern.
All others by the author.
Cover photo:
Monastery, Cholula, Mexico (Karl Kummels/SuperStock)

Acknowledgments

No author is an island. A number of individuals deserve credit
for their roles in the successful completion of this book, though
whatever shortcomings may exist in the text are my responsi-
bility alone. At the top of the list, I would like to thank Dottie
Kern for accompanying me on numerous trips to Mexico and for
introducing me to that wonderful country and its people. Many
thanks also to Jeff Poole and Craig Miller for their timely and
indispensable computer help. Finally, I would like to thank my
wife and partner, Ginger Bloomer, for her support and patience
during this period.

Contents

Introduction

Mexico: Why Go?

Mention Mexico to any North American and they will almost certainly conjure up strong though likely very different mental images: bandits blowing up trains, white sand beaches lapped by turquoise seas, ancient cities half hidden by jungle, colorful fiestas blending Christian and non-Christian beliefs, modern cities ringed by slums, seemingly endless deserts broken only by distant blue mountains, Indian villages clustered along the shores of green lakes. All these images and more are part of modern Mexico—except for the "bandidos." But fans of John Huston and Sergio Leone will be pleased to know that black-clad anti-narcotics squads have taken their place.

Among all the countries in the world Mexico enjoys a special mystique, especially for Americans: so close and yet so different, so exotic. The settlers and pioneers of the United States largely exterminated and then marginalized the Native American people living here. But Mexico, both as a colony and as a country, tried, however imperfectly, to incorporate these people into its society.

The result is a culture that precedes the date of European arrival and conquest. It is an ancient land whose tropical colors and magic lure us. Mexico provides an adventure for the spirit as well as for the body. In Mexico reality is surreal, as though what we see is only the tip of the iceberg and a whole other world waits in the wrinkles on an old woman's face or the iridescent patterns of a butterfly's wing. All things are possible in a magic world.

On a more concrete level the history of the United States and that of Mexico are inextricably linked. Almost half of U.S. territory was originally part of Mexico and acquired by means of imperialist wars under the rubric of "Manifest Destiny." Even today a large plurality of citizens in the southwest U.S.

are of Mexican origin, many of them only one or two generations removed.

Mexico is also easily accessible. Getting to the U.S.-Mexico border is a piece of cake and once you cross that line you discover that Mexico has the finest transportation system in Latin America. Trains, highways, buses, and airplanes all work interchangeably to move you wherever you want to go.

Another plus for Mexico is that the national language, Spanish, is one of the easiest languages to learn, having wonderfully regular pronunciations. There aren't any words like "though" or "tough." And with a couple of weeks of serious effort, anyone can have a traveler's working knowledge of Spanish.

This Book

This book is intended to be a do-it-yourself manual for the Mexican train traveler. With it in hand you should be able to negotiate Mexico by relying almost exclusively on rail transport. The information allows you to plug into Mexico's rail network at any point and proceed from there.

Near the beginning of each chapter I have included a description of services offered on the particular route as well as a timetable and fare information. All fares are expressed in US dollars. It goes without saying that these times and fares are subject to change.

The book is organized by region: each chapter in the travel section is devoted to a particular part of Mexico and the train routes that service it. Brief geographical and historical information on each route are also provided. Then, within each route section, there is more detailed information on each major stop along that route: history, attractions, fiestas, regional foods, excursions, and other tidbits.

There is no list of recommended hotels and restaurants. There is a list of mid-range and low-budget hotels in the appendix but these are not specifically recommended. The list is mainly for those who find themselves in desperate straits: they need a place immediately and it's too late to shop around.

Get hold of a Spanish language cassette course for tourists and spend a week or two listening to it. Hugo's *Spanish at the Wheel* or *Latin-American Spanish in Three Months* (both available from Hunter Publishing) are good possibilities. Then pick up a Spanish phrasebook (the Latin-American version) for your trip.

•

It was dark and cold on the Mexican central plateau as our train rocked along through a winter night. Wrapped in a sleeping bag, I was warm, comfortable, and reluctant to expose myself to the chill night air. Necessity, however, eventually forced me to leave my refuge. I made my way slowly down the aisle, past sleeping passengers almost indistinguishable beneath piles of blankets. I walked carefully and balanced myself against the rolling and unpredictable motion of the train by grabbing seat backs for support. A blast of colder air hit me in the face as I opened the door to the landing between the cars. In the dim light I could see piles of human beings, huddled together for warmth and covered by not enough blankets. These were, truly, the cheap seats.

I stepped over a body and opened the door to the toilet. I thought about my flashlight buried somewhere in my backpack as I studied the pitch black space. I could make out no details and could feel no light switch on the wall. Turning to a man on the floor who seemed to be studying me, I whispered, "Excuse me, but do you know if there is a light in the toilet?" In a patient voice he said, "My friend, this is Mexico, not France."

Chapter 1

Train System Basics

Train Services

Officially, there are only two classes of train travel in Mexico: first class (*primera especial*) and second class (*segunda clase*). Previously, there existed a much wider range of services. As of mid-1992, however, the classes available were consolidated into only two.

Second class provides unreserved seating in cars without air conditioning. Most of these coaches are of fairly good quality having been "retired" from regular first class service over the last several years. Many have reclining seats. Occasionally, however, you get assigned to a car that belongs in a transportation museum rather than on a passenger train. In this situation I usually pass the time fantasizing about what caused the damage: "How did that seat get so ripped-up, what knocked that hole in the floor, where is the other half of that window?"

Not too long ago second class travel was noted for overcrowding, short courses in animal husbandry, and toilets from hell. With the exception of the toilets, second class is considerably improved. No longer are tickets sold beyond the seating capacity of the car. Everyone gets a seat even though, since seating is unreserved, you may not get to sit where you want. Second class travel is also much cheaper than first class. Tickets are generally one-quarter to one-third the price of first class.

The ultimate in comfort is special first class, *primera especial*. Although considerably more expensive than second class, this service provides the traveler with air conditioned cars (usually), reclining seats, nice lavatories with running water, and drinking water (again, usually). Boxed meals—breakfast, lunch, and dinner—are also included in the price of a ticket and while the

Passenger Rail

San Diego
Tijuana
Calexico
Mexicali
Tucson
Puerto Penasco
Nogales
Nogales
El Paso
Juarez
UNITE
Caborca
Benjamin Hill
Hermosillo
Cuauhtemoc
Chihuahua
Piedra
Empalme
Cd. Obregon
Creel
Delicias
Navojoa
Bahuichivo
Jimenez
Los Mochis
Sufragio
Culiacan
Torreon
BAJA CALIFORNIA
MEXICO
Mazatlan
Felip Pesca
Zacatecas
Aguascalientes
Tepic
Lagos de Moreno
Guana
Guadalajara
Cd. Guzman
Uruapan
Manzanillo
Colima
PACIFIC OCEAN
Lazaro Cardenas

System of Mexico

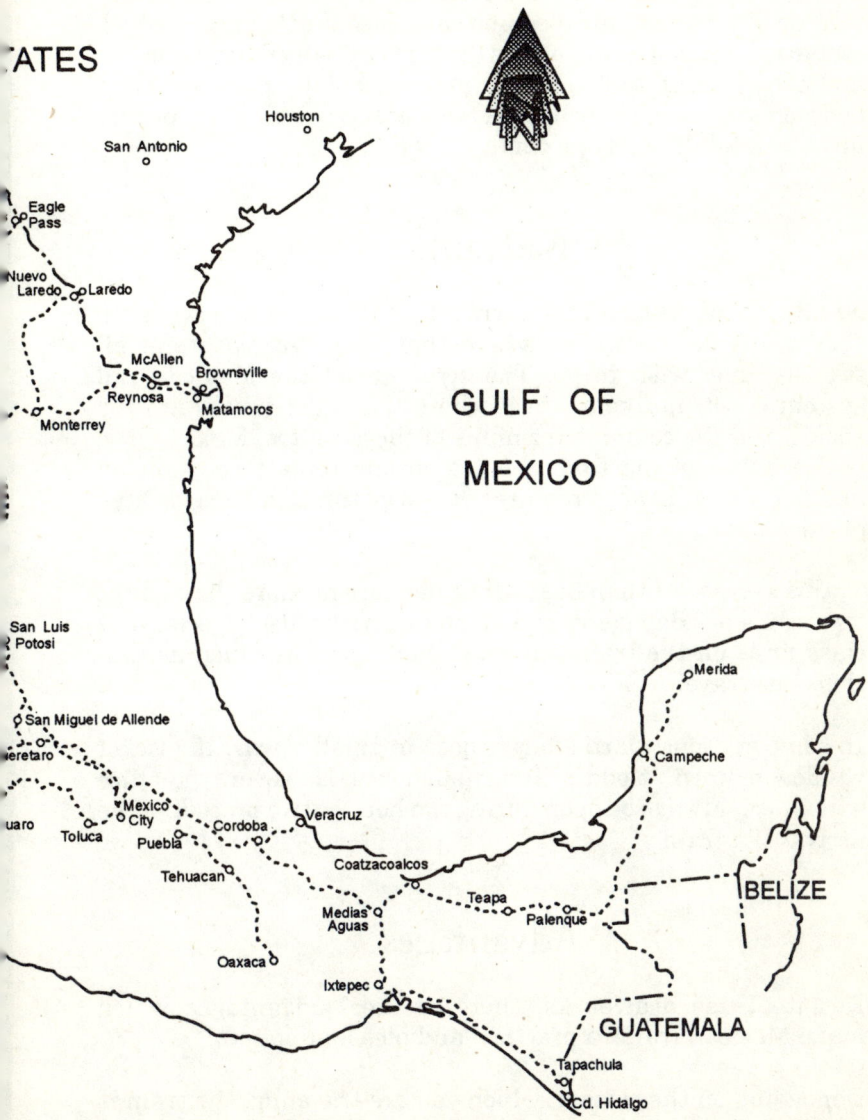

ATES

Houston

San Antonio

Eagle
Pass

Nuevo
Laredo Laredo

McAllen

Reynosa Brownsville

Monterrey Matamoros

GULF OF

MEXICO

San Luis
Potosi

Merida

San Miguel de Allende

Campeche

ueretaro

uaro Mexico
City Cordoba Veracruz

Toluca Puebla

Tehuacan Coatzacoalcos

Teapa

BELIZE

Medias
Aguas Palenque

Oaxaca

Ixtepec

GUATEMALA

Tapachula

Cd. Hidalgo

quality of these meals is quite variable they seem, at least, to be safe. My favorite is the fried turkey breast with macaroni salad that seems to pop up with regularity on the train to Zacatecas. Trains with special first class accommodations also sometimes include dining, bar, and sleeping cars. Sleeping facilities, which cost extra, consist of roomettes (*camarines*) which have one bed and can sleep up to two adults and one child (under five) and bedrooms (*alcobas*) which have two beds and can accommodate up to four adults and one child.

Disadvantages

Nothing is perfect and train travel in Mexico is no exception. The trains don't go everywhere that the off-the-beaten-trail traveler may wish to go. The structure of the Mexican rail system is set up like a wheel where the major routes are the spokes and the common terminus of these routes, Mexico City, is the hub. Getting from a point on one route to a point on another almost always requires you to go through Mexico City— or take a bus.

Trains are slower than buses and there are no more than one or two trains per day going in a given direction. Also, special first class fares on the train are about half again as much as first class bus travel.

In some stations, particularly those in small towns, the ticket window is open at odd or irregular hours. However, the office will almost always be open during the hour or two preceding the arrival of a train.

Advantages

Despite these drawbacks, there are real advantages which make Mexican trains a practical and pleasant option.

Depending on the class in which you are traveling, the train is more comfortable than the bus. You can move about, stretch your legs, and look at the scenery on both sides of the track through large windows. Buses, on the other hand, are often so crowded that walking in the aisles is impossible. The result is a feeling of cramped space and limited vistas.

This ability to move around in the train facilitates not only comfort but also the bicultural mixing which for many travelers is the chief incentive to travel. Oftentimes on the bus you are too crowded to get to know anyone except the person leaning over you, or over whom you are leaning.

Riding the rails also eliminates the fear, hassle, and potential disaster of driving your own car through Mexico. A car with foreign plates is an easy and usually lucrative target for vandals, thieves, and underpaid police forces. Some city police are notorious for stopping foreign motorists on the pretext of a traffic violation and extorting money. A friend was stopped six times and paid six bribes in a single day as he tried to negotiate Mexico City. Leave the car home and you also leave behind the hassles of driving in Mexican cities, trying to park on crowded colonial streets, and looking for hotels with parking facilities. You also leave behind the fear of accidents, theft, and vandalism. When you need a car for local transportation you will find that taxis are cheap and rental cars are available.

The Mexican rail network does provide access to virtually all regions of Mexico and, when used in conjunction with local bus service, this composite system is flexible enough to satisfy almost any traveler's needs. In most Mexican towns the train station is convenient to downtown, while new bus stations are increasingly being constructed in the remote, underpopulated, and generally uninteresting suburbs—an important consideration for the traveler afoot.

Regulations

• Children under 5 who do not occupy a separate seat are free when traveling with a ticketed adult. Children between 5 and 12 years of age are charged half the adult fare when traveling with a ticketed adult.

• Up to 110 pounds of baggage for each full fare ticket and 55 pounds for each half fare ticket can be checked on the baggage car free of charge. This is only advisable if you are traveling throughout Mexico on a serious shopping expedition or perhaps have brought along your mountain bike and folding kayak for another kind of expedition. If you're traveling with only one or two bags, you can store them on the luggage rack above your seat where your belongings will be more secure and accessible.

• Up to 2 adults and 1 child under 5 years old are allowed to stay in one roomette or up to 4 adults and 1 child are allowed in one bedroom.

• A bedroom compartment requires the purchase of a minimum of 2 adult first class tickets, while a roomette requires a minimum of 1.

Making Reservations

Reservations are usually not necessary if your timetables are flexible and you are not traveling at a particularly busy time of the year. However, if you are certain about your schedule or face some time constraint then you should reserve your tickets. Requests for reservations should be made in advance in writing and should include the exact dates of travel, the type of accommodations desired, the number of passengers, and the ages of any children. Requests should be addressed to one of the following agents, depending on where you plan to begin your trip.

• For trips from Mexico City to any point in the country or for trips to Mexico City from Monterrey, Veracruz, Chihuahua, Uruapan, or Guadalajara: Mrs. Juana Nava Pérez, Chief Commercial Passenger Department, National Railways of Mexico, Buenavista Grand Central Station, 06358 Mexico, D.F., Tel. 547-86-55.

• From Matamoros to Reynosa, Monterrey, and Mexico City: Mr. Juan Alberto Peña García, Ticket Agent, Calle Hidalgo entre 9 y 10 s/n, Col. Centro, Matamoros, Tamps. Mexico, Tel. 667-06.

• From Piedras Negras to Saltillo and Mexico City: Mr. Jesús Carreon Hernández, Cashier and Ticket Agent, Calle Zaragoza y Boulevard, Piedras Negras, Coah. Mexico, Tel. 200-87.

• From Ciudad Juárez to any point: Mr. Abelardo Barraza Silva, Commercial Agent, National Railways of Mexico, Ciudad Juárez, Chih. Mexico, Tel. 225-57, or P.O. Box 2200, El Paso Texas 79951.

• From Nogales to Sufragio, Culiacán, Mazatlán, Tepic, Guadalajara, and Mexico City: Mr. Luis Mejía Wagner, Commercial Agent, Calle Internacional No. 10, Nogales, Son. Mexico, Tel. 200-24.

• From Guadalajara to Mexico City, Tepic, Mazatlán, Culiacán, Sufragio, Nogales, and Mexicali: Mr. Donato Pacheco Vega, Person in Charge of Regional Passenger Department, Calle Enrique Díaz de León 336, Sector Juárez, Guadalajara, Jal., Mexico, Tel. 12-43-96.

• From Mexicali to Sufragio, Culiacán, Mazatlán, Tepic, Guadalajara, and Mexico City: Miss Evangelina Delgadillo Jauregui, Person in Charge Assignation Booth, P.O. Box 231, Calexico, CA, Tel. 57-23-86.

• From Chihuahua to Los Mochis and back (Copper Canyon): Mr. Oscar Luevano Ceniceros, Chief, Regional Passenger Department, P.O. Box 46, Chihuahua, Chih. Mexico, Tel. 15-77-56.

As regards payment, the agent you contact will send you a confirmation of your reservation stating the amount owed and a time limit within which this amount must be paid. Payment must be made by either a cashier's or certified check in Mexican currency and made payable to Ferrocarriles Nacionales de Mexico. If payment is not made within the time limit, the reservations will be cancelled.

Travel Tips and Warnings

It should come as no surprise that traveling in Mexico, however you do it, is considerably different from traveling in any of the industrialized countries of North America or Europe. Aside from language and climate, the most important differences derive from the fact that Mexico is a poor country with a non-European culture. In 1990 Mexico's per capita gross national product was US $2,220, while that of the United States was $22,088, a tenfold difference. Though not the poorest of the poor, Mexico still does not have the resources to spend on public transportation that some nations have. You should not expect Mexican trains to be as comfortable, timely, or fast as their European counterparts. Still they are often about as comfortable as Amtrak in the United States.

At least as important as financial resources in determining the character of Mexican train travel is Mexican culture. This culture is a mix of Indian, Spanish, and modern western values. As regards train travel in particular, Mexico offers the visitor an amalgam of the Indian's casual timelessness, the colonial Spaniard's love of bureaucracy, and a modern affection for published timetables. The result is a fascinating and often perplexing system that moves you around the country almost in spite of itself.

Here are a few tips which may smooth out, or at least prepare you for, potential rough spots on your Mexican train trip.

• On overnight trips during the winter or at high elevations always carry a blanket, sleeping bag, or something else for warmth. Similarly, when traveling through the *tierra caliente*, carry something with which to fan yourself. This applies to travelers in special first class as well as those in second class. I've been on trains where the air conditioning ran all night, forcing me into my sleeping bag, and then promptly broke-down the next morning as the Mexican sun began to make the cacti sweat.

• Take along your own toilet tissue and carry it in a convenient place. Trains will often start out with toilet tissue but it will be gone within the hour. It'll be no mystery as to where it's gone for you will probably find it scattered all over the floor. Rather than throw yours on the floor, put it in the trash basket—not in the toilet.

• No areas are reserved for non-smokers on Mexican trains. Nevertheless, cigarette smoke is rarely a problem unless you happen to be sitting near affluent teenagers traveling alone. On a related note, Mexicans do not have the same sense of personal space as North Americans and Northern Europeans. If a certain critical mass of children is present, the youngsters may use the aisles to play tag, with your backpack as cover in a game of hide-and-seek. I once sat in the midst of a group of girl scouts and I enjoyed listening to their songs until about 10 p.m., at which time I covered my head with a blanket and stuffed an amazing amount of material into my ears. My fitful sleep was troubled by nightmares containing the musical refrain, "*gracias por el pan.*"

• Carry some of your money in small bills and change so that you will be able to buy snacks and food from vendors along the route.

• If you are getting on the train in a border town, you must go through Mexican immigration and obtain a tourist card before boarding the train.

• If you have little flexibility in your plans, it is wise to make reservations before arriving in Mexico. If your itinerary and timetable are flexible you can make your reservations after arriving in Mexico. You may have to spend a day or two exploring Mexico City while you make arrangements, but you will probably not have to wait too many days and it will be time well spent. The only times of the year when this casual approach is a bad idea are the months of July and August and the period of mid-December to mid-January.

• If you are trapped in Mexico City and unable to buy tickets, take a bus to the nearest town which is on the route of interest and buy tickets there for the remainder of the journey. Each town along the route has a certain number of tickets reserved for it to sell and tickets can usually be purchased on short notice more easily than in Mexico City. However, these intermediate stops often have no sleeping car space to sell.

• Be patient and try to avoid really tight schedules. Occasionally there will be unexpected stops and inexplicable delays. Go with the flow. Take a plane when time is of the essence. Take a train when you want to see Mexico. ¡*Buen Viaje*!

Nuts & Bolts For The Visitor

Immigration

If you plan to go any distance beyond the Mexican border, you must carry appropriate documentation of your citizenship and obtain the appropriate paperwork from the Mexican authorities. Citizens of the United States and Canada should obtain and fill out a tourist card. This form can be picked up in the *Migración* (Immigration) office at the border, at Mexican government tourist offices or consulates, at some travel agencies, and on international airline flights into Mexico. Travelers must present this completed card along with either a passport, birth certificate, or voters' registration card (this last for U.S. citizens) to the officials at *Migración* . They will validate the tourist card, usually for a 90-day stay in the country, and give you a copy. You <u>must</u> carry this copy with you at all times. Visitors who are under 18 years of age and traveling without one or either parent must present a notarized letter of permission signed by the absent parent(s).

Years ago when I was a novice at traveling in Mexico I carelessly managed to get on a train without first getting a tourist card. Several days and a thousand miles later on Mexico's west coast, I spent most of an afternoon explaining to a Mexican anti-drug officer that I was not a smuggler, just a fool. It was a rocky time for my self-esteem.

There are *Migración* offices in each of the 24 crossing points along the U.S.-Mexico border as well as in the airports of all Mexican cities served by international airline flights. A number of these towns are located on the Mexican rail system: Mexicali, Nogales, Ciudad Juárez, Piedras Negras, Nuevo Laredo, Reynosa, Matamoros, Mazatlán, Manzanillo, Guadalajara, Mexico City, Monterrey, and Mérida, among others.

Customs

You can take almost anything into Mexico, although firearms require a lot of paperwork and medicines require prescriptions. Technically, you are only allowed one camera, 12 rolls of film, one video camera and 12 cassettes per person but I've never heard of this being enforced.

As for taking things out of Mexico and back home, the laws vary from country to country. As regards U.S. law, travelers returning from Mexico can bring back up to $400 worth of merchandise duty-free which can include no more than one liter of alcohol, 200 cigarettes, and 100 cigars. For all practical purposes no fresh fruit, vegetables, meats, plants, or pets can be imported. Also, products made from endangered or protected animal species cannot be brought into the U.S. Avoid anything made from coral, sea turtle shell, crocodile, or wildcat.

Accessing the Mexican Rail Network

Getting on Mexico's train system is easy and can be accomplished by air or land. Arguably the easiest way to make a connection is by flying to one of several Mexican cities served by both rail and international airlines. Presently, the major cities in this category are Mexico City, Guadalajara, Mazatlán, Manzanillo, Mérida, and Monterrey but a number of other, smaller cities are also served by international flights. For current information contact a travel agent.

Land connections with the train system can be made at the border towns of Mexicali, Nogales, Ciudad Juárez, Piedras Negras, Nuevo Laredo, Reynosa, and Matamoros. All of the U.S. cities opposite these rail heads are served by either local or national bus lines while several of the Texas border crossings—El Paso, Laredo, and Brownsville—are served by regional airlines. Also, El Paso is directly on an Amtrak route while Nogales, Arizona, is only a 90-minute bus ride from the Amtrak station in Tucson, Arizona.

If you arrive at the border by car but do not plan to take your car deep into Mexico it is quite easy to find long-term parking for a fee on either side of the border. Locally owned and operated motels or restaurants are your best bet. Avoid fancy chain hotels.

In the I'll-believe-it-when-I-see-it category, there are very preliminary studies under way to evaluate the feasibility of building a high speed rail connection between San Antonio, Texas, and Monterrey, Nuevo León, Mexico.

Local Transport

Presumably you plan to do most of your traveling by train but situations requiring other types of transport will arise. Taxis are generally cheap but very few have or use meters so determine the cost of the trip **before** you depart—"*Cuanto cuesta para ir al centro?*" (How much does it cost to go downtown?) The yellow and green VW bugs and Datsuns in Mexico City have meters but just make sure that the driver turns it on when you get in.

Another word of warning: taxis which depart from airports, train stations, or bus stations will often be much more expensive than taxis going the same distance but in the opposite direction–that is, to the station. The reason is clear: the drivers see the people at the station or airport as a captive audience desperate to get to their hotel rooms and willing to pay to get there quickly. But if you're on a budget every expenditure matters, so it pays to look for a cheaper alternative. And a cheaper alternative usually exists. Local buses and *colectivos* always run to or very near the stations and cost about a tenth or less of what a taxi costs. Both are also useful for maneuvering around town cheaply, though discovering what route they run usually requires some experimentation. Both buses and *colectivos* are usually identified by a route number and a list of destinations written on the windshield.

The differences between local buses and *colectivos* are a matter of cost, size, and speed. The latter are usually smaller buses or VW vans which cost slightly more, make fewer stops, and therefore are faster than city buses. Usually *colectivos* only stop at designated stands (*paradas*) while buses can be flagged down at any corner. To get off *colectivos* say "*Baja, por favor*" (Down, please). Buses usually have either a bell cord or button.

It's also possible to rent cars in most larger Mexican cities. Rental agencies will include the majors like Hertz and Avis as well as local companies. The latter are usually cheaper but rarely accept credit cards. And don't expect rentals to be cheaper in Mexico. Often they are more expensive.

If you are interested in an excursion to a particular destination, an option which may be cheaper than a rental car but more time efficient than public transportation is a tour group. Check with a travel agent or the tourism office in the town nearest the site.

The lifeblood of Mexican transportation is the nation's system of intercity buses. There are officially two classes of bus service: first class and second class. Both classes run between major towns and cities but small towns and villages are served by only second class buses. The differences between the two are mostly a matter of cost, comfort, and speed. In theory first class buses are more comfortable, more expensive and, because they make fewer stops, faster. Second class buses are liable to be flagged down by would-be passengers anywhere along the roadway. Both types usually leave from the same station, although in some towns they have separate stations. Within both classes of travel there are buses called *local*, which indicates that the bus route originates in that town and *de paso,* meaning that the route's origin is in some other town. This distinction is important because while the number of seats available on a *local* bus is easily determined, the number available on a *de paso* is not and you often find out whether there are seats only after the bus arrives in the station. Generally, if you are in a large town you will have plenty of *local* buses to choose from. But if you are trying to make connections from a small town you may have to deal with *de paso* buses, especially if you want to travel first class.

Although they serve a limited geographic area, ferries provide a significant embellishment to the Mexican rail network. Specifically, the ferry system provides the train traveler with easy and cheap access to Baja California from several locations on the west coast of Mexico. All these locations are on or very near a major rail route and are therefore convenient for the train traveler. The ferry schedule is below.

Ferry Routes	Departures	Duration
La Paz-Mazatlán	daily at 5 p.m.	16 hours
Mazatlán-La Paz	daily at 5 p.m.	16 hours
La Paz-Topolobampo	daily at 8 p.m.	8 hours
Topolobampo-La Paz	daily at 10 a.m.	8 hours
Santa Rosalia-Guaymas	Tues-Sun at 11 p.m.	8 hours
Guaymas-Santa Rosalia	Tues-Sun at 11 a.m.	8 hours

With the exception of the holiday season there is rarely a shortage of tickets and if you don't mind waiting a day or so then you can just buy your ticket when you arrive at the departure point. Otherwise, for more information and reservations, contact the "Grupo Sematur de California" at the appropriate location:

•Guillermo Prieto #1495, La Paz, B.C.S., Mexico
•Muelle Fiscal, Apdo. Postal 72, Santa Rosalia, B.C.S., Mexico
•Muelle Fiscal, Guaymas, Sonora, Mexico
•Circunvalación #103-2, Mazatlán, Sinaloa, Mexico

Currency Exchange

Before the nationalization of the banking system in 1982 it was an occasional hassle changing dollars into pesos, especially changing travelers' checks. Every bank seemed to have different rules and procedures. The nationalization seemed to produce at least a procedural uniformity. Today, you can walk in to almost any bank in the country and change cash or travelers' checks. You can also change money in *casas de cambio*, private currency exchange companies which offer exchange rates slightly better than the bank rates. Some hotels and travel agents will also change money but generally at less favorable rates.

Banks are open from 9 a.m. to 1 or 1:30 p.m. To facilitate your currency exchange transactions stick with name brand travelers' checks. Also, major credit cards are accepted at more expensive hotels, restaurants, and travel agencies. I usually take a credit card for emergencies and hope that I won't have to use it. The most widely accepted are Mastercard and Visa.

Crime

On balance there is no more crime in Mexico than in the United States and very possibly less. Our perception is affected by the fact that whenever something bad happens to a foreigner in Mexico reports of the event fill our national media. We don't hear reports about the millions of visitors to Mexico who enjoy a pleasant stay. Having traveled in Mexico at least 40 times I've never had a knife or gun pointed at me. By taking sensible precautions you can avoid being a victim.

• Don't get drunk in a Mexican bar and it's best not even to set foot in one unless it's a "Ladies Bar," which means that women are allowed in. Other bars are hangouts for Mexican *machos* who might be decent enough stone sober but who undergo weird and sometimes dangerous personality changes under the influence of alcohol.

• Avoid resort areas or, if you can't avoid them, take extra precautions. Don't walk around at night in isolated areas. Professional thieves gravitate to areas frequented by relatively wealthy North American tourists.

• If you ride the Mexico City Metro (subway) at rush hour, carry your valuables in a hidden pocket beneath your clothes or, at the very least, in a breast pocket. Thieves have been known to slash backpacks or clothing with razors to retrieve goodies. There are also ordinary pickpockets. In the unbelievable crush of rush hour you can hardly move, let alone defend your possessions.

• Exercise caution when camping near population centers.

• Don't look too affluent. Leave the jewelry and the Rolex at home. Most crime is in pursuit of property.

• Avoid drugs and definitely do not purchase illegal substances from any stranger. Chances are it's a set-up. In recent years the United States government has forced Mexico to pursue drug dealers, traffickers, and users more aggressively. Irritated by the heavy-handedness of this international pressure, Mexicans gain a certain self-satisfaction when they are able to jail North Americans for drug offenses.

Health

Health problems of Third World traveling are the stuff of jokes and even movies. The reality is far from humorous, though. Becoming ill while traveling can ruin a vacation. Nothing will guarantee well being but a few precautions will increase the odds in your favor. The first thing to do is to check with your doctor. The only immunization Mexico requires is yellow fever and then only when the traveler is coming from an infected area. A tetanus booster should be considered as well as a gamma globulin shot for Hepatitis A.

Malaria is also endemic throughout most of rural Mexico below

1,000 meters. You run little risk of contracting the disease in the coastal resort cities but if you plan to be out in rural areas during the mosquito-abundant rainy season then you should consider malaria prophylaxis medication. At the very least you should wear mosquito-protective clothing and use insect repellent.

As of mid-1992 there was a cholera epidemic working its way through Latin America including Mexico. Cholera is spread by consumption of contaminated water and is most dangerous in poor rural areas with inadequate (usually non-existent) sewage facilities. In Mexican towns and cities you should just follow the same precautions you would to avoid other problems. If you travel in Mexico's back country, be fastidious about purifying your water and food.

Now let's consider a problem you are more likely to face: diarrhea. In its most benign form diarrhea is caused when the traveler encounters a bacterial regime different from that in his home country. This version is called travelers' diarrhea or, in Mexico, *turista*. It usually lasts only two or three days and goes away without treatment. An effective preventative treatment is the consumption of one Pepto Bismol tablet four times a day. Nevertheless, you should talk with your doctor about this or any prophylaxis. If you come down with *turista* just let the illness run its course. Rest, drink bottled water and fruit juice, and eat only bland, non-dairy foods such as bread and saltine crackers. If you have to travel then you might consider taking a diarrhea suppressant like Imodium or Lomotil. Keep in mind, though, that while these substances suppress the diarrhea they also interrupt and delay the process of your recovery. If your diarrhea lasts for more than four days and you have blood and/or mucus in your stools then you probably have something more serious than *turista*, possibly amoebic or bacillary dysentery. You should get to a doctor immediately. Diarrhea suppressants should not be taken if you suspect dysentery.

A traveler with severe diarrhea, of whatever cause, needs to replace lost fluids and electrolytes. To do so, prepare two glasses with 8 ounces of fluid each. In the first glass put fruit juice with 1/2 teaspoon of honey and a pinch of salt. An alternative is Gatorade, though it should be diluted to half its strength. In the second glass put water with 1/4 teaspoon of baking soda. Use boiled or bottled water. Take alternate swallows from each glass and supplement with additional fluids. Some writers earnestly recommend that the traveler, in order to minimize the chances of gastroenteric problems, consume no tap water, iced drinks, dairy products, unpeeled vegetables or fruit, or anything cut by a knife on which a fly could have landed. I'm sure that when I'm asleep and snoring flies routinely land in my mouth. All I can say is I've never had anything more serious than *turista* in Mexico and here's what I advise:

• Never consume tap water, not even to brush teeth.

• Eat in restaurants popular with locals, not with tourists.

• In these restaurants eat any fruit or vegetable that has been peeled or cooked, consume dairy products and iced drinks, and trust that water given in a glass is safe.

• Hardly ever eat lettuce and if you ever have a bad feeling about a dish, however vague, don't consume it.

I believe that eating in Mexico is one of the joys of traveling there. Incorporate a sensible routine into your eating habits but don't sit down to every meal expecting it to be your last.

Finally, much of Mexico's territory is higher than 1,500-meters above sea level. For example, Mexico City is over 2,200 m elevation. People who have been transported to these high altitudes from their lowland domiciles should allow sufficient time to acclimatize before engaging in strenuous activities.

Hotels and Restaurants

A list of hotels is included in the appendix of this book. Hotels are ranked according to price and no top end hotels have been included. This compilation does not constitute a list of recommended hotels. It is simply a list of hostelries whose price and location are favorable. Selecting from the list is your job, not mine. I would encourage you to shop around before you settle on a hotel and be sure to check the room before paying.

While some travel books list and recommend restaurants, I've found that to be a waste of time. Finding good restaurants, like finding good hotels, is something that only the traveler herself can do effectively and dependably. This search is part of the adventure of traveling. My criteria for selecting a restaurant are safe, cheap food and plenty of it. When a place is new to me, I examine the clientele. If the restaurant is full of working and middle-class Mexicans then that is a real plus. On the other hand, a room full of gringo tourists in Hawaiian print shirts is a real minus. My simple reasoning is that the locals, who also want a safe meal and a good deal, know more about their town than any number of tourists. And when I find a good place I generally stick with it for the duration of my stay.

Most restaurants in Mexico offer a bargain mid-day meal variously called the *comida corrida* or *comida comercial* and travelers on a budget should take advantage of it. *La comida* is sold generally between 1 p.m. and 4 p.m. and is a fixed-price, multi-course meal. Typically, the courses include a soup, rice or pasta, an entree, and a dessert. The diner gets to choose from among two or more offerings within each course category.

Food

The triumvirate of the Mexican diet consists of corn, beans, and chiles. Corn is usually ground up into meal and formed into flat, pancake-like *tortillas* which can be eaten alone or used to make other dishes. Corn meal dough is also used to make *tamales*. Street vendors often sell whole ears of corn roasted or boiled and smeared with mayonnaise, chili powder and/or lime juice—one of the safest and tastiest treats on the street. Beans are ubiquitous but you never find plain, boiled beans. Occasionally you find boiled beans that have been mashed into a paste. Most often, however, beans are served in a refried format which means that the bean paste was fried in lard. Most places in Mexico serve beans with every meal. The third god of Mexico's culinary pantheon is the *chile*. While most people think of *chiles* as being fiery hot, in reality they range from sweet to volcanic and in color from yellow to black. They are eaten alone, in cooked and raw sauces, and stuffed. If you want to ask whether a dish is spicy, ask, "Is it hot?" or "Is it very hot?" (*Es picante? Es muy picante?*).

Tourism Offices

Every Mexican town of any size and with any sort of tourism appeal has at least one tourism office. The larger cities may have two or three, at least one of which will be a state tourism office and another a federal tourism office. Usually, these offices will be convenient to the center of the city but occasionally, and especially in resort areas, they will be far from a town's main plaza. There is also considerable variability in the quality of services offered. Some offices are overflowing with pamphlets, maps, and personnel who speak English, while others are so spare that the part-time office worker is reduced to drawing city maps on napkins from the restaurant next door. When functioning at their best, these offices are an excellent place to get information on local buses, tours, maps, medical facilities, and cultural activities.

There are also several Mexican Government Tourism Offices in the United States and Canada. You can contact these offices for information, maps, and tourist cards. Their addresses are:

• 233 N. Michigan Ave., Suite 1413, Chicago, IL 60601
• 2707 N. Loop W., Suite 450, Houston, TX 77008
• 10100 Santa Monica Blvd., Suite 224, Los Angeles, CA 90067
• 1 Place Ville Marie, Suite 2409, Montreal, Quebec H3B 3M9
• 405 Park Ave., Suite 1002, New York, NY 10022
• Centre Plaza Bldg., 45 N.E. Loop 410, Suite 125, San Antonio, TX 78216
• 181 University Ave., Suite 1112, Toronto, Ontario M5H 3M7

Chapter 2

History & Culture of Mexico

Pre-Conquest

Humans began migrating into North America around 40,000 years ago across a then-existent land bridge between Siberia and Alaska. The earliest evidence of human beings in Mexico has been dated to between 20,000 and 24,000 years ago.

During the **Archaic Period** (5000-1500 B.C.) these early Mexicans laid the foundation for later civilizations by discovering agriculture. Corn, beans, squash, and *chiles* are just a few of the crops cultivated and hybridized.

The **Formative Period** (1500 B.C. to 150 A.D. and also often called the **Pre-Classic**) saw the rapid proliferation of people and villages across Mexico, the intensification of ceramics and textile skills, and the development of the region's first and most mysterious civilization, the **Olmecs**. Other cultures which began during the Late Formative in their respective parts of Mexico and Mesoamerica were **Teotihuacán, Monte Albán**, and the **Maya**.

The **Classic Period** (150-900 A.D.) represents the Golden Age of Mesoamerican history when the great civilizations of the central highlands, the Valley of Oaxaca, and Mayaland all rose to their zenith and then collapsed. The most dominant of these was Teotihuacán which was already a powerful economic and ceremonial center by the beginning of the Classic. This city-state, located in the northern end of the Valley of Mexico, was Mesoamerica's first metropolis and had a population of perhaps 200,000 people in 600 A.D. Its influence extended from Guatemala in the south to northern Mexico. Yet by 700 A.D. the city lay pillaged and abandoned.

The **Zapotec** culture in Oaxaca also reached its peak florescence during the Classic. The spectacular site at Monte Albán is the most famous center of Zapotec culture and, like Teotihuacán, had its origins in the late Formative. Again like Teotihuacán, Monte Albán was largely and mysteriously abandoned by 700 A.D. in favor of lowland and less magnificent Zapotec towns in the valleys.

The Maya did not have one preeminent ceremonial center. Instead, there were a number of independent city-states scattered throughout Guatemala, Belize, Honduras and southern Mexico. These regional powers waxed and waned throughout the Classic but toward the end of this period there was an almost universal collapse of organized city life in the Maya area. Powerful cities such as **Palenque** in Chiapas and **Tikal** in Guatemala were abandoned. Only a few centers in the Yucatán– Chichén Itzá, Uxmal, and Cobá among them–managed to escape this catastrophic decline and extend their history into the next period.

The **Post-Classic Period** (900 A.D.-the Conquest) saw the rise of a new phenomenon in Mexican history: the militarized imperial state. The **Toltecs**, who ruled from their capital of **Tula**, were the first exponents of this concept. Originally a semi-barbaric tribe which migrated into the Valley of Mexico in the 9th Century, the Toltecs ruled an empire consisting of most of central Mexico from 950 to 1150 A.D. They were also prodigious practitioners of human sacrifice, believing that blood was the best food for their gods.

There is irrefutable evidence of Toltec influence in the Maya center of Chichén Itzá beginning in the late 10th Century. This contact led to a cultural and political renaissance in the Yucatán and may have been the result of the arrival of a group of Toltec exiles led by Topiltzin-Quetzalcóatl. These benefits only lasted a few hundred years, for by 1200 A.D. Chichén had been abandoned and the Yucatán had degenerated into factional and usually warring Maya cities.

In southern Mexico the Valley of Oaxaca had been usurped from the Zapotecs by a group of invaders known as **Mixtecs**. These people began moving into the Zapotec areas in the 9th Century and gradually, through marriage and war, took control of most of the region. The Mixtecs excelled at pottery, painting, and smithing and built their chief ceremonial center at **Mitla**.

The collapse of the Toltec empire opened up central Mexico, allowing barbarian tribes from the north to move into the civilized heart of Mexico. The most famous of these migrants were the **Mexica** or, as they are more popularly known, the **Aztecs**. These people arrived in the Valley of Mexico in the late 12th Century and found a region politically fragmented into a number of small city-states.

During the first two hundred years of their residence in the Valley, the Aztecs marginally survived by selling their mercenary services to various cities and by scavenging along the shores of Lake Texcoco. They founded their capital, **Tenochtitlán**, on some marshy islands near the lake's western shore and gradually expanded their little kingdom by building *chinampas* (floating islands) over the lake bed.

In the mid-15th Century the Aztecs formed an alliance with the city-states of Texcoco and Tlacopan and began the construction of their empire. By the time of the Spaniards' arrival in 1519 the Aztec empire included almost all of central Mexico from the Pacific to the Gulf coasts and south to Oaxaca. Their capital, Tenochtitlán, grew to 200,000 inhabitants and absorbed tribute from the far reaches of the empire. The Aztecs were the fiercest warriors in Mexico and were single-minded in their devotion to war and militarism. From infancy Aztec males were taught that death in battle was the highest of honors and was rewarded by the most pleasant of afterlives. While Aztec leaders almost uniformly embodied this same pre-occupation with conquest, as fate would have it the man who occupied the Mexica throne in 1519 was totally different.

Moctezuma Xocoyotzin (the Younger) was a complex man and, although a capable military leader, he was also given to meditation on religious and philosophical matters. One of his preoccupations was with the Toltec heritage his people claimed and one of the elements of that ancient heritage was the prophecy of Topiltzin-Quetzalcóatl that he would return to reclaim Mexico. **Hernán Cortés** arrived in 1519, which was the year predicted for the return of Quetzalcóatl. This and other portents convinced Moctezuma that the god had returned. By the time the Aztecs realized that the Spaniards were just men, it was too late.

The Conquest

When Cortés landed on Mexico's Gulf Coast in 1519, his was actually the third Spanish expedition to reconnoiter this area. But he was by far the boldest and proved it by burning his ships so that there would be no option of retreat to the Spanish colony of Cuba. The Spaniards were left with no choice but to march inland to the Aztec capital. On the way the Europeans enlisted the support of Indian groups opposed to the Aztecs, notably the Totonacs and the Tlaxcalans. By the time Cortés reached Tenochtitlán, he not only had over 400 Spanish troops but also thousands of Indians allies.

Still convinced that the Europeans were somehow divine, Moctezuma received them as friends, housing them in his father's palace. Surrounded by hundreds of thousands of enemies, Cortés decided to gain some security by taking Moctezuma hostage. The Aztec ruler, convinced that destiny was against him, put up with the indignity and allowed the Spaniards to use him as a puppet while they plundered the Aztec treasury.

This situation had continued for several months when Cortés received word of the arrival of another Spanish expedition on the Mexican coast. This group, led by Pánfilo de Narváez, had been sent by the governor of Cuba to arrest Cortés and assume his mission. With his typical audacity, Cortés left half of his forces in Tenochtitlán and led the remainder on a quick march to the coast. There Cortés defeated the much larger force under Narváez and then managed to convince most of these troops to accompany him back to Lake Texcoco where wealth and glory awaited them.

What actually awaited them was a riot. The Spanish force under **Pedro de Alvarado** had attacked and killed several thousand Aztecs during a religious ceremony and now the entire city was up in arms against the invaders. Cortés with his augmented forces managed to enter the city and reunite with Alvarado but then they found themselves trapped. Cortés forced the resigned and depressed Moctezuma to address the angry crowds but the Aztecs no longer recognized the authority of their former leader. During this confrontation Moctezuma suffered a fatal injury, whether from the Spanish or the Aztecs is unclear, and with his death the conquistadors were forced to make a run for it. Their escape resulted in the loss of over half the Spanish troops and thousands of Tlaxcalans. That night, June 30, is known as the **Noche Triste**. The remnants of Cortés' army made it to Tlaxcala where they spent several months recuperating and preparing for the final assault on Tenochtitlán. In January, 1521, with hundreds of thousands of Indian allies, the Spaniards besieged the Aztec capital. The Aztecs were led by **Cuauhtémoc** but their forces had been severely weakened by an outbreak of smallpox. Nevertheless, Tenochtitlán held out until August, 1521, and was only taken after a valiant but doomed house-by-house defense of the city. Tenochtitlán fell on August 13, 1521.

Colonial Mexico

What Cortés had wrought became the colony of **New Spain** and Mexico City, built on the ruins of Tenochtitlán, became its capital. At first Cortés administered the Spanish king's new possession and parcelled out properties and Indians to his followers and friends. But the Spanish king and his bureaucrats did not like or trust the conquistadors and soon placed control of New Spain in the hands of royally appointed administrators.

Beginning in 1535 with **Antonio de Mendoza**, New Spain was ruled by a succession of viceroys. These men were all Spanish-born and were of highly variable quality, generally reflecting on the quality of the royalty which appointed them. The viceroy ruled in place of the king and, while he technically had authority over the Catholic archbishop of Mexico City, in reality they were essentially equal. Each administered his part of a dichotomous New Spain, one for the king of Spain and the other for the Pope. To help him administer this vast, unknown land the viceroy had below him a large bureaucracy of civil servants, also Spanish-born and appointed by the crown. Most of these posts were seen by their holders as opportunities for profits. Many office-seekers, in fact, purchased their offices and regarded the money spent as an investment. With such a foundation it makes sense that the administration of New Spain would be predicated on greed and self-interest.

Meanwhile, by defeating the Aztecs the Spaniards assumed de facto control over most of their empire. But much of Mexico's indigenous population refused to accept Spanish hegemony and most of the remainder of the 16th Century was spent by the Europeans trying to destroy native resistance to their rule. Some regions and tribes were easier to subdue than others. The first attempt to conquer the Maya of the Yucatán took place in the late 1520s but temporary success wasn't achieved until the late 1540s. Despite this there continued to be periodic uprisings in Mayaland with the most serious being the **Caste War** of the 19th Century. This rebellion almost succeeded in eliminating all whites from the peninsula. The **Mixton War** took place in 1541 in the region around Guadalajara. This area had been conquered by the rapacious and bloodthirsty Nuño de Guzmán in the early 1530s and, although he had gone to a prison in Spain, continued exploitation led to this short-lived rebellion.

Longer-lived was the **Chichimec War** which lasted from around 1550 to 1600. The spark which set off this conflagration was the discovery of silver at Zacatecas in 1546. Ill treatment of the Indians by mine and hacienda owners led to this uprising by several Chichimec tribes of the arid Mexican altiplano.

Ultimately, it was not the weapons, horses, or self-righteous religion that allowed the Spanish to conquer and hold New Spain. It was their diseases: measles, mumps, typhus and, the most deadly, smallpox. When the Europeans arrived in Mexico there were an estimated 25 million indigenes in the area. By 1600 there remained only about 1.5 million, most of the difference representing victims of periodic epidemics of European diseases.

The economy of New Spain was based on mines and haciendas, a fact which boded ill for the Native Americans. Both types of enterprises required labor and the haciendas additionally required land. The Native Americans had both. Since the Spaniards hadn't come to New Spain to work as manual laborers, various mechanisms were employed to deprive the Indians of both their land and their labor. Throughout Mexico, until the Mexican Revolution in the 20th Century, Indians were at best serfs and at worst slaves.

Along with the conquistadors looking for gold came Catholic missionaries looking for souls. To the Franciscans, Dominicans, and Jesuits New Spain was a rich vein of pagan souls begging for evangelical mining. Many of these early religious workers were selfless and sincerely interested in the physical and spiritual redemption of the Indians. Many tried to protect their native congregations from the worst excesses of the mine owners' and hacendados' greed. Others performed the first scientific observations of both the people and lands of New Spain. Despite these virtues the missionaries at the same time made every effort to destroy Native American culture and replace traditional with more "catholic" beliefs. Priests burned indigenous books containing the history and customs of the people and used the natives' forced labor to construct grand colonial churches on the ruined foundations of Mexican temples. More insidiously, the missionaries tried to teach the Indians a passive acceptance of life with its pain and subjugation in anticipation of a heavenly reward.

As the colonial period wore on the well-intentioned missionaries were replaced by secular priests whose primary intention was to live as comfortably as possible in whatever parish they found themselves. Many of these priests charged outrageous fees for weddings, baptisms, and confirmations, putting the sacraments out of reach for most peasants. By the 19th Century the conservative Catholic church was the single most powerful institution in New Spain with an estimated half of all arable land in the colony and three-quarters of the available capital.

Virtually all positions of political power in New Spain were reserved for men born in Spain, *gachupines* or *peninsulares*. *Criollos*, people of pure Spanish blood born in the colony, were excluded from most important offices and almost all political power. While the Crown felt it could trust the European, it saw the loyalty of the provincial as problematic.

For the first 200 years of New Spain's history this policy caused few problems. But as the country grew, so did the wealth and expectations of the *criollo* class. Not wedded to the staid traditionalism of the *peninsulares*, these native-born whites saw the liberal and revolutionary philosophies that were sweeping Europe and North America in the 18th Century as justification for their emancipation and assumption of the political power to which they were entitled. Hypocritically, few of these *criollo* leaders saw those same philosophies as mandating the emancipation of the Indian and *mestizo* masses.

The *mestizo* race was born when the first Spanish soldier raped an Indian woman. Embodying a mixture of Spanish and Indian blood, *mestizos* comprised a majority of New Spain's population by the late 18th Century but occupied a rung on the socio-economic ladder only slightly higher than the Indian.

By the early 1800s *criollos* were gathering together in small "literary" societies to discuss in secret dangerous literature banned by the Spanish government. In time, these literary groups became, mostly in name only, revolutionary cells which brainstormed ways to overthrow the outdated Spanish colonial regime. One such group was meeting in Querétaro in 1810 and counted among its members **Miguel Hidalgo y Costilla**, a *criollo* priest from the town of Dolores, and **Ignacio Allende**, a *criollo* military officer. They were discovered, so Hidalgo incited his peasant parishioners to rise up to overthrow the regime which they hated even more than the *criollos* hated it. After initial successes, Hidalgo lost the will to fight, was captured, and executed.

The cause of independence was taken up by another priest, **José María Morelos**, who was not only a better tactician but was also a *mestizo*. He understood better than Hidalgo that the independence struggle, to have any meaning, had to be a struggle to enfranchise the peasants, both Indians and *mestizos*, and not a struggle just to replace one ruling class with another. Although Morelos came close to ousting Spain from Mexico, ultimately he was defeated, captured, and executed in 1814.

The War for Independence had become something that the *criollos* hadn't envisioned and didn't want. What they had wanted was a simple change of personnel: *peninsulares* out, *criollos* in. But Hidalgo and Morelos had released social forces driven by anger and desperation centuries old. These forces threatened to snatch the fruits of victory out of white *criollo* hands and put them into the brown, calloused hand of the *mestizo*. Faced with a common foe, native-born and foreign-born whites united to prevent independence.

Finally, in 1821, independence came to Mexico but only because the Spanish government became more liberal than the Mexican elites could countenance. To any objective observer independent Mexico looked identical to colonial New Spain: a powerful Catholic church, wealthy mine and hacienda owners, and impoverished Indians and *mestizo*s.

Independent Mexico

With independence in 1821 Mexico found itself in possession of territories stretching from Guatemala in the south to modern day Texas and California in the north. But Mexico was far from being a real nation. For the most part its people lacked a sense of national identity, seeing themselves as citizens of villages, cities, or regions rather than of a nation. This fragmented national consciousness made it easy for local bosses, known as *caciques* or *caudillos*, to achieve and hold power in the disparate parts of the new republic. This political fragmentation weakened the national government and made it easy prey for the more powerful *caudillos*.

In Mexican history much of the 19th Century is a period of political instability with one *caudillo* replacing another in quick succession as the head of Mexico's government. This instability had tragic consequences, for it was exploited not only by Mexicans hungry for power and wealth but also by foreign powers hungry for territory. The first major event of this kind began in 1836 when the Mexican province of Texas, inhabited mostly by settlers from the United States, declared its independence and it ended in 1848 with the defeat of Mexico in the **U.S.-Mexico War**. Under the terms of the **Treaty of Guadalupe Hidalgo** Mexico was forced not only to recognize Texas as independent but also to cede over half its territory–modern day California, Arizona, New Mexico, Nevada, and Utah–to the United States for a mere 15 million dollars.

The second major intervention came in the 1860s when France under Napoleon III decided that another empire would be just like a return to the good old days. At the same time Mexican conservatives–chiefly the Catholic Church and large land-owners–were casting about Europe for a good aristocrat who would lead their country out of the chaos and godlessness spawned by democracy. Their real motivation was that they were then engaged in a losing battle with Mexican liberals led by **Benito Juárez**, a battle which threatened to deprive the conservatives of their perks and privileges.

Between 1862 and 1867 Napoleon tried to install and maintain Maximilian of Hapsburg, an Austrian archduke, as emperor of Mexico. Under the leadership of Juárez, Mexico ultimately defeated and executed the hapless Maximilian but not before 50,000 Mexicans lost their lives.

With the expulsion of the French, the power of the traditional conservative elite was irreparably damaged. Under Benito Juárez Mexico finally settled into a pattern of peace, progress, and democracy and the foundations were laid for the modern-ization of Mexico. But Juárez's death in office in 1872 set the stage for Mexico's longest running individual dictator, **Porfirio Díaz**. Díaz had served as an officer in the struggle against the French and assumed the office of president in 1877. For the next 34 years he ruled Mexico and presided over a period of rapid modernization and economic growth as well as deepening pov-erty and worsening social conditions.

British, American, French, and German capital was enticed into the country and it quickly came to dominate the fields of mining, manufacturing, utilities, and transportation. More and more of Mexico was owned by foreign interests. Simultaneously peasant land holdings and communal Indian lands were gobbled up at an increasing rate by the wealthy and powerful, both foreign and Mexican. By 1910, of the ten million Mexicans who lived off agriculture, nine and a half million were essentially landless, while half of Mexico was owned by only 3,000 families. An estimated one-fifth of Mexico's total land, 96 million acres, was owned by 17 people. While modernization was widening the gap between rich and poor, it was also creating other changes in the social structure, specifically, a growing middle class of professionals and intellectuals. These people were nationalists who objected to Díaz's policy of selling Mexico's resources to the highest foreign bidder. They were also ambitious; they wanted to participate in directing the organization of society, that is to say, in politics. But the **Porfiriato** was a dictatorship and political participation was permitted to very few. That left only one option for this new class of Mexican nationalists: revolution.

The Mexican Revolution

The War for Independence had started with demands for a transformation of Mexican society but ended simply with one elite replacing another elite. In the mid-18th Century the Liberals led by Benito Juárez held the naive, romantic notion that it was only necessary to make the political system more democratic and the ballot would cure the peasant of his ignorance, the Indian of her poverty. But nothing really changed for a century.

By the early 20th Century the new middle class wanted a piece of the action. It didn't want to redistribute land or wealth, to recognize or promote labor unions, or to nationalize industry or natural resources. But social forces that had been building for hundreds of years made short work of the desires of men.

Francisco Madero first assumed leadership of the nonexistent movement when, in 1908, he published a political tract opposing the reelection of Porfirio Díaz. Two years later he announced his candidacy for the presidential election of 1910 but was arrested, jailed, and then exiled for his trouble. From his exile in Texas Madero proclaimed himself provisional president of Mexico and called for a general insurrection to oust Díaz. Amazingly, Mexicans began to comply.

In the northern states of Chihuahua and Sonora revolutionary bands under the leadership of **Pancho Villa** and **Pascual**

Orozco began to harass federal troops and eventually captured the town of Juárez opposite El Paso, Texas. Meanwhile, in the south arose the truest revolutionary of all, **Emiliano Zapata**. Fighting under the battle cry "Tierra y Libertad" (Land and Liberty), Zapata's army of *mestizo* and Indian peasants fought to regain the village lands that had been taken from them by the sugar plantation owners.

Toward the end of 1911, with opposition to his continued rule rising in all parts of Mexico, Porfirio Díaz went into exile. On October 2, 1911, Madero was elected president. But the revolution had only just begun. What followed was another nine years of assassinations, war, betrayal, chaos and, above all, death. By the time that Alvaro Obregón assumed the presidency in November, 1920, almost all of the other major figures of the Revolution were dead. As if to complete the cycle, Pancho Villa was assassinated in 1923 and Obregón five years later.

Following the Revolution, Mexico was a changed country. The social changes that occurred, while not as radical as they are sometimes advertised to have been, were far more extensive than the cosmetic changes Madero sought when he began his quixotic quest. The politicians and generals of the revolutionary period had to offer their peasant and worker armies something in order to get them to slaughter each other. Ultimately what the leaders offered the followers was the Constitution of 1917. There are two key provisions of that document that reflected the new social contract between Mexico's rulers and the ruled. The first, Article 27, contained itself two key principles. The first was the idea that all the natural resources of Mexico belong to Mexico and that private exploitation of these resources is temporary and conditional. The second was that private property is secondary to the public welfare and may be expropriated by the state to provide land for landless rural workers.

The second provision of significance was Article 123. This provided for the protection of both urban and rural workers by mandating a minimum wage, an eight hour day, the abolition of peonage and child labor, the right to organize unions and to strike, workers' compensation and other protection.

Modern Mexico

While Mexican presidents from Obregón on enforced the empowering provisions of the constitution with great variability, one administration stands out in the post-revolutionary history of Mexico for its commitment to those provisions. That was the presidency of **Lázaro Cárdenas**, 1934-1940. During his administration Cárdenas greatly accelerated the land reform program by distributing 45 million acres of land to the landless, more than twice as much as all previous administrations had distributed. He gave his sympathy and support to striking workers and brought peasant and labor groups into the National Revolutionary Party (PNR). In March, 1938, after the foreign oil companies had refused to follow a government directive, Cárdenas nationalized their operations. Lázaro Cárdenas is still the most revered Mexican figure, political or otherwise, of this century.

The depression of the 1930s and the world war that followed accelerated Mexico's drive toward industrialization. The presidents that followed Cárdenas prioritized industrial growth over all other issues. So while these politicians still paid lip-service to the ideals of the Revolution, in reality the concerns of the poor and working classes grew ever more distant from their minds.

In the 1970s huge reserves of petroleum were discovered in Mexico. With the price of oil going higher every year, Mexico's economic future seemed bright. The discovery launched a boom period fueled by money borrowed from international bankers who could not conceive of a better credit risk. When oil prices collapsed in the early 1980s, so did Mexico's economy. Mexico spent most of that decade in a recession, struggling to make interest payments on its $100 billion foreign debt.

Recent Mexican presidents have continued to move the country's politics rightward. Both **Miguel de la Madrid** (1982-1988) and **Carlos Salinas de Gortari** (1988-1994) tried to counter the "decade of no growth" by attracting foreign capital, especially in the form of border assembly plants. These plants convert imported semi-finished goods into finished products for export.

Aside from the **Constitution of 1917**, there were two other significant byproducts of the Mexican Revolution. The first was pride, the simple pride of being Mexican. Most of Mexico has always been non-white but its leaders had always aped some other culture–Spanish, French, American. Neither the Indian, the conquered race, or the *mestizo*, the bastard race, were considered to have any culture of value. With the Revolution, however, things Mexican were suddenly elevated to the apex of art, anthropology, sociology, and political discourse. An idyllic pre-Hispanic past was celebrated by authors and muralists, while artisans scurried to learn the quickly disappearing crafts of indigenous people. Native American leaders such as Cuauhtémoc who had led the doomed opposition to the Spaniards became national heroes.

The other byproduct was the political hegemony of Mexico's ruling political party, the **Institutional Revolutionary Party (PRI)**. The PRI is only the latest incarnation of a political party that was formed in 1929 as the **National Revolutionary Party (PNR)**. It incorporated all the major political and military actors of the Revolution and was formed to create stability in the Mexican political process. The stability achieved by the PNR and later the PRI is legendary. Since its establishment in 1929 the PNR/PRI has controlled Mexican politics at all levels. There have been numerous elections through the years but the PRI has won virtually all, sometimes with fraud, most of the time without it. The other Mexican political parties have been small, often sectarian, and sometimes even created by the PRI to give the political process the appearance at least of democracy.

Recently, opposition to the PRI has stiffened. The **National Action Party (PAN)**, which is pro-business and pro-U.S., had won a couple of governorships as of 1992. Meanwhile, on the left, is the populist challenger, the **Party of the Democratic Revolution (PRD)**. This party embodies more the tradition of Lázaro Cárdenas, and why not? Its leader is Cuauhtémoc Cárdenas, the son of the former president. Cárdenas ran against Salinas de Gortari in the 1988 presidential election and most objective observers believe Cárdenas won. But the PRI fraud machine came through. After many delays and irregularities, Salinas was declared the winner by the smallest electoral margin in history. Many speculate that the PRI has permitted the PAN to win a few elections as a public relations move but that it will never allow the PRD any measure of the same success because the PRI fears Cuauhtémoc Cárdenas and his populist message. There still remain millions of unfulfilled hopes in Mexico 80 years after the Revolution.

Mexican Culture

The Mexicans. Most of the Mexican population is *mestizo*, a term used originally by the Spanish to designate people of mixed Spanish and Indian blood. Today the term has a broader meaning for there is not only European and Indian in Mexico's racial mix but African and Asian as well. During the colonial period black slaves were imported to work on the plantations of Veracruz and Guerrero and in the mines of Zacatecas and Guanajuato. Later, in the 19th Century, Asian workers were brought into the country for large-scale construction and agricultural projects on the west coast. But for the most part Mexico's people see themselves as a mixture of Spanish and Indian, a fact which is at the source of the *mestizo*'s identity problem. To claim the Native American side of his history the Mexican must acknowledge not only that 25 million Indians were defeated by a few thousand Europeans but also that some of the Indians, by allying themselves with the Spanish, were traitors. For *mestizo*s choosing the Indian side of their history seems also to involve choosing weakness and duplicity. To claim the European side of his history the Mexican must embrace the conqueror, the rapist, the exploiter, the race which obliterated entire cultures to serve the god of gold.

Machismo. The unconscious choice that many Mexican men have made is to be macho. Machismo is a well-known term and is commonly thought to be synonymous with exaggerated masculinity. Perhaps symptomatically it is, but it really reflects a heritage-based conclusion that in this life one is either a victim or victimizer. Given this choice, the Mexican male prefers to be the master of the situation, not its pawn. While machismo is overrated, it is real and can pop up at any time. An innocuous example of it may occur when you are trying to take care of a transaction in a bank or at a border crossing. If you let the male clerk know that you're impatient then what was a neutral relationship becomes a confrontation and both honor and history demand that the clerk "win" that confrontation. At that point you might as well just take out a book and get some reading done. Machismo can also lead to dangerous situations, especially when alcohol is involved. The most important rule: never impugn a man's character in a bar.

Women. Perhaps it goes without saying but Mexican women are not "macha." They have had no experience at being the dominators, but plenty at being the dominated. Until the last couple of decades their role was strictly delimited by a male-dominated society. However, the world-wide student movement of the 1960s and the feminist movement in the 1970s created the space and consciousness for a traditional feminist movement in Mexico. This movement is not large and is composed mainly of educated, middle- and upper-class women.

The recession of the 1980s and the earthquake that hit Mexico City in 1985 led to the mobilization of a different group of women, the working class. Faced with worsening social and economic conditions, these women organized for family, neighborhood, and community issues: jobs, public transportation, nutrition, and crime among others.

Native Americans. Today over 50 indigenous ethnic groups survive in Mexico. By definition all these groups still speak their native language but maintain other elements of their traditional culture and belief systems to varying degrees. While the numbers are somewhat uncertain, there may be as many as 10 million Indians in Mexico. The groups whose cultures have been least altered are those who live in the most inaccessible areas: the **Tarahumara, Cora**, and **Huichol** in the rugged Sierra Madre Occidental and the **Tzotzil, Tzeltal**, and **Lacandón** in the mountains and forests of Chiapas. Other groups, such as the **Yaqui** of Sonora and the **Nahua** of central Mexico, show a more pronounced blend of indigenous, Spanish, and Mexican elements in their political, social, and religious activities.

Despite revolutionary rhetoric in praise of Mexico's indigenous roots and cultures, the Indian remains at the bottom of the

Mexican social ladder and is ridiculed and discriminated against by *mestizo* society. The land reform has given some indigenous communities an element of economic independence but, with little political power, they are often victimized by powerful logging, mining, and tourism interests.

Death. The Mexican attitude toward death is definitely non-Western and reflects the mixture of cultures that is Mexico. Death is as likely to be celebrated as dreaded, mocked as feared, sung about as prayed over. But it is never hidden or ignored. For pre-Hispanic cultures in Mexico death was not an end but the beginning and guarantor of new life. Death in battle, on the sacrificial altar, or at birth guaranteed the dead one a place of honor in the Mexican afterlife. It was the blood which flowed from human sacrifice that kept the gods strong, the rains falling, the volcanoes silent, and the world from collapsing into the maw of chaos. For the indigenous Mexicans death was life and part of an eternal cycle in which the living were always connected to the spirits of their ancestors.

The Spanish brought conquistadors and Catholicism and both added to the modern attitude toward death. The Spanish soldier, fighting for god and king, faced death bravely and uncomplainingly. Whatever their shortcomings and vices, it cannot be said that the conquistadors were afraid of death. Much as with the Indians, death served a spiritual, as well as temporal, end and guaranteed the soldier residence in heaven.

The Catholic Church brought its conception of the immortal soul and, more importantly, a framework within which the Indians could continue to celebrate their beliefs. In the Catholic religion, November 1 and 2 are, respectively, All Saints Day and All Souls Day. The indigenous people of central and southern Mexico have transformed these days into both a spectacular and a spiritual affirmation of their roots. It is called *El Día de los Muertos* (The Day of the Dead). *El Día* is officially November 2 but the celebrations and memorials often extend to several days around that date. Actual customs vary from region to region but the theme is the same: remembrance of the dead. During this time vendors sell foods and candies in the shape of skeletons and skulls. With gusto children bite the sweet heads off spun-sugar cadavers while mothers bake bread in the shape of human beings; **pan de muerto** (bread of the dead) it is called. In home and store windows dioramas and figurines appear. These figures mimic the events and activities of daily life–riding a bicycle, dancing, walking in the park–but the catch is that all the figures are skeletons–adults, children, even pets. Kids play with skeleton puppets and toy coffins whose cadavers pop out when a string is pulled.

Everywhere death, and life by inference, is laughed at, belittled, and embraced. But there is a serious side to this time as well, a time when departed family members are remembered with love and longing. Families prepare *ofrendas* or memorials in their homes and decorate them with flowers, candles, pictures, maybe a favorite toy, items that the departed treasured in life. And always there is food, the dead one's favorite dish, and maybe a bottle of liquor.

November 1, All Saints Day, is the day when the souls of little children return briefly to their families. Usually less elaborate memorials are built for these tiny spirits. That evening, especially around midnight, preparations are made for the return of adult spirits: foods and special treats for the dead are laid out while the survivors pray, retell old stories about the dead, and watch for signs of the return. In some locales these festivities take place in people's homes, while in other areas the entire community gathers in the cemetery to conduct the same rites. It's an eerie sight, a candlelit picnic in the graveyard. At dawn, the food and drink is gathered up and the families return home where they spend the rest of the Day of the Dead eating, drinking, and enjoying themselves because they know that death may be waiting for them tomorrow. But, hey, this is today!

The Stage

Geography. Mexico is shaped like a giant, twisted funnel with its broad mouth to the north and its narrow end bending east and then north into the Yucatán Peninsula. Variations in land elevations and climate give the country a variety of climatic zones–alpine conditions on the highest volcanoes, tropical rainforests in the south, temperate deserts in the north, scrub brushlands in the northeast, hardwood and conifer forests throughout the highlands.

Mexico is a very mountainous country. In the north the Sierra Madre Oriental roughly parallels the Gulf Coast and consists of low, highly folded limestone ranges. On the other side of the country the higher and more rugged Sierra Madre Occidental runs in a broad band along the west coast. These mountains are an extension of the Rockies in the United States. Both ranges terminate in the volcanic belt of central Mexico. Here there are a series of volcanoes, among them the highest peaks in the country, in a broad east-west belt across the mid-section of Mexico. Scattered among the volcanoes are fertile, high altitude basins. Between the Sierras Madre Oriental and Occidental is Mexico's high central plateau, the altiplano. A few short mountain ranges break up the surface of this semi-arid tableland, all of which is at least 1,500 m above sea level.

East of the Sierra Madre Oriental is a broad, flat coastal plain running along the margin of the Gulf of Mexico. This plain extends south from the Texas border all the way to the state of Tabasco, where it curves east and then north into the Yucatán Peninsula. Along the west coast is a much narrower coastal plain which is occasionally obliterated by encroaching mountains. From the state of Nayarit south the coast is very mountainous until you reach eastern Oaxaca and the state of Chiapas. West and south of Mexico City is a crumpled, mountainous landscape dominated by the Sierra Madre del Sur in the southwest and the Sierra Juárez in the east. In the northern part of this region, especially in the states of Morelos and Puebla, are large, fertile, flat-floored basins while the southern part is an almost unrelieved landscape of low mountains and rugged canyons. East of this mountainous area is the narrowest part of Mexico, the Isthmus of Tehuantepec. The isthmus is a low-lying neck of land between mountain ranges in eastern Veracruz and Oaxaca and has been considered as the site for an inter-oceanic canal.

Continuing east from Tehuantepec is the state of Chiapas. It is dominated by two paralleling mountain systems, the Sierra de Chiapas along the Pacific Coast and the Sierra del Norte de Chiapas, and by a broad, linear valley nestled between the ranges. Northeast of Chiapas is the low, flat, limestone platform of the Yucatán Peninsula.

Climate. As far as rainfall goes, most of Mexico follows a simple rule: rainy summers, dry winters. Along Mexico's Gulf Coast, however, considerable rainfall is also possible in the winter when strong cold fronts sweep south and contact the moist coastal air. Northern Mexico experiences hot summers and cold winters. Temperatures below freezing are common. The central Mexican highlands, including Mexico City, benefit from the moderating effects of high altitude and low latitude. Here the summers are warm with cool nights and winters are mild with occasional cold spells. Temperatures rarely drop below freezing.

Mexico's coastal climate varies with latitude. The northern coasts have hot summers and cool winters. As you move south past the Tropic of Cancer the climate quickly becomes subtropical to tropical with hot, humid, insect-ridden summers and slightly less hot, less humid winters. The real difference between the seasons is in the insect population.

The Yucatán Peninsula is oppressively hot, humid, and rainy during the summer. Winters are warm but much less humid and rainy. The southern Mexican highlands show little temperature variation between summer and winter, though the former season does produce most of the region's rainfall. Temperatures are generally mild, though at night, during either season, temperatures can drop quite low.

Chapter 2

Mexico City & The Valley Of Mexico

Pre-Hispanic History

The Valley of Mexico has always been at the heart of power. Every civilization that laid claim to a Mexican empire was seated here: Teotihuacán, Tula, Tenochtitlán, Mexico City. No one can understand Mexico without spending time here where so much of Mexico's history was born.

Valley of Mexico. The valley is a physiographic feature, a high altitude basin sitting at over 2,200 meters above sea level and surrounded by volcanoes. It measures about 100 kilometers from north to south and 65 kilometers east to west.

Human beings have lived in the Valley of Mexico for at least 12,000 years, lured there by the game which frequented the margins of the valley's numerous lakes. With the discovery of agriculture around the fifth millennium before Christ these early Mexicans could directly exploit the region's fertile volcanic soil. The population of the valley grew but it would still be 5,000 years before the first, and perhaps greatest, of central Mexico's civilizations would arise.

Teotihuacán. Sometime before 200 B.C., a settlement was founded at the north end of the Valley of Mexico. Somehow, from these humble beginnings, there developed an entity for which there was no precedent in Mexico: an urban metropolis. By 500 A.D. the city-state of Teotihuacán contained a population of as many as 200,000 and covered over nine square miles. Teotihuacán's influence extended throughout most of central and southern Mexico, reaching as far south as Guatemala. The city's art, architecture, and theology spread throughout the country, carried either by armies, traders, priests, or all three.

Around 600 A.D. a long period of decline began, probably precipitated by the exhaustion of the city's local resources or by drought. Finally, around 700 A.D., Teotihuacán was destroyed and burned.

Tula. With the collapse of Teotihuacán, the Valley of Mexico entered a chaotic period marked by war and massive migrations. Tribes of barbarians from the northern wastelands moved into the power vacuum, conquering and appropriating the cultures of sedentary, civilized Indians. These barbarians were known by the generic term "Chichimeca" and one of the tribes that entered central Mexico around 900 A.D. was the Tolteca-Chichimeca. They eventually established their capital at Tula, at the northern margin of the Valley of Mexico.

Between 950 and 1150 A.D. the militaristic Toltecs subjugated and ruled an empire spanning Mexico from coast to coast. During this period Tula grew to a population of maybe 50,000. But in the middle of the 12th Century a series of droughts combined with civil war to topple the empire. Bands of Toltecs migrated away from the dying city, spreading their culture and the memory of their greatness throughout Mexico.

Tenochtitlán. After the fall of Tula another period of upheaval convulsed the Valley of Mexico. Mini-states rose and fell while new bands of Chichimecs entered and settled in the basin. One of the last tribes to arrive was the Aztecs, also known as the Mexica. From their arrival in the mid-13th Century until the mid-14th Century, the Aztecs lived a generally miserable hand-to-mouth existence in the swamps of Lake Texcoco. Despised by the other people of the Valley for their bloody and cruel customs, the Aztecs were left to their own devices in the wasteland, a condition which fueled their stoic militarism and gave them a sense of their historic purpose. They founded their capital of Tenochtitlán on land reclaimed from the lake.

In 1427 the Aztecs overthrew their former overlord, the city of Atzcapotzalco. In less than a hundred years the Spanish would lay waste to the Aztec empire but not before that empire covered most of civilized Mexico. Tenochtitlán grew like a fantasy on Lake Texcoco, connected to the mainland by wide causeways. In 1519, when the Spaniards first looked upon the splendors of

Tenochtitlán, many of them thought the city a wonderful dream. By 1522 the "dream" had been destroyed.

Mexico City

Mexico City, known simply as Mexico to most Mexicans, rose from the ashes of Tenochtitlán. Most of the first Spanish buildings were built with the stone and brick from razed Aztec structures. And the laborers who built these structures were the enslaved Mexica. It was no accident that Cortés built the capital of New Spain on top of Tenochtitlán. It satisfied a pattern of domination to which the Indians of Mexico had become accustomed, namely being ruled from the Valley of Mexico. The valley was the traditional seat of power, a power that was as much mythic and religious as military and political.

From its founding in 1522 to independence in 1821 Mexico City served as the political and religious capital of New Spain. The viceroy ruled from Mexico, translating the Spanish king's will into colonial policy. Despite frequent floods from overflowing Lake Texcoco and occasional food shortages, Mexico City continued to grow, but took 300 years to achieve the size of its Aztec predecessor.

Mexican independence in 1821 weakened somewhat the capital's domination of the country. Without a king and a royal bureaucracy to impose a political hierarchy, centrifugal forces developed, producing regional strongmen or *caciques*. New Spain had been a colony, never a country and the newly emergent Mexico was, in the minds of its people, not a country either. As the country unravelled, Mexico City became almost irrelevant.

The U.S.-Mexico War in the 1840s and the French Intervention in the 1860s generated a powerful wave of Mexican nationalism that forged for the first time a bona fide Mexican consciousness and nation. Under first Benito Juárez and later Porfirio Díaz, Mexico City became the opulent capital of a modern nation with a fast growing economy. During the 34-year reign of Díaz public works projects transformed the city into a veritable European capital with numerous monuments, broad landscaped boulevards, and French neoclassical government buildings.

The Mexican Revolution put the capital's growth on hold. But not for long. Spurred by the world-wide depression of the 1930s and war in the 1940s, the Mexican government embarked on a program of national industrialization and most of the new factories built were in or near the capital. Mexico City grew quickly. Modern office buildings went up and trapped colonial relics in their shadows. By the 1960s rapid economic growth coupled with political corruption and domination by the PRI led to a series of protest demonstrations in Mexico City. The culmination of this unrest occurred at the Plaza of Three Cultures in 1968 when a student rally was encircled and attacked by government troops. As many as 400 unarmed protesters died. Hundreds were arrested.

In the aftermath of the massacre relative calm returned to the city. The discovery in the 1970s of vast new Mexican reserves of petroleum created an economic boom throughout the country. Then, in the 1980s, the oil industry collapsed and Mexico's economy went bust. The effect of the depression on Mexico City was immediate. With economic opportunity at zero or less in the countryside, hundreds of thousands of people migrated to the capital every year looking for a way to survive. But the economic slump meant that public revenues were down and that there was no money to provide services for Mexico City's new immigrants. The result was a growing suburban wasteland of squatter communities in the capital, communities without water, sewage, electricity, or public transportation.

Today Mexico City is, arguably, the largest city in the world, with 25 million people in its metropolitan area. It covers the Federal District and its tentacles reach into the neighboring state of Mexico. The city also has the world's most polluted urban atmosphere. Thirty years ago residents could still see the snow-capped volcanoes that ring their once paradisiacal valley, but no more. Thermal inversion layers during the winter create deadly conditions for inhabitants with bronchial problems. At last, however, the government is taking Mexico's environmental crisis seriously and real solutions are being proposed and implemented. But don't expect to see the volcanoes this decade.

The economic crisis of the country and the overwhelming population pressure in the city have created a worsening crime problem. Despite this, Mexico City is no worse than any other large urban area in North America.

Why Go? I used to travel all over Mexico but would studiously avoid Mexico City. My only associations with it were unpleasant: paying bribes to cops, sleeping on the floor of the airport, being trapped on a bus in a flooded drainage ditch. If I were making a connection in Mexico City I would hole up in the bus or train station, reluctant to venture outside. And if I were driving, I'd go an additional 400 miles out of my way just to bypass Mexico City.

Those days are long gone. I now love the megalopolis and can't wait to be back beneath its yellow sky. The city is vibrant and exciting and possesses a wealth of culture, history, and activities that I am nowhere near exhausting. And if the city itself isn't enough, then within a short day trip of Mexico is a potpourri of sights ranging from snow-covered volcanoes and national parks to pre-Hispanic ruins and colonial churches.

Tourism Office. The first thing to do in Mexico City is to go by the **Federal District Tourism Office** at the corner of Ambres and Londres in the **Zona Rosa**. Here you can pick up a free map of the city as well as whatever brochures are out on the shelves. The office is open daily from 9 a.m. to 8 p.m. and is located two blocks north of the "Insurgentes" station on Metro Line 1.

Information on tourism throughout the republic can be obtained at the ministerial-level **Secretary of Tourism (Sectur) office** at Av. Presidente Mazaryk 172. Every time I've visited this office, the personnel have been extremely friendly and helpful. This tourism office is open 9 a.m. to 8 p.m. and is located three blocks east of the "Polanco" station on Metro Line 7. Sectur also operates a 24-hour, English hot line for tourist information and hotel reservations: 250-0123 or 250-0151.

Getting Around. The key to enjoying the biggest city in the world is being able to get around in it. Fortunately, that is pretty easy. There are a variety of transportation media to choose from, street layout is fairly regular, and many of the points of

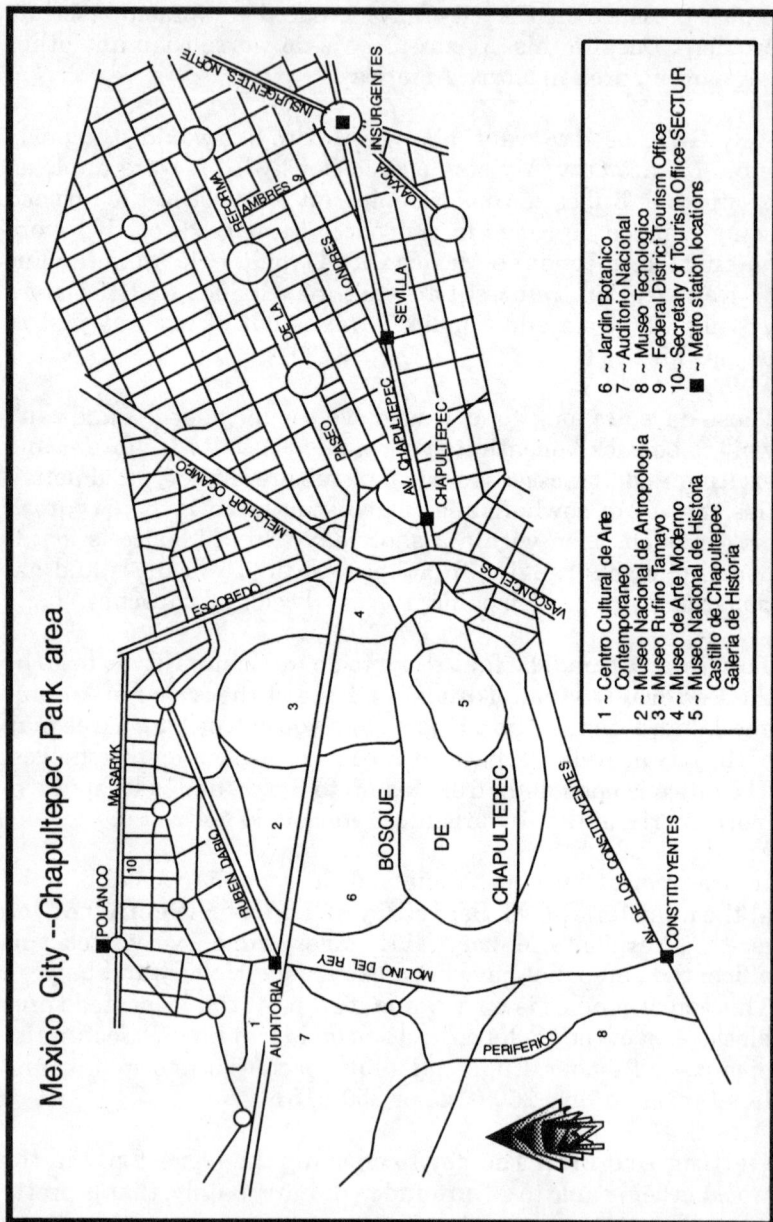

Mexico City --Chapultepec Park area

1 ~ Centro Cultural de Arte
    Contemporaneo
2 ~ Museo Nacional de Antropologia
3 ~ Museo Rufino Tamayo
4 ~ Museo de Arte Moderno
5 ~ Museo Nacional de Historia
    Castillo de Chapultepec
    Galeria de Historia
6 ~ Jardin Botanico
7 ~ Auditorio Nacional
8 ~ Museo Tecnologico
9 ~ Federal District Tourism Office
10~ Secretary of Tourism Office-SECTUR
■ ~ Metro station locations

interest tend to be clustered together within easy walking distance.

The easiest and fastest method of transport is the cab. Cabs in Mexico City are among the cheapest in the entire country and much, much cheaper than cabs in the United States. Stick with the yellow or green VW bugs or Datsuns and make sure that the driver turns on his meter. Otherwise, your ride will be costly.

Mexico City is full of buses and if you're familiar with them they can take you anywhere. There are both diesel and electric buses. You can get information and even, occasionally, route maps at the tourist office. I have always found the buses in Mexico City confusing, slow, and crowded. In their favor, they are cheap. Two useful route numbers are: **17**, which goes north and south along Av. Insurgentes from San Angel to Indios Verdes, and **76** which travels from the Anthropology Museum, along the Paseo de la Reforma, past the Alameda, and to the Zócalo. As always, watch for pickpockets on crowded buses.

My favorite way to get around Mexico City is the subway, which is known here as the **Metro**. It's fast, cheap, goes just about everywhere, and simple. For about 13 cents U.S. you can go across the length and breadth of Mexico City. Ask at the tourist office or at the ticket window in the Metro for a map of the Metro system (*"una mapa del red del Metro"*). I have reproduced one here but their maps are in color.

You can see from the map how simple yet comprehensive the system is. Specific Metro lines are identified by their color, number, and their end points. If you want to go west on Line 1 then enter a subway station on that route and follow the signs saying "Observatorio." If you want to go east, look for signs saying "Pantitlán." Most stations are on only one line. Some, however, are located at the junction of two or more routes. In these latter stations you can switch from one line to another without having to purchase another ticket. You can see how powerful mastery of the Metro is.

There are a few drawbacks to the Metro. First, you are not allowed to take large pieces of luggage on the trains which means that usually you cannot take them to and from the train or bus station. Second, as in most crowded places in Mexico City, there is the danger of thieves and pickpockets. Keep an eye on your valuables or, better yet, don't even take them on the Metro. Finally, during rush hour on certain lines, men and women are segregated in different cars. This policy was initiated because some men were taking advantage of the rush hour crowds to "grope" the women near them. If you're traveling in a group of mixed sexes then you need to make sure everyone knows where to get off the Metro and where to rendezvous.

Another way to get around to some of the sights in Mexico City is with a tour group. While it certainly costs more than riding the Metro, going with a tour is time efficient and this is important if you're on a time budget. You can ask at the tourism office about tours. Or contact "Panoramas Universales" at 658-74-76 and located in the Torre Latino Americana (Latin America Tower). Panoramas conducts tours of the city as well as excursions to such places as Teotihuacán, Cuernavaca, Taxco, and Puebla.

Getting Away. The **train station** is called the Estación Central de Buenavista and is located two kilometers north of the Alameda at the intersection of Av. Insurgentes Norte and Mosqueta. The No. 17 bus runs beside it on Insurgentes, and there is a Metro station (Guerrero on Line 3) four blocks east of the train station. If you come out of the train station looking for a cab, ignore those drivers clustered on the front steps. Go out to Mosqueta or Insurgentes and flag down a VW bug with the "Libre" sign on in the windshield. Your ride will cost half as much.

There are four **bus stations** in Mexico City and which one you choose depends on where you are going. The largest is the **Terminal del Norte** located on Av. de los Cien Metros near its intersection with Insurgentes Norte. Beside it is the "Autobuses del Norte" Metro station (Line 5). Buses leave here for all destinations north of Mexico City including the U.S. border and Guadalajara.

The **Terminal de Autobuses de Pasajeros de Oriente (TAPO)** is located on Av. Ignacio Zaragoza near the "San Lázaro" Metro station (Line 1). Buses depart from here for destinations in south and southeastern Mexico: Puebla, Oaxaca, Chiapas, Veracruz, and the Yucatán.

The **Terminal Central del Sur** is at Av. Tasqueña 1320 about four blocks from the "Tasqueña" Metro station (Line 2). Buses depart from here for destinations on the Pacific coast or on the way to the coast: Cuernavaca, Taxco, Acapulco, Ixtapa.

Finally, the **Terminal Poniente** is at the intersection of Calle Sur and Tacubaya right beside the "Observatoria" Metro station (Line 1). This small station serves only Toluca with direct buses but also Morelia and Guadalajara with slow, indirect buses.

If you are coming into Mexico City from one of the above regions, you will of course arrive at the corresponding station. If you want to take a taxi from the bus station, you buy tickets at a booth, paying an amount which is a function of the distance to your destination. You then wait in a line and present your ticket to an authorized cabby when your turn comes.

Crafts. While Mexico City as a cultural region is not known for a particular style of crafts, it is possible to find here a variety of arts and crafts, both locally and externally produced, that is unequalled anywhere else in the country. Many of the millions of immigrants in this city are craftspersons. At the same time Mexico City offers an incredibly large potential market for artisans and the highest quality crafts end up here to be sold to tourists or wealthy Mexicans. Strictly for arts and crafts, there are two excellent markets. The **Plaza de la Ciudadela** is on Av. Balderas two blocks north of the "Balderas" Metro station (Lines 1 & 3). Prices are reasonable and the selection is enormous. Also, the **Saturday crafts market in San Angel** is huge. It is located in the Plaza San Jacinto and is open from about 9 a.m. to 6 p.m.

Although not markets, the **Fonart** shops offer a wide variety of *artesanía*. These crafts are always more expensive than their counterparts in the markets but they are almost always of higher quality. These shops are run by a government agency whose purpose is to promote Mexican arts and crafts and which operates stores throughout the republic. The crafts sold come from all parts of Mexico. There are two Fonart shops on Av.

Mexico City
Metropolitan Area

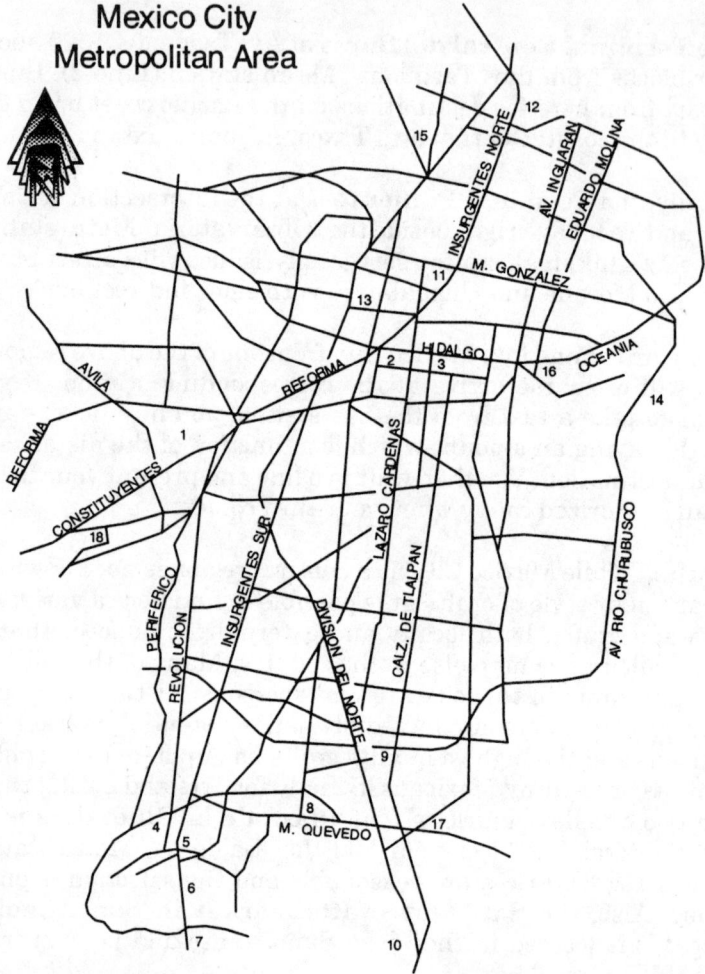

1 ~ Bosque Chapultepec	10 ~ Museo Anahuacalli
2 ~ Alameda	11 ~ Tlatelolco
3 ~ Zocalo	12 ~ Basilica de Guadalupe
4 ~ San Angel	13 ~ train station
5 ~ Copilco	14 ~ airport
6 ~ Ciudad Universitaria	15 ~ bus station–north
7 ~ Cuicuilco	16 ~ bus station–east
8 ~ Coyoacan	17 ~ bus station–south
9 ~ Museo Nacional de las Intervenciones	18 ~ bus station–west

Juárez south of the Alameda: at Juárez 89 and at Juárez 44 in the Museo Nacional de Arte e Industrias Populares. There is another shop at Londres 136 in the Zona Rosa. The shops are open 10 a.m. to 7 p.m., closed Sundays.

Sights

This will be a somewhat abbreviated look at the points of interest in Mexico City. Entire books have been written about this town and there is no point in my recapitulating them, especially since much of the pleasure of Mexico City is about what you discover in going from one sight to another. Use this section as the skeleton of your explorations in Mexico and flesh it out with things that spontaneously occur to you. Your trip will be more memorable for it. Fortunately for the traveler many of Mexico City's attractions occur in clusters. And that is the way this section will deal with them, cluster by cluster. Basically, the nuclei which interest us are the Alameda, the Zócalo and Chapultepec Park. The highlights of northern and southern Mexico City can't really be said to cluster, so we'll look at them one by one.

Before examining Mexico City's sights, let's get oriented. Downtown is dominated by roughly three geographic districts: Chapultepec Park on the west side of the center, the Zona Rosa immediately to the east of the park, and the Centro Historico, which includes the Alameda and the Zócalo, a little further east still. Running north-south through the middle of central Mexico and bisecting the entire city is the immensely long Av. Insurgentes. Insurgentes Norte passes by or near the train station, the northern bus station, and the Basílica de Guadalupe, while its southern extension (Insurgentes Sur) passes by the neighborhoods of San Angel and Coyoacán, the university, and the pyramid of Cuicuilco.

The other major thoroughfare of central Mexico City is the Paseo de la Reforma. Often compared to the Champs Élysées, this lovely street was built during the reign of Emperor Maximilian. Its length is marked by numerous statues and monuments commemorating Mexican heroes and events. The Paseo cuts through Chapultepec Park and the Zona Rosa, crosses Insurgentes, angles eastward to the Alameda, then turns north.

Alameda. Formerly the place where the Spanish Inquisition burned heretics, today the Alameda is a pleasant city park filled with paths, benches, monuments, fountains, and people. It is also conveniently located between the historic center of Mexico City, the Zócalo, to the east and the Zona Rosa/Chapultepec Park complex to the west. It is bounded on the south by Av. Juárez and on the north by Av. Hidalgo.

Opposite the west end of the park is the **Museo Mural Diego Rivera**, also called the **Museo de la Alameda**. This museum contains the remains of a Diego Rivera mural that formerly graced the Hotel del Prado. The hotel was virtually destroyed by the 1985 earthquake but the mural, entitled "Dream of a Sunday Afternoon in the Alameda," survived. The mural was moved to this building a couple of years after the quake. Rivera uses the Alameda as a stage for virtually all the personalities of Mexican history, the famous and infamous, hero and villain. Rivera himself is present, but as a child between his daughter and mother. While the mural contains the wonderful Mexican colors for which Rivera is celebrated, it mostly lacks the political commentary for which he is also famous.

Beside the mural museum is the **Pinacoteca Virreynal** (Vice-regal Art Museum) containing a collection of religious paintings from the colonial period. It is open Tues-Sun, 10 a.m. to 5 p.m. At Calle Balderas #71, one block west of the Alameda, is the **Instituto Nacional de Estadistica Geografia e Información** (National Institute of Statistics, Geography, and Information). In this government office you can buy topographic maps of any part of Mexico, which is really only useful if you plan on hiking or backpacking.

Opposite the south side of the Alameda at Av. Juárez 44 is the **Museo Nacional de Artes e Industrias Populares** (National Museum of Popular Arts and Industries). There is actually both a museum and a store here and both contain some of the finest examples of Mexican folk art to be found anywhere. It is not cheap, though. The museum is open Mon-Fri, 9 a.m. to 3 p.m., while the store is open Mon-Sun, 9 a.m. to 6 p.m.

At the far eastern end of the Alameda is the unmistakable, and unmissable, **Palacio de Bellas Artes** (Palace of Fine Arts).

Palacio de Bellas Artes

This extravagant building was designed by the Italian architect Adamo Boari and built of white Carrara marble. Begun in 1901, it was scheduled for completion in 1910. However, subsidence in Mexico City's soft subsoil and the Mexican Revolution delayed its inauguration until 1934.

With an art deco interior reflecting the style of the 1920s, the Palacio serves multiple purposes, housing government offices, a fine theater, and equally fine art collections. The spectacular theater with its Tiffany glass curtain is the site of numerous fine arts performances but is most famous as the home of the **Ballet Folklorico**. This dance troupe performs regional dances from throughout Mexico. There are several performances weekly.

The upper floors of the Palacio contain temporary and permanent art exhibits. More impressive than the exhibits are the spectacular murals which cover the walls and stairwells of these floors. All of Mexico's great muralists are represented by panels here: Diego Rivera, David Alfaro Siqueiros, José Clemente Orozco, and Rufino Tamayo. The art exhibits are open Tues-Sun, 10:30 a.m. to 6:30 p.m. The "Bellas Artes" Metro station (Line 2) is on Av. Hidalgo near the Palacio.

Mexico City -- Historic Center

1 ~ train s
2 ~ Plaza
3 ~ Alame
4 ~ Museo
    Pinaco
5 ~ Museo
    y Indu
6 ~ Palaci
7 ~ post o
8 ~ Museo
9 ~ Torre

1

MOSQUETA

MAGNOLIA

GUERRERO

REVOLUCION

23

EDISON

D C

22

21

INSURGENTES NORTE

REFORMA

HIDALGO

LA

4

BELL

JUA

DE

G MADRID

PASEO

JUAREZ

INDEPENDENC

AYUNTAMIENTO

VICT

2

A

ROMA

BALDERAS

REVILLAGIGEDO

MOYA

B

BALDERAS

SALTO
DE AGU

10 ~ Zocalo
11 ~ Cathedral
12 ~ Monte de Piedad
13 ~ Palacio Nacional
14 ~ Museo de las Culturas
15 ~ Templo Mayor
16 ~ Templo de la Santisima
17 ~ Suprema Corte de Justicia
18 ~ Museo de la Ciudad
19 ~ Secretaria de Educacion Publica
20 ~ Escuela Nacional Preparatoria

21 ~ Monumento a la Revolucion
      Museo Nacional de la Revolucion
22 ~ El Fronton Mexico
23 ~ Museo de San Carlos
A ~ Hotel Conde
B ~ Posada de Don Enrique
C ~ Hotel New York
D ~ Hotel Carlton
E ~ Hotel Hidalgo
F ~ Hotel La Avenida
G ~ Hotel Regente
■ ~ Metro station locations

adela

go Rivera
rnal
de Artes
lares
Artes

de Arte
ricano

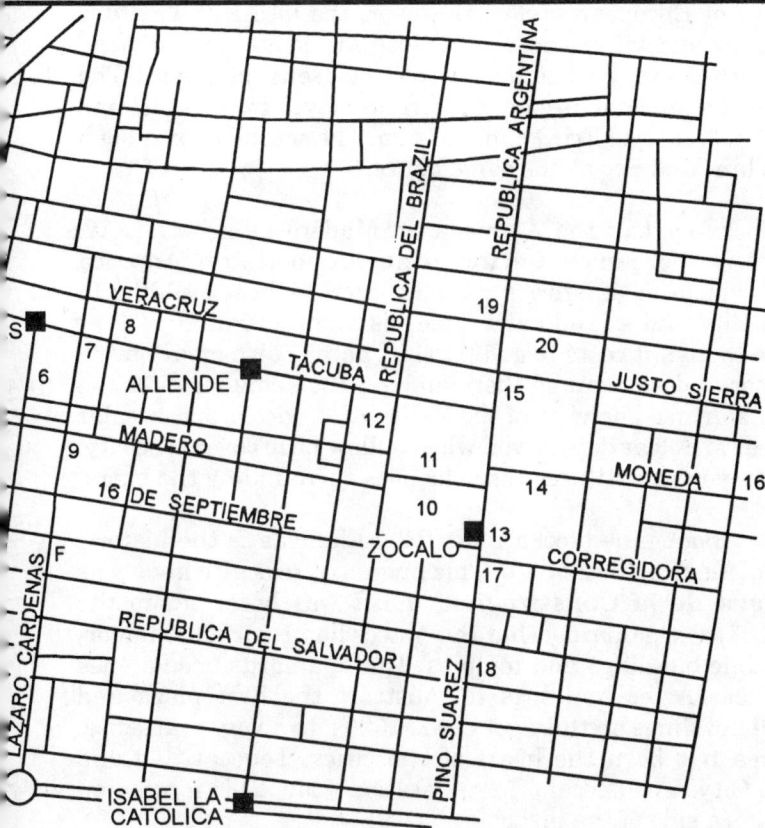

VERACRUZ
8
7
6
ALLENDE
TACUBA
MADERO
9
16 DE SEPTIEMBRE
12
11
10
ZOCALO
13
17
19
20
15
JUSTO SIERRA
14
MONEDA
16
CORREGIDORA
REPUBLICA DEL SALVADOR
18
LAZARO CARDENAS
F
REPUBLICA DEL BRAZIL
REPUBLICA ARGENTINA
PINO SUAREZ
ISABEL LA CATOLICA
S

Immediately behind the Palacio de Bellas Artes is the **Correo Mayor** (Main Post Office). This intricate and eclectic building was also designed by the Italian Adamo Boari and opened for business in 1907.

Just north of the post office on Tacuba is the **Museo Nacional de Arte.** Fronted by the statue "El Caballito," designed by Manuel Tolsa, this building contains a huge collection of Mexican art, mostly paintings, covering all periods of history: pre-Hispanic, colonial, independence, and modern. Most of it is imitative of European styles. However, the late-19th Century landscapes and village scenes by José María Velasco and the entire 20th Century collection give a strong sense of Mexico. The floors in the museum are open alternate days. The first floor is open Sun, Wed, and Fri, 9 a.m. to 7 p.m. The second floor is open Tues, Thur, and Sat at the same hours.

Two blocks east of the Alameda on Madero (which was Av. Juárez) is the **Torre Latino Americano** (Latin America Tower) which, at 42 stories, is the second highest building in Mexico City and a landmark. There is an observation deck at the top, though it costs to go up to it. There is also a bar on the 41st floor and you can go there and get the same view for the price of a drink. The view of the Valley of Mexico is spectacular on those rare clear days. Even when yellow haze covers the city, however, you can still see the volcanoes surrounding the basin.

Zócalo. About nine blocks east of the Alameda is the historic center of Mexico, the **Zócalo.** This huge square is also known as the **Plaza de la Constitución** and it was here, before the arrival of the Spaniards, that the Aztecs had their most important public buildings and temples. The Spaniards used stones from these Aztec buildings to construct the first plaza and colonial buildings on this spot in the 1520s. In a very real sense, this area has been the heart of two cities, Tenochtitlán and Mexico City. The "Zócalo" Metro station (Line 2) is located on the eastern side of the plaza.

On the north side of this huge plaza is the **Cathedral.** The first church on this site was begun only a few years after the Conquest. The present structure was begun in 1573 and its final additions were not completed until 1813. A mix of architectural

Cathedral and the Zocalo

styles were employed but the overall effect is one of immense severity. The interior was damaged by fire in 1967 and still shows the effects.

Next to the Cathedral is the parish church, **El Sagrario**. Originally built as a storage place for sacred objects and materials in the 18th Century, the church has intricate Churrigueresque facades which contrast with the rather plain exterior of the Cathedral.

Just west of the Cathedral is the **Monte de Piedad**, Mexico City's huge national pawn shop. It was founded in 1775 by the Count of Regla, a man made rich by silver mines in the state of Hidalgo. Inside you will find an amazing assortment of pawned items. The "Monte" is open daily except Sunday.

Opposite the east side of the Zócalo is the **Palacio Nacional** with its immense facade stretching the length of the plaza. This was originally the site of Moctezuma's house. Later, after razing the Aztec structure, Cortés built a palace here for himself. Most of the present building was constructed in the 18th Century and it currently houses several government offices, including that of the president, a small museum dedicated to Benito Juárez, and some wonderful murals by Diego Rivera. Access to the Juárez museum is through the northernmost gate. The museum consists of the room that he died in and some personal effects. It is open Tues-Fri, 9 a.m. to 6 p.m. and Sat-Sun, 10 a.m. to 2 p.m. Diego Rivera's murals are, however, the prime attraction here. To find them, go through the center gate. The paintings are located in the stairwell in the northwestern corner of the courtyard and on the walls around the first floor (not the ground floor). The series of murals depict Mexican history from an idyllic Native American past through the brutality of the conquest. Painted in the 1920s and 1930s, this is some of Rivera's best work.

Just around the corner from the Palacio Nacional on Calle Moneda is the **Museo de las Culturas** (Museum of the Cultures), which contains exhibits devoted to the art, anthropology, and customs of various non-Mexican cultures. Almost as interesting as the exhibits is the building which was constructed in 1567 and served as the "Casa de la Moneda," the mint. The museum is open Tues-Sat, 9 a.m. to 6 p.m., Sun, 9 a.m. to 4 p.m. Just north of the Palacio Nacional are the remains of the principal Aztec temple, the **Templo Mayor**. For many years this temple was thought to lie under the massive Cathedral but when excavations at the present site in 1978 uncovered an eight-ton, carved stone disk, that opinion changed. Excavations since that date have revealed the base of the main temple and several buildings around it. There are raised, wooden walkways which allow you to examine every part of the site from above. There is also a **museum** beside the Templo which displays some of the artifacts that have been found. The site is open Tues-Sun, 9 a.m. to 5 p.m.

A couple of blocks east on Calle Moneda from the Museo de las Culturas is the **Templo de la Santisima**. Built in the mid-18th Century, this church boasts one of the city's finest and most intricate Churrigueresque facades.

Immediately south of the Palacio Nacional on Av. Pino Suárez is the **Suprema Corte de Justicia** (Supreme Court), an otherwise unremarkable building save for the three mural panels inside painted by José Clemente Orozco.

Two blocks further south on Pino Suárez is the **Museo de la Ciudad** (City Museum). These fascinating exhibits trace the geological, anthropological, and political evolution of the Mexico City area. There are intriguing scale models of Tenochtitlán and the Valley of Mexico as well as old photographs, documents, and maps. The colonial building which houses the museum was built in the 1520s with further elaboration in the 18th Century. The museum is open Tues-Sun, 9:30 a.m. to 7:30 p.m. and is near the "Pino Suárez" Metro station (Lines 1 & 2).

If your appetite for murals is still undimmed then there are two sites north of the Plaza de la Constitución which merit your attention. The **Secretaría de Educación Pública** (Ministry of Public Education) is located three blocks north of the Cathedral on Av. Argentina. One of the finest and most farsighted public servants in Mexican history, Education Minister José Vasconcelos, commissioned Diego Rivera to paint the ministry's hallways. Between 1923 and 1928 Rivera covered 1,585 square meters of wall space with 239 mural panels. This constitutes the most extensive exhibit of Rivera's work in the world. The building is open Mon-Fri, 9:30 a.m. to 6 p.m.

About one block east of the Secretaría de Educación Pública at San Idelfonso 33 is the **Escuela Nacional Preparatoria** (National Preparatory School) with another set of fine murals, again commissioned by Vasconcelos, which includes the work of Rivera, Fernando Leal, Siqueiros, and others. But it is Orozco's work in the stairwell and around the upper floors that is the most impressive, passionate, and cynical of the lot. The building is open Mon-Fri, 9:30 a.m. to 6 p.m.

Paseo de la Reforma. Running at an oblique angle just west of the Alameda, the **Paseo de la Reforma** is a sight in itself. With 10 lanes of traffic, this is the chief artery in downtown Mexico City, passing through Chapultepec Park, the Zona Rosa, and the heart of the city's business district. Up and down its tree-lined length there are periodic traffic circles known as *glorietas* which are usually marked with a monument to some Mexican hero or idea. Among the entities so honored are Cuauhtémoc, Columbus, Quetzalcóatl, and Tetlepanquetzal. But the most striking monument is the golden Angel of Independence standing on top of a 50-meter marble column. *El Angel*

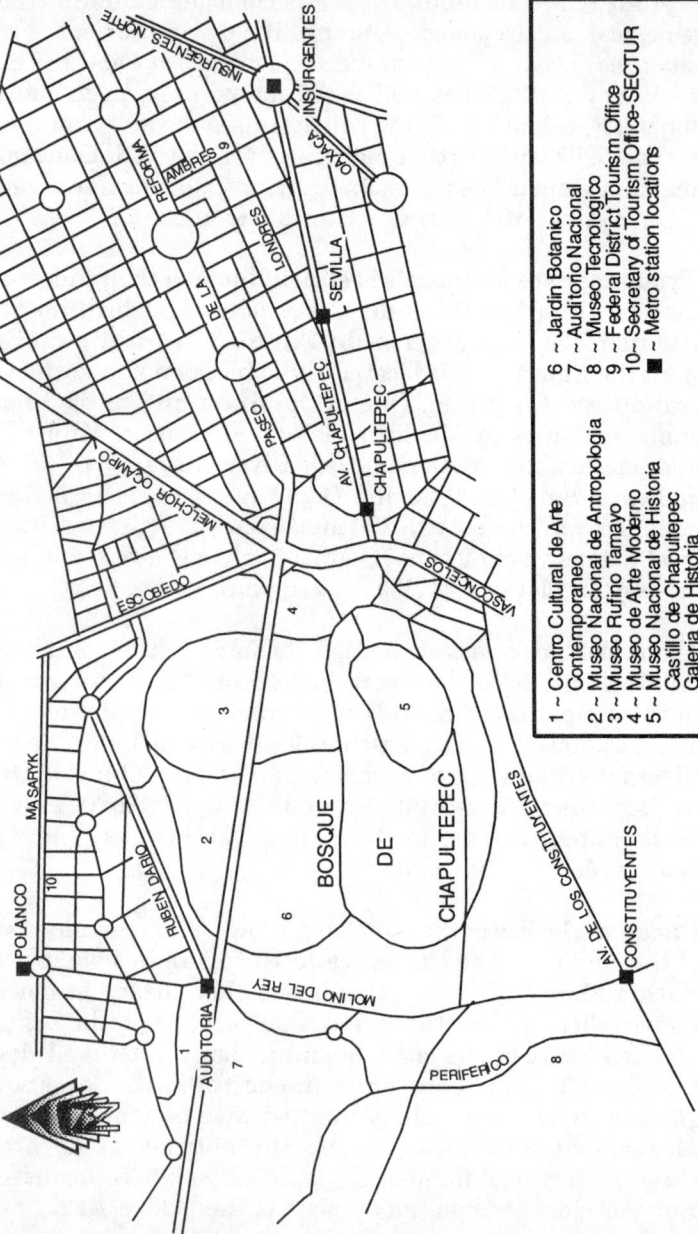

Mexico City --Chapultepec Park area

1 ~ Centro Cultural de Arte
    Contemporaneo
2 ~ Museo Nacional de Antropologia
3 ~ Museo Rufino Tamayo
4 ~ Museo de Arte Moderno
5 ~ Museo Nacional de Historia
    Castillo de Chapultepec
    Galeria de Historia

6 ~ Jardin Botanico
7 ~ Auditorio Nacional
8 ~ Museo Tecnologico
9 ~ Federal District Tourism Office
10~ Secretary of Tourism Office-SECTUR
■ ~ Metro station locations

marks the halfway point between the Alameda and Chapultepec Park and also marks the heart of the Zona Rosa.

About five blocks west of Reforma and almost exactly opposite the Alameda is the huge **Monumento a la Revolución** (Monument to the Revolution) located in the **Plaza de la República**. Back in the early 1900s Porfirio Díaz originally intended this to be the site for a new legislative building but the Revolution interrupted those plans and gave the Mexicans something to commemorate. Hence, the monument. The remains of several revolutionary heroes are contained in the base of the structure. Below the Monument is the little-visited but quite excellent **Museo Nacional de la Revolución**. The exhibits here try to express what life was like in Mexico at the turn of the century using dioramas and antiques. There are also photographs, documents, and artifacts which relate more directly to the Mexican Revolution itself. The museum is open Tues-Sun, 9 a.m. to 6 p.m. The monument is about three blocks south of the "Revolución" Metro station (Line 2).

On the north side of the Plaza de la República is **El Frontón Mexico** which is a jai-alai arena. Matches are played most evenings, though I've never figured out how to bet on the games. Two blocks east of the "Revolución" Metro station on Puente de Alvarado is the **Museo de San Carlos**. Housed in an 18th Century neoclassical building, this art museum contains mostly European art of the 17th and 18th centuries. The museum is open Tues-Sun, 10 a.m. to 5 p.m.

Chapultepec Park. The Bosque de Chapultepec is a 900-acre park located in the hectic heart of Mexico City. This tree-filled expanse is home to museums, a zoo, gardens, and monuments and it daily provides refuge for hundreds of thousands of Mexicans looking for green space in the megalopolis.

Getting to the park is easy. The Paseo de la Reforma passes east to west through the park and is plied by countless buses from all parts of the city. There are also three Metro stations on Chapultepec's borders: Auditorio (Line 7) on the north side, Constituyentes (Line 7) on the south, and Chapultepec (Line 1) on the east.

Aztec relic, part of a modern walkway in Chapultepec Park

There are three attractions in the sliver of the park north of Reforma and all are accessed via the Auditorio Metro station: the **Centro Cultural de Arte Contemporáneo** (Cultural Center of Contemporary Art), the **Museo Nacional de Antropología**, and the **Museo Rufino Tamayo**. The Centro Cultural hosts temporary and often very interesting art exhibits and boasts an excellent art bookstore. It is just northwest of the Metro station.

The jewel in the crown of Mexican museums and, by all accounts, one of the finest museums in the world is the Museo Nacional de Antropología or Anthropology Museum. Designed by Mexican architect Pedro Ramírez Vásquez and built in the 1960s, this museum contains essentially two floors of exhibits. The lower floor is devoted to pre-Hispanic civilizations and archeology while the upper floor contains ethnography exhibits covering the indigenous cultures existent in Mexico today. There is no way to see all this museum in one day and two days pushes me to exhaustion. Fortunately, each room is devoted to a particular culture or region (e.g., the Aztecs or Oaxaca) so you can, if your time is limited, concentrate your attention on those areas that especially interest you or to which you will be traveling. Also, your ticket allows you to leave and return to the museum during the day of purchase for no extra charge. The Anthropology Museum is open Tues-Sat, 9 a.m. to 7 p.m. and Sun, 10 a.m. to 6 p.m. Admission is free on Sunday.

As you enter the building the superb bookstore/giftshop is on the left and a room for temporary exhibits on the right. To the side of the bookstore is a checkroom where you can leave coats, bags, or whatever. Ahead and to the right is the ticket office and beside the office is a desk where guided tours in your native language can be arranged for a small fee. Opposite the ticket office is the entrance to the **Sala de Orientación** where a multimedia orientation presentation, in Spanish, takes place. Even if you don't speak Spanish, you learn something from the visual images. The rest of the ground floor consists of salons arranged around a central courtyard. Each room deals with a particular pre-Hispanic culture or area and the layout is such that the chronological order is counter-clockwise beginning with Room 1 to the right of the courtyard.

Room No.   Description
First Floor
 1   introduction to anthropology
 2   introduction to Mesoamerican civilization
 3   earliest evidence of humans in Mexico
 4   Pre-classic cultures: Tlaltilco, Cuicuilco
 5   Teotihuacán
 6   Toltec
 7   Aztecs/Mexica
 8   Oaxaca:Zapotec, Mixtec
 9   Gulf Coast of Mexico
10   Maya: Yucatán, Chiapas
11   Northern Mexico
12   Western Mexico: Colima, Michoacán, Nayarit

Second Floor
13   introduction to Mexican ethnography
14   Cora, Huichol: Jalisco and Nayarit
15   Tarascan/Purépecha: Michoacán
16   Otomí: Querétaro
17   Puebla
18   Zapotec, Mixtec: Oaxaca

19   Totonac, Huastec: Gulf Coast
20   Maya: Chiapas
21   Tarahumara, Yaqui: northern Mexico
22   Nahua: Veracruz, Hidalgo, Morelos, Tlaxcala, Mexico

Just east of the Anthropology Museum is the **Museo Rufino Tamayo**. The core of this modern art museum consists of the private collection of, and many pieces by, the Mexican artist Rufino Tamayo whose work was considerably less political and generally more abstract than that of Rivera, Siqueiros, or Orozco. Many of the artists represented are either American or European, among them Picasso, Henry Moore, Miro, Andy Warhol, De Kooning, and Francis Bacon. The museum is open Tues-Sun, 10 a.m. to 6 p.m.

The remainder of the sights in Chapultepec are to be found south of the Paseo de la Reforma. At the eastern end of the park are the **Museo de Arte Moderno**, the **Museo Nacional de Historia**, and the **Galeria de Historia**, all located near the "Chapultepec" Metro station. The Modern Art Museum contains contemporary Mexican and Latin American art including works by Frida Kahlo, Orozco, Rivera, José María Velasco, Siqueiros, and Remedios Varo. It is open Tues-Sun, 10 a.m. to 6 p.m.

Just southwest of the Art Museum is a rocky hill which from time immemorial has been called **Chapultepec**, meaning "Hill of the Grasshoppers." This spot served as a temporary refuge for the barbarian Aztecs when they were still living off bugs and carrion on Lake Texcoco and later as a summer resort for Aztec royalty after the tribe had come into its own. The building on top of the hill today is the **Castillo de Chapultepec** (Chapultepec Castle). It was built in the late 18th Century as a retreat for the Spanish Viceroy and in various incarnations served as palace, military school, warehouse, and now museum, the **Museo Nacional de Historia**. Although there are a few Aztec artifacts, most of the exhibits cover Mexico's colonial and independence periods. Many rooms contain period furniture and housewares from the times when the castle was occupied by Maximilian and Carlota. There are also murals by Orozco and Siqueiros, but the best are drawn by Juan O'Gorman. The museum is open Tues-Sun, 9 a.m. to 5 p.m.

On the road up to the Castillo de Chapultepec is the **Galeria de Historia**, also called the *caracol* because the path through the exhibits follows a snail-like spiral. The history portrayed by these dioramas and maps covers the period from independence through the revolution. It is open Tues-Sun, 9 a.m. to 5 p.m.

In the north central part of the park on the west side of Lago Antiguo (Old Lake) is the **zoo** and beside it the **Jardín Botánico** (Botanical Garden). Across Av. Molino del Rey from the zoo is the **Auditorio Nacional** where performance arts events frequently take place.

Going south on Molino del Rey leads to the "Constituyentes" Metro station and just northwest of this station are the *juegos mecanicos*, or what we would call an amusement park. Beside the amusement park is the **Museo Tecnológico** with a rather unimpressive display of science and technology exhibits. It is open Tues-Sun, 9 a.m. to 5 p.m. Finally, in the far southwestern corner of the park is the **Museo de Historia Natural**. The exhibits here offer a nice introduction to Mexico's natural history: geology, biology, the environment, and other natural sciences. The museum is open Tues-Sun, 10 a.m. to 5 p.m.

Northern Mexico City

There are few attractions north of the city's center but these few are worth mentioning. One is **Tlatelolco**, also called the **Plaza de las Tres Culturas** (Plaza of the Three Cultures), about two km north of the zócalo up Av. Lázaro Cárdenas. Here one can see three Mexican cultures represented by their architecture side by side: the foundations of the main temple of the Aztec city of Tlatelolco, the Spanish Church of Santiago, and assorted modern Mexican government buildings and housing projects.

Both Tlatelolco and Tenochtitlán were Aztec cities but they were ruled by essentially different clans. Different until one day in 1473 when Tenochtitlán forcibly annexed the other. Today, the ruins exposed in the excavation are all that remains of what must have been a huge pyramid/temple. What happened to part of that temple can be seen in the center of the plaza: the Church of Santiago, built in 1609. This church replaced an earlier

Franciscan monastery on the same site. Both were built with stone from the nearby Aztec temples.

In 1968 this plaza was the scene of a violent encounter between protesting students and government troops. That year Mexico was hosting the summer Olympic games and the government had been embarrassed by a series of student demonstrations against authoritarianism and corruption in the government. So on October 2 when unarmed protestors gathered at the plaza, government security forces moved to block the avenues of retreat and began firing into the crowd. Several hundred people were killed.

The best way to get to the Plaza of the Three Cultures is to go to the "Tlatelolco" Metro station (Line 3), go out to Av. Manuel González, turn right and then take another right on Lázaro Cárdenas.

Another point of interest on the north side is the **Basílica de Nuestra Señora de Guadalupe** (Basílica of Our Lady of Guadalupe). There are actually two churches and a bunch of chapels. The older of the two churches was built in 1533 and remodeled several times since then. Now, however, it is in disrepair and has been replaced by the modernistic new church which was completed in 1976.

The hoopla about this spot derives from its history. The hill behind the older church is Tepeyac Hill and it was on this hill that the Virgin appeared to the Indian, Juan Diego, in 1531. In his native tongue she told him to tell the bishop to construct a church on this site. Juan Diego told Bishop Zumarraga of the vision and the order but the priest did not believe him. Several days later the Virgin reappeared to Juan Diego and told him to pick the roses growing on the hill and to take them to the bishop as a sign. Diego gathered the roses, wrapped them in his cloak, and took them to Zumarraga. But when he opened his cloak instead of flowers there was an image of the dark-skinned Virgin which has since become Mexico's religious icon. Whether Zumarraga believed this event to be a miracle or whether he saw this merely as a way to make Catholicism more appealing to Mexico's indigenous people, we'll never know. Regardless, he ordered a church built on the site. Juan Diego's cloak hung in that church for hundreds of years and has been the objective of countless pilgrimages over the centuries. Today, the cloak hangs in the new church behind the altar and you can see it up close by riding a moving sidewalk beneath and behind the altar. To get to the Basílica take the subway to the "Basílica" station (Line 3) and walk six blocks east on Av. Montiel. Or get off the Metro at the "La Villa" station (Line 6) and walk straight north two blocks.

Southern Mexico City

What is today southern Mexico City evolved as separate towns and villages that were only in this century enveloped by the irresistible urban surge of Mexico City's growth. Although overwhelmed by the larger city's growth and changed from towns into neighborhoods, these communities retain many of their traditional characteristics which distinguish them from the surrounding urban sprawl. They are islands of charm in an often graceless sea.

San Angel is one such community. As recently as 1950 it was separate from the megalopolis but no longer. This suburb's origins lie far back in the colonial period and when you walk its cobbled streets surrounded by colonial mansions and churches it's easy to forget that you're still in the largest city in the world. Exploration of the area could begin at **Plaza San Jacinto**, a small, lovely square surrounded by old houses. Many of these houses have been converted into restaurants and stores. One of the more notable of these is the **Bazaar Sabado**, a high-quality but expensive Mexican crafts shop. The entire plaza becomes a crafts market on Saturdays when it fills up with artisans selling their wares. On the west side of the plaza is the **Iglesia de San Jacinto**, a lovely 16th Century church. On the north side of the plaza is the **Casa del Risco** which contains a rather eclectic museum focusing on colonial art and home furnishings. It is open Tues-Sun, 10 a.m. to 3 p.m.

One block east of Plaza San Jacinto on Av. Revolución is the **Plaza del Carmen** and facing it is the **Museo del Carmen**. Built in the early 17th Century, this building served formerly as a Carmelite monastery but serves today as a religious art museum. You can also see the mummies in the crypt–always a plus. More impressive than the art is the architecture, especially the building's colorful tiled domes and exuberant gardens. The museum is open Tues-Sun, 10 a.m. to 6 p.m.

Three blocks north of the museum on Av. Revolución is the **Museo de Arte Carrillo Gil**. This is a fine collection of contemporary Mexican and international art. Among the artists represented are Orozco, Rivera, Rodin, Picasso, Siqueiros, Villon, and others. The museum is open Tues-Sun, 11 a.m. to 7 p.m.

To get to San Angel, catch any bus or *colectivo* going south on Insurgentes which is labelled "San Angel,""Ciudad Universitaria," "CU," or "UNAM." All will go at least as far as the suburb. The nearest Metro station is "Quevedo" (Line 3) which is about three-quarters of a kilometer east of San Angel. The "Barranca del Muerto" Metro station (Line 7) is on Av. Revolución about one km north of the Museo de Arte Carrillo Gil. Taxis to San Angel from this point are cheap.

The archeological site of **Copilco** is just south of San Angel and on the east side of Av. Insurgentes Sur. This early village was inhabited from approximately 1500 B.C. to 400 B.C. and around 100 B.C. covered by a lava flow from the volcano Xitle. There is a small museum displaying some of the artifacts found in the excavations. It is open Tues-Sun, 10 a.m. to 5 p.m. The "Quevedo" Metro station is about three-quarters of a kilometer northeast of the site.

The **Ciudad Universitaria** (University City) is two kms south of San Angel on the east side of Av. Insurgentes Sur. Built over a period of just five years (1950-1955) this university, "Universidad Nacional Autonoma de Mexico" or "UNAM," represents a remarkable artistic, architectural, and engineering achievement. With almost 400,000 students, UNAM is the largest university in Latin America. It is also the oldest in the Western Hemisphere, having been chartered in 1551. The highlights on campus are the murals: Juan O'Gorman's mosaic on the main campus library building, David Alfaro Siqueiros' mosaic mural on the Rectory Tower, José Chávez Morado's glazed mosaic in the auditorium of the science building, and Rivera's stone mosaic on the wall of the Olympic Stadium (located on the other side of Insurgentes Sur from the campus). Buses marked "UNAM" or "Ciudad Universitaria" run south on Av. Insurgentes to the University City. The closest Metro station is "Copilco" (Line 3) at one km from the center of campus.

Four kilometers south of Ciudad Universitaria at the intersection of Av. Insurgentes Sur and the Periferico Sur is the archeological site of **Cuicuilco**. This was apparently the largest city in the Valley of Mexico in its time and was occupied at the time of the Xitle eruption. The resulting lava flow covered most of the site and the settlement was abandoned. Although archeologists have made some excavations, the only structure visible at the site is the circular pyramid which rises above the *pedregal* or lava flow. There is a small museum which displays artifacts from this and nearby sites. It is open Tues-Sun, 10 a.m. to 5 p.m. To get there take a bus south on Insurgentes marked "Villa Olímpica" or "V. Olímpica" (the Olympic Village is on the opposite side of Insurgentes Sur from Cuicuilco), take a cab (expensive), or go with a tour group. An alternative is to take the Metro to the southern part of the city and then catch a cab—much cheaper than a cab from downtown.

Coyoacán is, like San Angel, another colonial town that was finally absorbed by Mexico City this century. It remains quaint and picturesque but the air is often full of pollutants driven south from factories on the north side of the city. The neighborhood's zócalo is the **Plaza Hidalgo** which is pleasantly lively, especially on weekends. On the north side of the plaza is the **Casa de Cortés**, built by the chief conquistador himself and said to be the place where the last leader of the Aztecs, Cuauhtémoc, was tortured and killed. Appropriately, there are two Rivera murals in the building, one of which represents the torture of the Aztec. On the south side of the plaza is the 16th Century **Iglesia de San Juan Bautista** and just east of the square on Hidalgo is the **Museo de Culturas Populares**. A variety of temporary exhibits are housed here, all of which deal with Mexican popular culture. Its hours are variable but it is usually open Tues-Sun, 10 a.m. to 4 p.m.

About five blocks north of the plaza on Calle Londres is a bright blue building which houses the **Museo Frida Kahlo**. This was Kahlo's house and the house she shared with her husband,

Diego Rivera, from 1929 until her death in 1954. Rivera gave the house to the Mexican government in 1955 in memory of his wife. Although she lived in Rivera's shadow, Frida Kahlo was an exceptional Mexican artist whose work often contained an expression of the physical and emotional pain she suffered in her own life. In addition to polio, she suffered serious injuries in a car accident. Much of her short life was spent in wheel chairs or the hospital. The Frida Kahlo Museum is as much a gallery as museum. There are paintings, drawings, and statuary by artists such as Rivera, Klee, Kahlo, Orozco and others as well as fine examples of Mexican folk art and crafts. See, in particular, her absolutely wonderful Mexican kitchen. The museum is open Tues-Sun, 10 a.m. to 2 p.m. and 3 p.m. to 6 p.m.

Three blocks away at the corner of Viena and Morelos is the **Museo y Casa de Trotsky** (Museum and House of Trotsky). This fortified and forlorn building commemorates the final days of the famous Russian revolutionary. Exiled from the Soviet Union and under a death sentence from Stalin, Trotsky lived in Mexico from 1937 until his death in 1940. Much of his time was spent in this fortress. The first attempt on his life came on May 24, 1940, when a group of men, one of whom was the artist David Alfaro Siqueiros, fired several hundred rounds of ammunition into his house. Trotsky survived that attempt but not the one on August 20, 1940, when a trusted associate killed him with an icepick in Trotsky's study. Today, the house is a memorial and the study remains as it was on the day of Trotsky's assassination. It is open Tues-Fri, 10 a.m. to 2 p.m. and 3 p.m. to 5:30 p.m., Sat-Sun, 10 a.m. to 4 p.m.

On the eastern margin of Coyoacán is the **Museo Nacional de las Intervenciones** housed in the **Ex-Convento de Churubusco**. In 1847, this convent was the site of a valiant though doomed defensive stand by Mexican troops against the superior invading forces of the United States. Eventually the Mexicans ran out of ammunition and the convent was taken only after a hand-to-hand battle. It's appropriate then that this museum is dedicated to the history of foreign interventions in Mexican affairs. The exhibits concentrate on Mexican wars with Texas and the United States, but French and Spanish interventions are treated as well. It's an intriguing introduction to imperialism from the receiving end. The museum is located just north of

Calle 20 de Agosto about one-half kilometer northwest of the "General Anaya" Metro station (Line 2). It's about 1.5 km northeast of the Plaza Hidalgo in Coyoacán.

On the even more distant southeastern margin of Coyoacán is the **Museo Anahuacalli**. This striking and unusual museum was designed and built by Diego Rivera to house and display his collection of pre-Hispanic art and artifacts. The building, which sits on a rugged lava flow and is built of the same material, is loosely designed to represent an Aztec temple. The museum exhibits pieces from several Mexican cultures but has an especially excellent collection of work from Mexico's western cultures in Colima, Michoacán, and Nayarit. Anahuacalli is open Tues-Sun, 10 a.m. to 6 p.m. To get there take the subway to "Tasqueña" Metro station (Line 2). From here you can either take a taxi or make connections with the light rail train (*tren ligero*) and take this train to the "Xotepingo" station. The museum is about a half-kilometer southwest of the station. There are signs.

Finally, in the far southeastern corner of the Federal District is the suburb of **Xochimilco**, famous for its flower market and extensive canal system. One of the great traditions in Mexico City is a weekend family excursion to Xochimilco and a boat ride on the canals. The canals are actually the remains of a lake. Since before the time of the Aztecs the people of Xochimilco have built *chinampas* to increase the amount of land available to grow food. The *chinampas* begin as rafts of lake mud and reeds. Trees are planted around the periphery of the raft and food or flowers are grown in its fertile interior. The trees' roots quickly grow into the lake bottom, effectively anchoring the "raft" and over several decades sediments fill in beneath the structure. Soon it is no longer a raft but an island. For centuries this process has gone on in Xochimilco, so that now there the lake has been replaced by over 100 km of canals. You can do as Mexicans have done for 800 years–take a boat ride on the canals. To get a boat, go to the plaza and follow the signs which say "Embarcaderos." Prices are per boat per hour so the more people to share costs the better. Weekends are incredibly busy here while weekdays are very slow. Prices are supposed to be fixed but bargaining is possible on weekdays. Alas, the canals are quite polluted. Try to concentrate on the brightly decorated boats, the floating flower and taco stalls, and the history of Xochimilco rather than the deltas of trash accumulating everywhere.

To get to Xochimilco take the metro to "Tasqueña" Metro station (Line 2) and then take the light rail train (*tren ligero*) to its final stop, "Estación Xochimilco." Alternatively, at the Tasqueña station catch a bus marked "Xochimilco" running south on Calzada Tlalpan.

Fiestas

Although the city is host to many celebrations, there are three that stand out. One is **Diez y Seis de Septiembre** (16th of September). This is Mexico's Independence Day celebration. Every year at 11 p.m. on September 15 the president reads Miguel Hidalgo's *Grito de Dolores* to crowds which fill Mexico City's huge zócalo. There are also fireworks, music, food, and games which reach a climax the next day, September 16.

The other celebration is **El Día de Nuestra Señora de Guadalupe** (The Day of Our Lady of Guadalupe), specifically December 12. This is the official day of the holy pilgrimage to the Basílica of Guadalupe in honor of Mexico's patron saint. On this day thousands of pilgrims can be seen crawling on their knees across the stone plaza and church floor only to stop finally before the venerated cloak of Juan Diego with its image of the dark-skinned Virgin. There are other festivities–including music and parades–taking place during the week surrounding December 12.

Another important festival is **Día de Santiago** on July 25. Santiago, or Saint James, was the rallying cry of the conquistadors as they conquered Mexico. On the Sunday following the 25th there are dances and a market at the Plaza de las Tres Culturas and dances as well in Xochimilco.

Classes

The Instituto Mexicano Norteamericano offers classes in Spanish (all levels), Mexican history, and foreign language instruction. Contact:

Francisco Lozano or Susan Guzmán
Spanish, IMNRC
Hamburgo 115, Col. Juárez
06600 Mexico D.F., Mexico

Another institution which offers classes in Spanish language
and in Mexican and Latin American culture is Universidad
Iberoamericana. Contact:

Mtra. Esperanza Wilson
Intl. Div., Foreign Programs
Universidad Iberoamericana
Prolongación Paseo de la Reforma No. 880
Col. Lomas de Santa Fe, Del. A. Obregón
01210 Mexico DF, Mexico

Climate

At an elevation of over 2,200 m (7,000 ft), Mexico City enjoys a
mild climate year round with temperatures rarely exceeding 29°
C (85°F) in the summer or falling below 4°C (40°F) in the winter.
May to October constitutes the rainy season when afternoon
thunderstorms are likely most days. Pollution is at its worst
during the winter, when thermal inversions trap contaminant-
rich air in the Valley of Mexico. The almost daily showers during
summer have a cleansing effect on the atmosphere.

Excursions

The town of **Valle de Bravo** is 153 km west of Mexico City on
Hwy 15. Extremely crowded on weekends when the wealthy of
Mexico City and Toluca retreat to their country houses here,
this picturesque village seems almost deserted during the week.
Valle de Bravo is a town of red-tiled roofs and cobblestone
streets built on the sloping edge of a man-made lake. Pine clad
hills surround the town and a cobalt-blue sky overhangs it. The
lake and the countryside which surrounds it offer numerous
recreational opportunities such as boating, sailing, wind surf-
ing, hiking, hang-gliding, camping, and swimming. This area is

also part of the **Monarch Butterfly Sanctuary**. Several rivers and waterfalls around the town offer wonderful backpacking and camping possibilities.

While the town has several hotels, rooms are scarce or non-existent on weekends. Also, because this is a resort area, prices are higher than the average in Mexico. Sunday is market day when Otomí, Nahua, and Mazahua Indians from neighboring villages bring their products to town to sell. To get to Valle de Bravo, catch a bus at the Terminal de Autobuses de Poniente in Mexico City. The trip takes three hours.

South of Mexico City on the road to Acapulco is the city of **Cuernavaca**, the capital of the state of Morelos. Since the time of the Aztecs Cuernavaca has served as a retreat for the wealthy and powerful. Moctezuma had a house here as did Cortés. They were followed by the silver millionaire José de la Borda whose mansion and gardens were later appropriated by the Emperor Maximilian and Carlota. Cuernavaca can claim with more justification than most the title "City of Eternal Spring." Its year-round temperate climate and showy lavender jacarandas and fuchsia bougainvilleas give it the look and feel of a tropical garden. Or **would**, were it not for the environment-destroying urban and industrial growth which has overtaken the city in the last decade. Only 90 minutes from Mexico City by modern highway, Cuernavaca has succumbed to businesses and residents eager to escape the capital's out-of-control growth. So, they've transferred a smaller version of that growth to this formerly idyllic town.

Despite this increasing congestion, Cuernavaca is still an interesting and pleasant destination for a day trip from Mexico City. Most of the city's attractions are within walking distance of the zócalo, the **Plaza de Armas**. Just east of the plaza is the **Museo de Cuauhnahuac**, also known as the **Palacio de Cortés**. Built by Cortés in the 1520s, this building today serves as a museum dedicated to the pre-Hispanic Indian cultures of Mexico, including the Tlahuica who have inhabited this area since before the Aztecs. The highlight of the museum is a 1930 Diego Rivera mural on the upper floor which chronicles the history of the region from the conquest to the revolution. The museum is open Tues-Sun, 9:30 a.m. to 7 p.m.

Just south of the museum is the **Plaza de las Artesanías** (Handicrafts Plaza) where vendors sell arts and crafts from around the state. Two blocks west of the zócalo is the **Cathedral**. Begun by the Franciscans in 1529, this fortress-like church has a surprisingly delicate, though spare, gold and white interior. The remains of 16th Century murals decorate some walls.

Across Av. Morelos from the Cathedral is the **Jardín Borda** (Borda Garden). This garden and mansion were built by the silver millionaire José de la Borda in the 18th Century. Later, this place served as a residence for Maximilian and Carlota. Nowadays the gardens are rather run down.

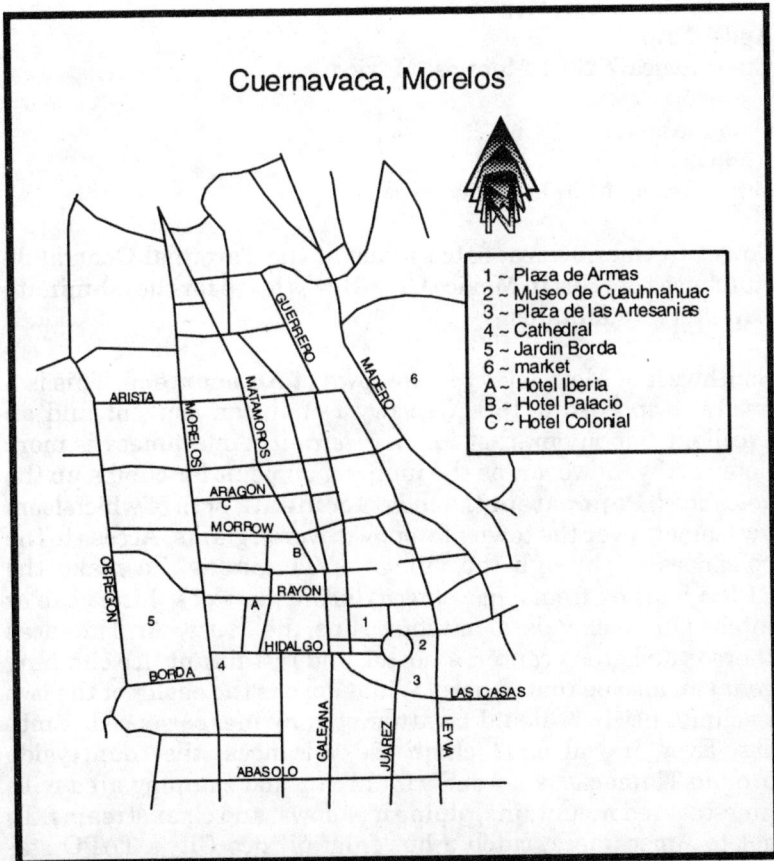

Cuernavaca, Morelos

1 ~ Plaza de Armas
2 ~ Museo de Cuauhnahuac
3 ~ Plaza de las Artesanias
4 ~ Cathedral
5 ~ Jardin Borda
6 ~ market
A ~ Hotel Iberia
B ~ Hotel Palacio
C ~ Hotel Colonial

The **state tourism office** is at Morelos Sur 802, about eight blocks south of the Jardín Borda. This is the place to get maps and information about tours and language schools.

Cuernavaca is popular with North American retirees and language students. The city probably has ten Spanish language schools, several of which offer other courses on Mexican culture, history, and politics. Some of the most popular schools are:

Cuauhnahuac
Apdo. Postal 5-26
Cuernavaca, 62051 Morelos, Mexico

I.D.E.L.
Moises Cano, Director
Apdo. 1271
Cuernavaca, 62001 Morelos, Mexico

Cemanahuac
Apdo. 21-C
Cuernavaca, Morelos, Mexico

To get to Cuernavaca, catch a bus at the Terminal Central de Autobuses del Sur in Mexico City. Buses leave for the 90-minute trip every 10 minutes.

Southwest of Mexico City is the town of **Amecameca**. This is a lovely town with a 16th Century Dominican convent and an excellent Sunday market full of *artesanía*. Amecameca is more noteworthy, however, as the jumping off point for climbs up the volcanoes, **Popocatépetl** and **Iztaccíhuatl**, both of which loom awesomely over the town like snow-covered giants. Access to the volcanoes is through the village of **Tlamacas**. To make the 21-km journey from Amecameca during the week, hire a cab or hitch. On weekends a minibus runs the route. At Tlamacas there is a visitor's center, a hostel, and restaurant. Ice climbing gear can also be rented here. While Popo is the easier of the two to climb, neither should be attempted by inexperienced climbers. Even if you don't climb the volcanoes, the countryside around Tlamacas is a wonderful hiking and camping area with pine-covered mountains, alpine meadows, and clear streams. To get to Amecameca, catch a bus from Mexico City's TAPO station. Buses leave about every two hours for the two-hour trip. Another easy and fascinating excursion is to the archeological site of **Teotihuacán**, the most visited such site in the country. The name, "Teotihuacán," was given this place by the Aztecs and means, "the place where men became gods." Its original name and the origins of the people who built and inhabited it are lost in antiquity for the city had been abandoned for 600 years before the Aztecs first saw it. Teotihuacán was the greatest city in the pre-Hispanic history of Mesoamerica. At the height of its power the city had a population of 200,000 people, covered an area of 156 square kilometers, and influenced other cultures from Guatemala in the south to the present-day state of Sinaloa in the northwest. Settlement at the site spanned over 1,000 years, from around 600 B.C. to 700 A.D., but the development of the city as a ceremonial center began in earnest around 100 B.C. with the construction of the Pyramids of the Sun and the Moon.

The growth of Teotihuacán and the spread of its influence throughout Mexico continued unabated from that point until

Teotihuacan, Mexico

1 ~ La Ciudadela
    Templo de Quetzalcoatl
2 ~ Pyramid of the Sun
3 ~ Pyramid of the Moon
4 ~ Plaza de la Luna
5 ~ Palacio del Quetzalpapalotl
6 ~ Tepantitla
7 ~ Tetitla

about 650 A.D. This growth was conditioned upon the proximity of productive and strategic local resources: fertile land, forests, abundant water, and obsidian. While the former three resources were used by the population to satisfy their immediate consumption needs, the latter, obsidian, was extremely valuable as an item of trade. Lacking metals, the Mesoamericans depended on stone, wood, and bone for all their tools and weapons. And nothing could hold a sharper edge than obsidian. By controlling a large part of the trade in this commodity, Teotihuacán assured for itself wealth and power. Beginning in the 7th Century, however, drought, the exhaustion of local resources, or a combination of the two, led to the collapse of the Teotihuacán culture. By 700 A.D. the city had been abandoned.

Even in death the city continued to influence at least the mythologies of subsequent cultures. The Aztecs considered the city holy and conducted regular ceremonial pilgrimages to the ruins. Because Teotihuacán was not inhabited at the time of the Spaniards' arrival, it was spared the destruction which they visited upon every other "profane" site they encountered.

Today, the site stands in the middle of barren terrain, probably made barren by the Teotihuacanos themselves. The bus drops you off in the parking lot beside the Unidad Cultural where there is a restaurant, several small shops, and a forgettable museum. Just east of the parking area is the **Calle de los Muertos**, a roughly north-south street which was the main axis of the ceremonial heart of the ancient city. Now only two km long, the Street of the Dead originally ran for four km.

On the east side of the Calle de los Muertos opposite the Unidad Cultural is **La Ciudadela**, the Citadel. This large sunken quadrangle appears to have been an administrative and ceremonial center for the city. On one side of the square is the **Templo de Quetzalcóatl** which is impressively decorated with hundreds of heads of Quetzalcóatl, the plumed serpent, and Tlaloc, the rain god.

North of the Ciudadela and two-thirds of the way up the Calle de los Muertos is the unmistakable **Pirámide del Sol** (Pyramid of the Sun). This structure dominates the site and is the second largest pyramid in Mexico, second only to that at Cholula. It was built around 100 A.D. on top of an even older temple. In 1971 a natural cave was discovered beneath the pyramid and this is undoubtedly the reason why the structure was located where it was. Caves were very important in Mexican religion and cosmology and examinations of this cave show that it was used for ceremonial purposes. Unfortunately, it is closed to the public.

At its north end the Calle de los Muertos terminates in the **Pirámide de la Luna** (Pyramid of the Moon). This structure is smaller and was built later than the Pyramid of the Sun. It also seems more elegant than the larger pyramid and offers a great view of the site from its summit. The Pyramid of the Moon is fronted by a nicely laid-out square, the **Plaza de la Luna**. On the west side of this plaza is the **Palacio del Quetzalpapálotl** (Palace of the Quetzal Butterfly). This well-restored structure appears to have been a residence for either priests or nobility. Its walls and columns are decorated with representations of birds and butterflies. In some of the chambers of the palace the remains of fading frescos survive.

The **Palacio de los Jaguares** and the **Templo de las Conchas** are beside and partially beneath the Palacio. Both were apparently residences and today contain some excellent fresco remnants.

One-third of a kilometer east of the Pyramid of the Sun is the residential structure known as **Tepantitla**. This building contains the remains of the famous mural representing the Teotihuacanos' heaven, a reproduction of which is in the Museum of Anthropology in Mexico City. Other frescos can be found at **Tetitla** about one km northwest of the Unidad Cultural.

Second class buses go directly to Teotihuacán from the Terminal del Norte in Mexico City. They leave every half hour starting at 6 a.m. There are also tours to the site organized by Panoramas Universales, located on the 23rd floor of the Latin American Tower in Mexico City (658-74-76). The archeological site is open Tues-Sun, 8 a.m. to 5 p.m.

Another archeological site within easy excursion distance of Mexico City is **Tula**, located three km from the town of Tula de Allende. The ruins here are not nearly as spectacular as those at Teotihuacán but the culture they represent had an influence in Mesoamerica almost as profound. Tula was built by the Toltecs and served as their capital from about 950 to 1150 A.D. The Toltecs were a semi-barbaric Chichimec tribe who migrated into the Valley of Mexico around the late 9th Century. After several other locations, the tribe settled on Tula for their capital.

The precise history of the Toltecs is confused by myths and legends. What is known is that the first leader of the tribe was Mixcóatl. He was later assassinated by his own brother but survived by his son, Topiltzin. Topiltzin was raised by his maternal grandparents far to the south and as he grew he became a priest of the god, Quetzalcóatl. Later, Topiltzin avenged his father's death, assumed the leadership of the Toltecs, and founded Tula. He became known by the name of the god he served, Quetzalcóatl, and preferred science and art to war and sacrifice. Eventually, he and his followers were driven out of the city by a militaristic faction devoted to the god of war, Tezcatlipoca. Topiltzin-Quetzalcóatl, depending on which legend you believe, either ascended into heaven and became Venus or sailed into the east on a raft. He also vowed to return and reclaim his kingdom. It was this vow that Moctezuma would remember when Cortés appeared.

Under the leadership of the militarists the Toltec empire expanded rapidly. But by the mid-12th Century a severe drought and civil war destroyed the city as a political power. The city was finally abandoned in the early 13th Century.

Today at the site there is a small but good **museum** beside the parking lot. Most of the excavated and restored structures are on top of a hill, which commands an excellent view of the surrounding countryside. The most impressive building at Tula is **Pyramid B**, also known as the **Templo de Tlahuizcalpantecuhtli** (Temple of the Morning Star). On the north side of the pyramid is the **Coatepantli** or Serpent Wall which is decorated with snakes devouring human skeletons. On top of the pyramid are four 4.5-m tall **Atlantes** representing stylized warriors. These, along with the columns behind them, once supported the temple roof. Immediately west of the pyramid is the **Palacio Quemada** (Burned Palace), which contains three patios. There are several other structures at the site, among them two ball courts, and many unexcavated mounds. None of the rest, however, are very intriguing.

Buses run to Tula from Mexico City, leaving every 20 minutes from the Terminal Central de Autobuses del Norte. The company is Autotransportes Valle del Mezquital and the bus drops you in the town of Tula de Allende. From here it is a three km walk or taxi ride to the ruins.

Chapter 3

Routes West &
Northwest of Mexico City

The train from Mexico City to the state of Michoacán departs at dusk from the most polluted city in the world, passing through neighborhoods the color of mud and rust, where the occasional living plant stands out like a juggler at a funeral. As darkness falls, a curtain on catastrophe, the train climbs out of the Valley of Mexico and rocks the traveler gently to sleep.

By dawn you're in Michoacán, a land of forested hills and waterfalls, where indigenous, colonial, and modern Mexico blend to form a rich cultural mix. It's a place where Indian towns dot the fertile valleys and crowd the shores of fish-rich lakes, where artisans transform wood, clay, and copper into works of art and utility. The train brings the wounded visitor here to heal in the garden state of Michoacán.

Train To Michoacán

The state of Michoacán is one of the very special areas of Mexico, a place where striking natural beauty combines with vibrant Indian and Mexican culture. Lakes, waterfalls, and forested hills form a lovely backdrop for numerous farming and fishing villages populated by Purepechan Indians. The Purépecha, also called Tarascans by the Spanish, are the descendants of a civilization that was never subjugated by the Aztecs despite the close proximity of the Valley of Mexico. On one occasion Moctezuma formed a great army and sent it west against the Purépecha. When the Purépecha force came within sight of their foes, they put a large quantity of food and drink on the ground and fled. The Aztecs started to give chase but stopped to consume the food. Later, after the Aztecs were stuperous from overconsumption, the Purépecha attacked and destroyed most of the Aztec army.

Rail Routes West and Northwest
of Mexico City

San Diego
Calexico
Tijuana
Mexicali

Puerto Peñasco
Tucson
Nogales
Nogales
Caborca
Benjamin Hill
SONORA
Hermosillo

Santa Rosalia
Guaymas
Empalme
CHIHUAHUA
Cd. Obregon
Navojoa
Alamos
Los Mochis
Sufragio
Topolobampo

La Paz
Culiacan
DURANGO
Durango

Mazatlan
ZACATECAS
AGUASCALIENTES

San Blas
Tepic
Guadalajara
JALISCO
GUANAJUATO
Cd. Guzman
Acambaro
Tula
Manzanillo
Colima
Morelia
Uruapan
Patzcuaro
Mexico City
COLIMA
Toluca
MICHOACAN
Cuernavaca
Lazaro Cardenas

~ train routes
~ ferry routes

The Purepechan confederation did not fare so well when confronted by the Spanish. Although the natives repelled the first Spanish invasion in 1522, a 1529 campaign led by the hated Nuño Beltran de Guzmán reduced much of the population to corpses or slaves. In his obsession with finding gold, this conquistador burned alive the Purepechan king, Tangaxoan. Soon after the conquest of the region, the Spanish crown sent Bishop Vasco de Quiroga to the Tarascans, both to Christianize the natives and to try to lessen their hatred of the Europeans. If Quiroga was unable to get the Indians to trust all Spaniards, he was at least able to get them to love and respect him.

The Bishop knew that the only thing that could keep the Tarascans from dying at hard labor in mines or on plantations would be skill as artisans. Fortunately, the people had a long history as craftspersons. It only remained for Quiroga to direct them into crafts in demand by the Spanish. Not only did he help in the selection of crafts, he also encouraged villages to specialize in the production of one commodity. This specialization resulted in higher quality products and allowed the producers to control better prices and quantity.

The rich heritage of crafts production and specialization that Quiroga encouraged over 450 years ago continues in Michoacán today. Certain towns are still noted for the production of certain crafts, among them: Santa Clara del Cobre for hammered copperware, Paracho for high quality guitars, Quiroga for leather goods, Tzintzuntzan for hand painted ceramics, and Pátzcuaro for lacquered boxes and trays.

The train leaves Mexico City and travels west, climbing over the pine-covered mountains that rim the Valley of Mexico. The route enters the state of Mexico and, at the capital city of Toluca, turns northwest. It cuts across a corner of Michoacán and enters southern Guanajuato state. At the town of Acámbaro the route turns southwest, skirts the eastern corner of Lake Cuitzeo, and re-enters the rolling terrain of northern Michoacán. The train reaches the state capital of Morelia and continues west through forested river valleys and past mist-shrouded corn fields to the Indian town of Pátzcuaro. West of Pátzcuaro the train begins its descent from the cool highlands to the subtropics, passing avocado and citrus groves as it ap-

proaches Uruapan. At Uruapan the route turns south and
enters a broad, well watered valley. The terrain quickly changes
to a drier, mountainous landscape through which the track
winds. As it approaches the coast the train enters the valley of
the Río Balsas and remains there until it reaches the coastal
port of Lázaro Cárdenas.

Train Services. Trains 31 and 32 ("Purépecha") connect Mexico City with Toluca, Acámbaro, Morelia, Pátzcuaro, Uruapan,
and Lázaro Cárdenas. This train has both special first class and
second class.

	Train 31		Train 32		1st.cl. Reserved	2nd.cl. Coach
Lv.	9:00 PM	Mexico City	7:30 AM	Ar.		
	11:10 PM	Toluca	5:05 AM		$ 3.03	0.61
	3:25 AM(+1)	Acámbaro	0:35 AM(+1)		8.65	2.39
	5:20 AM	Morelia	10:40 PM		11.23	3.10
	6:45 AM	Pátzcuaro	9:15 PM		13.19	3.65
	9:00 AM	Uruapan	6:10 PM		15.45	4.29
Ar.	4:00 PM	Lázaro Cárdenas	12:00 PM	Lv.	24.26	6.71

Toluca

At almost 2,800 m elevation, Toluca is the highest state capital
in Mexico. It is also a big, busy, industrialized city. The only
thing which recommends this city to the traveler is the huge
Friday *tianguis* (Indian market) with, among many other
things, crafts from nearby Nahua and Mazahua villages. Acco-
modations are very difficult to find on Thursday evenings.

Acámbaro

There is relatively little to see or do in this pleasant town.

Morelia

Despite a population of around 400,000, Morelia has managed
to remain charming and relaxed. Founded in 1541 by the first
viceroy of New Spain, Antonio de Mendoza, the city was originally called Valladolid. In 1828, seven years after the conclusion

Morelia, Michoacan

1 ~ bus station
2 ~ Plaza de Armas
3 ~ aqueduct
4 ~ Bosque Cuauhtemoc
5 ~ Museo de Arte Contemporaneo
6 ~ Palacio de Justicia
7 ~ Museo Michoacano
8 ~ Palacio Municipal
9 ~ Museo Casa Natal de Morelos
10~ Museo de Morelos
11~ Cathedral
12~ Casa de las Artesanias
     Iglesia de San Francisco
13~ Palacio Federal
     post office
14~ Palacio de Gobierno
15~ Colegio de San Nicolas
16~ Palacio Clavijero
     tourist office
     Mercado de Dulces
17~ Casa de la Cultura
A ~ Hotel Mintzicuri
B ~ Hotel Concordia
C ~ Posada Don Vasco
D ~ Hotel Casino

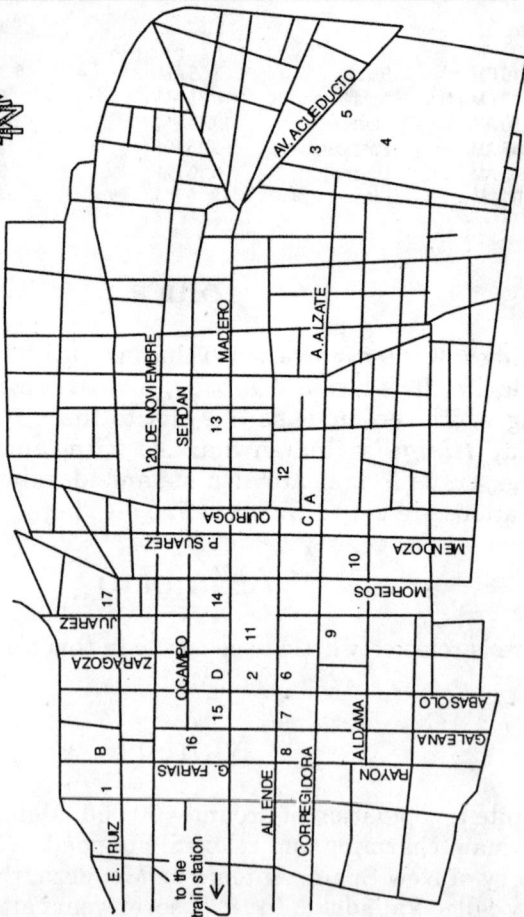

of the War of Independence, the name of the city was changed to Morelia in honor of the city's most famous son and hero of the independence struggle, José María Morelos y Pavón.

The modern city's center, the zócalo, remains a colonial master-piece with 16th and 17th Century homes, churches, and government buildings, all constructed of pink volcanic rock. Sometimes it is hard to tell colonial from modern buildings because federal law mandates that all new construction in the city conform to colonial architectural style.

Getting Around. The bus station is within walking distance of the zócalo, at the corner of Eduardo Ruíz and Gómez Farías. It is too far, however, to walk from the train station which is southwest of the main plaza. It is best to take a cab ($1 to $2) or share a minivan ($.50).

Sights. While the visitor to Morelia does not have to stray far from the **zócalo** (also called **Plaza de Armas** and **Plaza de los Martires**) to see most of the places of interest here, there are several important exceptions. A ruined **aqueduct** built in 1788 and consisting of 253 arches is about 13 blocks east of the Plaza de Armas. The two-km-long structure is an impressive sight, especially at night when it is lit by spotlights.

Just south of the aqueduct, **Bosque Cuauhtémoc** (Cuauhtémoc Forest) is a nice place to picnic and also contains the **Museo de Arte Contemporáneo** (Contemporary Art Museum) at its north end on Av. Acueducto No. 18 and an interesting display of orchids in the **Orquidiario** at the southern end of the park. Finally, a rather nice Mexican zoo can be found in **Parque Juárez**, a two-km walk south of the zócalo along Galeana.

Most of the remainder of Morelia's sights are found in the vicinity of the Plaza de Armas. Immediately south and west of the zócalo along Allende are, from east to west, the **Palacio de Justicia** (Palace of Justice), the **Museo Michoacano** (Michoacán Museum), and the **Palacio Municipal** (Municipal Palace). This latter building is where Miguel Hidalgo published his independence decree. The Michoacán Museum, open Mon-Sat from 9 a.m. to 7 p.m. and Sun 9 a.m. to 3 p.m., has a nice collection of pre-Hispanic artifacts, good regional natural science displays, and paintings dating from the colonial through the modern era. It also contains exhibits on Mexican history, especially the French and United States interventions, and a fine mural by Alfredo Zalce. The baroque 16th Century Palace of Justice is notable for a powerful courtyard mural by Agustín Cárdenas. There are two museums in town dedicated to the patriot Morelos. The **Museo Casa Natal de Morelos** (Morelos Birthplace Museum) is located one block south of the zócalo on Corregidora. It has a rather small display of Morelos memorabilia. A more comprehensive exhibit can be found in Morelos' former house, now the **Museo de Morelos** (Morelos Museum), which is just around the corner from his birthplace. This museum contains an extensive collection of the Mexican leader's personal effects as well as historical documents relating to his military and political activities.

Immediately east of the main plaza is the **Cathedral** with its twin 70-meter towers. Constructed in the 17th and 18th Centuries, this structure is a mixture of architectural styles with baroque predominating. Inside the Cathedral is probably the building's most interesting feature–a statue called "El Cristo de la Sacristia." This 16th Century sculpture is made of dried maize paste and topped by a gold crown donated by Spain's King Philip II (1556-98).

Three blocks east of the Cathedral at the end of Avenida Valladolid is the former convent of the Church of San Francisco which today is the **Casa de las Artesanías** (House of Handicrafts). Arranged by region, the arts and crafts displayed inside come from all over the state as well as all over Mexico. While the crafts for sale here are fairly expensive, the displays are very informative for the visitor to Mexico.

Immediately behind the Casa de las Artesanías is the **Iglesia de San Francisco** (Church of San Francisco). Built in the 16th Century, this church is one of the oldest in the city. One block north of the Casa de las Artesanías on Madero is the **Palacio Federal** (Federal Building) which houses the telegraph and post offices. West of the Federal Building and almost opposite the Cathedral is **Palacio de Gobierno** (Government House). Built in 1732 this building has a small collection of paintings and another historical mural by the Michoacán artist, Alfredo Zalce.

Two blocks west of the Cathedral at the corner of Avenida Madero Poniente and Nigromante is the **Colegio de San Nicolás**. This school was founded by Vasco de Quiroga in Pátzcuaro in 1540 but the main school was moved to Morelia in 1580, which is the date of this building's construction. The structure was remodeled in the 19th Century. The Colegio is the oldest continuously operating school of higher education in Latin America. It also offers summer classes for foreign students.

Opposite and a little north of the Colegio on Nigromante is the **Palacio Clavijero**. This impressive 17th Century baroque building was originally a Jesuit school. However, over the years the structure has served as a jail, Chamber of Deputies, and conference center. Today the Palacio houses several government offices including that of the state tourism department, a library, and an exhibit hall for art displays. Behind the building is the **Mercado de Dulces** (Candy Market). Here you will find all types, colors, and sizes of candies–so many sweets, so little time.

Three blocks due north of the Cathedral in the ex-Convento del Carmen is the **Casa de la Cultura** (House of Culture). Here there is a nice collection of masks from different regions of Mexico, some pre-Columbian artifacts, as well as a bunch of crucifixes and religious statuary.

Fiestas. May 18 is the anniversary of the founding of the city and the International Organ Festival. September 30 is the celebration of the birthdate of José María Morelos y Pavón.

Classes. Centro Mexicano Internacional offers both university affiliated programs in language, social sciences, and fine arts and unaffiliated intensive Spanish classes. Contact:

Mexico Programs
2626 North Mesa, Suite 355
El Paso, Tx 79902
1-800-426-1349

Climate. At 1,951 meters (5,850 feet) elevation Morelia is pleasantly mild. While winter nights can be quite cold, it rarely freezes. The rainy season is from May to September with the greatest amounts of rain in July and August.

Excursions. About 14 km southeast of Morelia is the spa **Cointzio** where a 37°C hot spring feeds two swimming pools and a wading pool. An admission fee is charged and the spa is quite crowded on weekends and holidays. Second class buses run from the bus station.

Pátzcuaro

Pátzcuaro is 67 km (40 mi) west of Morelia and has about 40,000 inhabitants. The town is located five km south of Lake Pátzcuaro. The site was originally settled about 1320 AD by the Purépecha chief, Curatame. According to their own oral history, the Purépecha accompanied the Aztecs on their migration toward the Valley of Mexico. At the command of their chief god, the Purépecha stopped to bathe in Lake Pátzcuaro. The Aztecs then gathered up their companions' clothes and possessions and left. This is a pretty unlikely story since the Aztecs and Purépecha speak totally different languages.

Whatever their origins, the Purépecha came to dominate all of northern Michoacán and parts of modern Jalisco and Guanajuato. The native economy was based on fishing and agriculture. With the death of King Tariacari in 1400 the Purépecha kingdom was divided in thirds with regional capitals in Pátzcuaro, Tzintzuntzan, and Ihuatzio. The new political configuration was that of a confederation among the three regions. This confederation lasted until the arrival of the Spanish conquistadors.

Following Nuño Beltran de Guzmán's brutal conquest of the Tarascans, the area was largely abandoned by the natives. Then, in 1540, Bishop Vasco de Quiroga resettled the town and surrounding area with 30,000 Indians and 28 Spanish families. Today there are few more picturesque towns in Mexico than Pátzcuaro. With its narrow cobbled streets, red-tiled roofs, and white-washed colonial buildings, the town is like a flashback to

Street scene in Pátzcuaro, Michoacán

the 16th Century–if you can ignore the cars, telephone lines, and occasional Los Angeles Raiders T-shirt. This very Indian town is also one of the friendliest places in Mexico. For their livelihood the people here rely on tourism, crafts, agriculture, and fishing. Sadly, pollution has seriously damaged water quality in Lake Pátzcuaro. At the same time, soil erosion caused by the deforestation of hills for logging and agriculture is causing the lake to silt up. This combination of crises has caused a serious, and possibly irreversible, decline in the fishing culture.

Getting Around. The **train station** is 1.5 km north of the Plaza Vasco de Quiroga on the Uruapan-Morelia highway. It's best to take a colectivo or taxi. The new **bus station** is one km west of the plaza on the Circunvalación, a loop around the town that goes to Santa Clara del Cobre. Take a taxi or walk.

Crafts. The markets and workshops of Pátzcuaro contain one of the finest collections of locally produced crafts in Mexico. Some of these crafts are produced in Pátzcuaro itself while others come from nearby villages. Pátzcuaro is well known for silver jewelry, especially earrings and necklaces. This silver-work employs traditional design motifs such as fish, birds, and

Patzcuaro, Michoacan

1 ~ train station
2 ~ bus station
3 ~ Plaza Gertrudis Bocanegra
4 ~ Exconvento de San Agustin/library
5 ~ post office
6 ~ public market
7 ~ Mercado de Artesanias
8 ~ Plaza Vasco de Quiroga
9 ~ tourist office
10 ~ Casa del Gigante
11 ~ Templo del Sagrario
12 ~ Iglesia de la Compania
13 ~ La Casa de los Once Patios
14 ~ Museo de Arte Popular
15 ~ La Basilica de la Virgen de la Salud
A ~ Posada la Basilica
B ~ Hotel Los Escudos
C ~ Hotel Concordia
D ~ Hotel Valmen

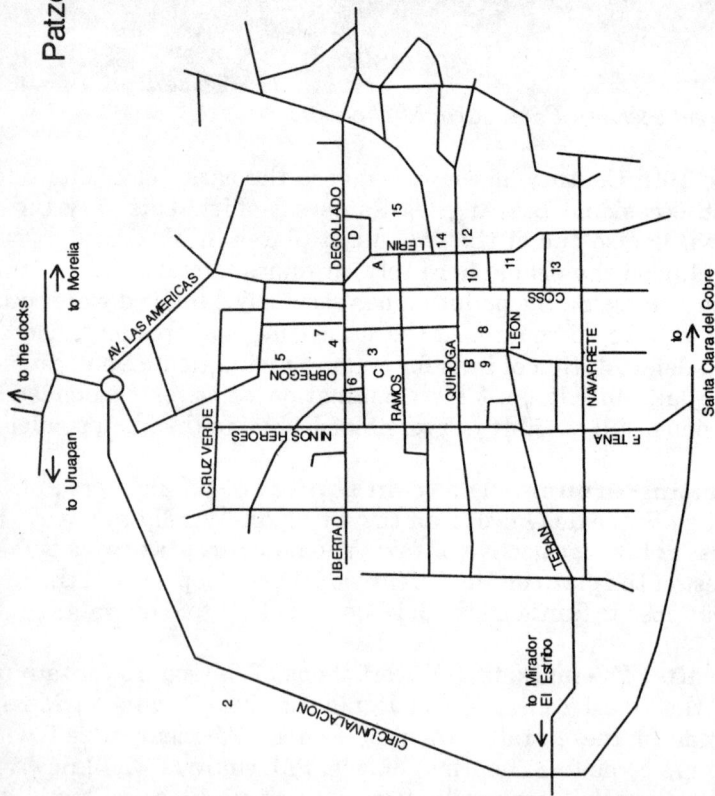

to the docks
to Morelia
to Uruapan
AV. LAS AMERICAS
CRUZ VERDE
OBREGON
NIÑOS HEROES
LIBERTAD
DEGOLLADO
LERIN
RAMOS
QUIROGA
LEON
COSS
NAVARRETE
F. TENA
TERAN
CIRCUNVALACION
to Mirador El Estribo
Santa Clara del Cobre
to

fruit. Other crafts include woven textiles, wooden furniture, and lacquerware. This latter product usually consists of gourds, wooden boxes, or wooden trays which are lacquered with a single color. This layer is then incised with designs which are in turn filled with different colors. This technique is also used to produce distinctive earrings and pins.

Comida Tipica. The most famous food found here is the *pescado blanco*, a small white fish found in the lake. It is usually fried with garlic. Another delicious dish unique to this area is *sopa tarasca*, a pureed bean/tomato soup served with cheese and fried tortilla strips.

Sights. There are two plazas in Pátzcuaro and almost everything of interest is within walking distance of them. The smaller and more northerly of the two is **Plaza Gertrudis Bocanegra**, named after a heroine of the War of Independence, who was executed by firing squad in Pátzcuaro. On the north end of this plaza is the 16th Century **Exconvento de San Agustín** which is now the town's public library. Inside the library is a good selection of English language books and a huge mural by Juan O'Gorman portraying the history of Michoacán. Around the corner from the library on Obregón is the **post office**.

There are two markets in the vicinity of Plaza Gertrudis Bocanegra. The **public market** wherein vendors sell mainly food items is just west of the plaza at Libertad and Obregón. The **Mercado de Artesanías** (Crafts Market) is on the east side of the library. Here you will find all those wonderful, frivolous, practical, and perplexing products for which craftspersons and towns around Pátzcuaro are justly famous. Friday is the day of *tianguis* (Indian market) when rural craftspersons bring their products into town to sell.

One block south of the Plaza Gertrudis Bocanegra is the larger **Plaza Vasco de Quiroga**. Opposite the west end of the plaza is the **tourist office** which is staffed by very friendly and helpful people. Opposite the east side of the plaza is **Casa del Gigante**. This well preserved piece of colonial architecture was originally built (1663) as a residence for a count and countess.

Just south of Casa del Gigante is the 17th Century **Templo del**

Sagrario and opposite it is **Iglesia de la Compañía**. This latter, built in the mid-16th Century, was the first church in Pátzcuaro.

In the next block south of these churches is **La Casa de los Once Patios** (The House of the Eleven Patios). Originally built by Vasco de Quiroga to serve as one of Mexico's first hospitals, the building was later converted into a convent. Today the colonial structure serves as a combination arts and crafts gallery, store, and production shop. In general, each room is devoted to a particular type of craft and often contains craftspersons working at their trade.

Two blocks north of La Casa de los Once Patios at the intersection of Vasco de Quiroga and Arciga is **Museo de Arte Popular** (Museum of Popular Art). The building which houses the museum was built in 1540 as the original Colegio de San Nicolás. Today, this museum contains the most extensive and comprehensive collection of Michoacán arts and crafts to be found anywhere. The displays are organized by region and this set-up works as a wonderful educational tool for the first-time visitor to Michoacán. The museum is open Tues-Sun, 9 a.m. to 1 p.m. and 3 p.m. to 5 p.m. Tour guides (Spanish speaking) are available.

One block north and slightly east of the Museo de Arte Popular is **La Basílica de la Virgen de la Salud**. This church was begun in the 16th Century by Vasco de Quiroga but was not finished until the 19th. Inside is a figure of the Virgen de la Salud (Virgin of Health). This statue, which is believed by many to have miraculous healing powers, was fashioned by local Indians from a ground corn cob and honey paste in the 1540s, almost 450 years ago. La Basílica also houses the remains of Vasco de Quiroga, benefactor of the Purépecha.

Fiestas. A regional fair in honor of **la Virgen de la Salud** is held from Dec 2 through 16. Traditional Tarascan dances are performed including Danza de los Viejitos (Dance of the Old Men), Moros y Cristianos (Moors and Christians), and La Camacua. La Danza de los Viejitos is performed by three to eight dancers wearing richly embroidered pants and a mask representing the face of an old man. In the days before the conquest this dance was dedicated to the god, Huehueteotl–and to some degree it still is. The celebration of the Virgin of Health also includes an agricultural and crafts fair with hundreds of vendors from all over the state displaying and selling their products. **La Bendición de los Animales** (the Blessing of the Animals) takes place on Jan 17. On this occasion people dress up their animals and take them to the Basílica for, you guessed it, the priest's blessing. **El Día de los Muertos** (the Day of the Dead) celebration begins at midnight, Nov 1, on the island of Janitzio in Lake Pátzcuaro. The celebration includes music, dances, and a procession. Nowadays, this event is very touristy but still interesting.

Climate. At 2,150 m (6,450 ft) above sea level Pátzcuaro enjoys a cool to temperate climate. Though below freezing temperatures are rare, winter nights are cold. Even summer days turn chilly when the rains start falling. Most of Pátzcuaro's 101 cm (40 in) of rain a year fall between May and September.

Excursions. The largest of five islands in Lake Pátzcuaro, **Janitzio** is a popular local excursion for many visitors to Pátzcuaro. On the island there are souvenir shops, restaurants, and a rather ugly monument to Morelos. The best part of the trip is the half-hour boat ride across the lake which offers the traveler memorable images of fishing villages clustered up against the lake shore and backed by forested, rolling hills. Boats leave the docks for Janitzio about every 20 minutes. To make the five km trip from Pátzcuaro to the lake, catch the bus labelled "Lago" from the market.

View of Lake Pátzcuaro from the top of Janitzio

If you like to walk, there is a hike to **Mirador El Estribo** with a spectacular outcome . This hill is four km west of

Pátzcuaro and offers a splendid view of the town and lake. Also, it is a good place for a picnic. Upon reaching the chapel of El Calvario, continue on the cobbled road, not the paths to the left.

Santa Clara del Cobre, 18 km south of Pátzcuaro, is famous for its copper crafts. There are numerous shops here where artisans, using the pre-Conquest technique of hammering the metal, transform copper into works of art and utility. Examples of this craft are housed in the small **Museo del Cobre** (Copper Museum) on the town's main plaza. Second class buses of the Flecha Amarilla line leave from the Pátzcuaro bus station for Santa Clara.

Roughly 15 km north of Pátzcuaro is the town of **Tzintzuntzan** whose name in Tarascan means "Place of the Hummingbirds." Before the arrival of the Spanish, this village served as the nominal capital of the Purépecha confederation. Today, the partially restored ruins of the Purepechan ceremonial center, **Yácatas**, can be found on a hill one km south of town and just east of the Pátzcuaro road. There are nice views of the town and the lake beyond from the site.

Potter decorating her work in the village of Tzintzunzan

Back in the town of Tzintzuntzan is the **Mercado de Artesanías** which contains extensive displays of the crafts typical of this village, notably painted ceramics and straw figures. On the south side of town are the remains of a 16th Century **Franciscan monastery** which includes two churches, the **Iglesia de San Francisco** and the **Templo de la Soledad**, and a grove of ancient olive trees. These were planted by Vasco de Quiroga in the 1530s. Flecha Amarilla buses run from the Pátzcuaro bus station to Tzintzuntzan several times daily.

Uruapan

The train to Uruapan from Pátzcuaro winds among the green
mountains of Michoacán, passing pine and hardwood covered
summits and descending through lake- and river-filled valleys.
Progress is slow but that just allows more time to take in the
beauty of this region. The train actually descends 500 m (1635
ft) between the two towns and, as you approach Uruapan, the
valleys become full of avocado and citrus trees heavy with fruit.
Before the Spanish conquest, the region around Uruapan was
conquered by the Tarascan armies. However, the land was so
lush and productive that the Tarascan rulers, following the
mandate of their god, Curicaueri, decided to allow the land to
return to its previous occupants so that it would be spared the
ravages of war and conflict.

The first Spaniard to settle in the area was Friar Juan de San
Miguel who founded the town in 1533. He was so impressed by
the lush growth of the area that he chose the name "Uruapan"
which in Tarascan roughly means "place of eternal spring."
Juan de San Miguel was a priest in the mold of Vasco de
Quiroga. He was less interested in exploitation of the natives
than he was in Christianizing and ensuring their survival. To
this end he encouraged the building of neighborhoods with their
own churches and tried to get Indians of different cultures to
work together. He also built schools, training centers, and hospitals for the poor and encouraged the learning of craft skills.

Today Uruapan is a city of 200,000 inhabitants located in a
well-watered and rich agricultural area. While a variety of
citrus and other fruits are grown in the area, the most important, economically, is the avocado. At least in Mexican brochures the city is called the "Avocado Capital of the World."
Also, tourists are fairly rare and the people are friendly.

Getting Around. The **train station** is 1.5 km southeast of
Jardín Morelos. Buses marked "Panteon" go there from the
plaza. The **bus station** is on the northwest side of town on the
Morelia highway. "Los Reyes" buses go there from the plaza.

Crafts. Artisans in and around Uruapan make lacquerware
similar to that found in Pátzcuaro but which exhibits more

Uruapan, Michoacan

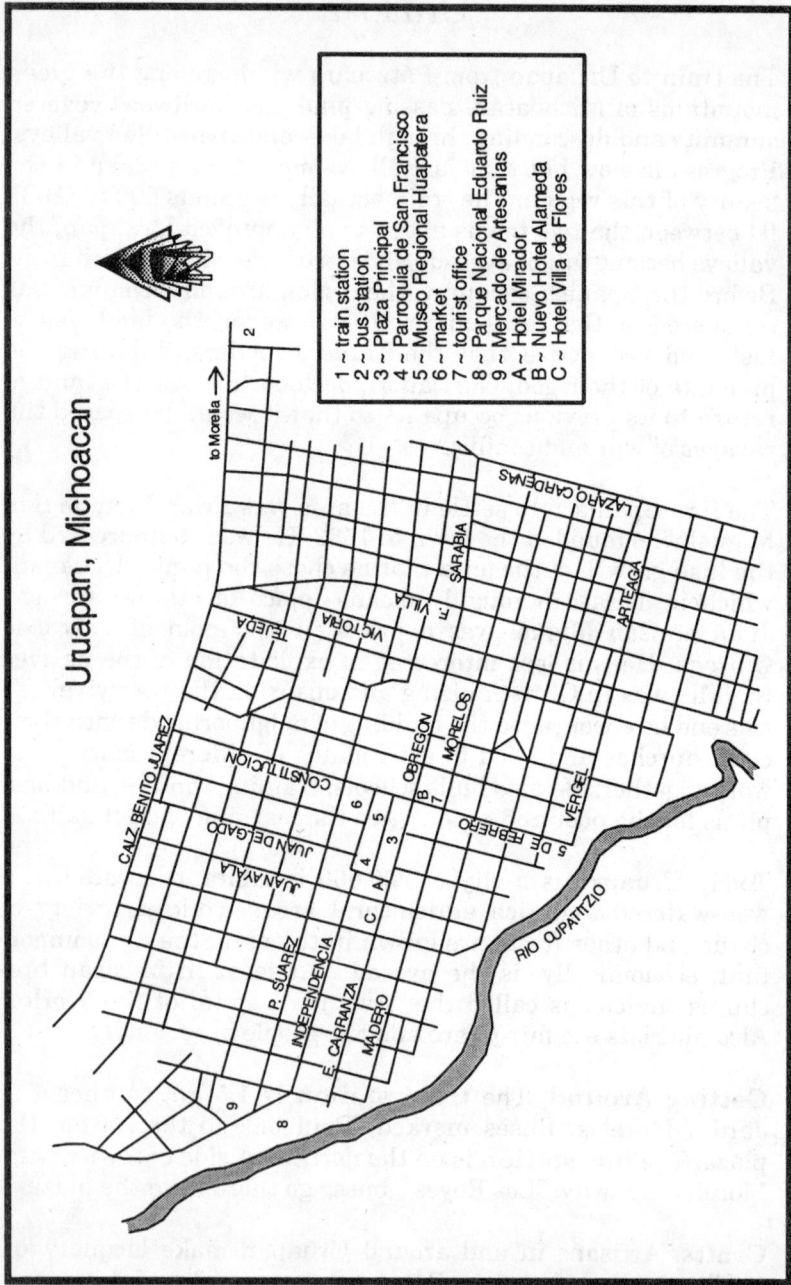

to Morelia →

1 ~ train station
2 ~ bus station
3 ~ Plaza Principal
4 ~ Parroquia de San Francisco
5 ~ Museo Regional Huapatera
6 ~ market
7 ~ tourist office
8 ~ Parque Nacional Eduardo Ruiz
9 ~ Mercado de Artesanias
A ~ Hotel Mirador
B ~ Nuevo Hotel Alameda
C ~ Hotel Villa de Flores

LAZARO CARDENAS

SARABIA

T. VILLA

VICTORIA

TEJEDA

CALZ BENITO JUAREZ

CONSTITUCION

JUAN DELGADO

JUAN AYALA

OBREGON

MORELOS

5 DE FEBRERO

VERGEL

ARTEAGA

RIO CUPATITZIO

P. SUAREZ

INDEPENDENCIA

E. CARRANZA

MADERO

traditional Mexican design motifs. Wood products, utensils, and housewares are also common here. During the Sunday *tianguis* in the nearby town of **Nuevo San Juan**, that plaza fills with craftspersons selling beautiful cross-stitched and embroidered blouses and dresses.

Comida Tipica. Coffee and cocoa beans are grown in the fertile soil around Uruapan and can be found in their processed forms locally. Coffee (*cafe*) is available whole, ground, or instant. The cocoa is combined with sugar and cinnamon and formed into tablets. These tablets can be dissolved in warm milk to make hot chocolate or eaten as they are.

Sights. Find the zócalo and you've found most of the points of interest in the city. At the west end of the plaza is **Parroquia de San Francisco**. The most interesting thing about this 17th Century church is that in the dome over the altar there are modernistic paintings of Christ, Mary, and God the father complete with atoms and chemistry beakers.

At the opposite end of the plaza is the **Museo Regional Huatapera** which contains displays of Tarascan crafts. It is not as nice as the Museo de Arte Popular in Pátzcuaro. The Huatapera building was built by Juan de San Miguel in the 16th Century and served as both a church and as the first hospital in Mexico. Next door is a crafts workshop. The museum is open daily 9 a.m. to 1:30 p.m. and 3:30 p.m. to 5:30 p.m.

Just north of the Museo Regional is the **mercado** which contains mostly food. Two blocks south of the mercado on 5 de Febrero in the courtyard of the former Hotel Progresso is the **tourist office**, open Mon-Sat. Little English is spoken.

At the west end of the city, about eight blocks from the zócalo is **Parque Nacional Eduardo Ruíz**. Contained in the over 1,000 acres of this fine park are springs, waterfalls, trails, picnic tables, lush tropical vegetation, and cool shadows beneath the forest's canopy. It is here that the Cupatitzio River rises, Cupatitzio being Tarascan for "river that sings." One can walk to the park or catch a local bus labelled "El Parque" at the plaza. Just outside the park one block north of the entrance is the **Mercado de Artesanías** where local crafts are sold.

Fiestas. The festival of **Domingo de Ramos** is celebrated on Palm Sunday with a procession and exhibits of Tarascan ceramics in the zócalo.

Climate. At 1,612 m (4,830 ft) elevation Uruapan can be cool at night. Generally, though, the climate is subtropical and quite warm especially in the summer. Most of the area's precipitation falls from June to August.

Excursions. About 30 km (18 mi) north of Uruapan on Federal Highway 37 is **Paracho** which is world famous for the quality of its guitars. Other musical instruments and wood objects are also made and visitors can watch the craftspersons at work. The town is served by second class buses of the Flecha Amarilla line.

The waterfalls of **Tzaráracua** are 13 km (8 mi) south of the city. Between 30 and 40 m high, these falls are actually a set of three different cascades formed by the Río Cupatitzio. The 1.5-km trail to the falls is well marked. Unfortunately, there are considerable deposits of trash along the bank of the plunge pool, all of which has washed down from upstream. A 2-km and less well-marked trail on the other side of the main falls leads to a smaller, cleaner, and strikingly beautiful cascade on a tributary to the Cupatitzio. To get to the falls from Uruapan, catch the bus marked "Tzaráracua" on Alvaro Obregón beside the zócalo. This bus will deposit you at the trailhead to the falls where you will be surrounded by people offering to rent you a horse.

Bell tower emerging from the lava field of Paricutín volcano

An interesting monument to the recent history of this area can be seen in the town of **Nuevo San Juan** about 12 km (7 mi) west of Uruapan. In 1943 the volcano Paricutín erupted and destroyed the town of San Juan. Fortunately this destruction took place slowly enough so that the inhabitants had time to escape. These refugees from the cataclysm founded the town of Nuevo San Juan. The church on the plaza was built in 1943 and contains the relics and altar from its destroyed predecessor. The basement has a photo display on the destruction of the old church and the construction of the new. On the ground floor over the altar is a figure of Christ reputed to have miraculous powers. On Sundays there is a good, cheap market in the plaza with beautifully embroidered blouses and dresses. To get there take the "Nvo. San Juan" bus from the corner of 5 de Febrero and Avenida Juárez in Uruapan. It's a lovely 40-minute bus ride.

North of Nuevo San Juan is the volcano **Paricutín**. What started in 1943 as a steaming fissure in a farmer's cornfield became a volcano which, over eight years, covered 20 square kilometers with lava. Today, the traveler can visit the 1/4 km-wide crater and the remains of the town, San Juan, which was overwhelmed by the lava flow. Actually, all that is visible of the town are the spires of the church, an amazing sight.

Horses and guides can be rented and hired in the town of **Angahuan**. The horse ride to the ruins of San Juan takes half an hour, while the trip to the volcano takes about six hours. Horse rentals run about $10, while guides usually offer their services for "whatever you wish to pay." While it is an easy hike to San Juan or Paricutín, please remember that the Purépecha Indians here have few income opportunities other than this volcano. The horse ride or hike to San Juan and Paricutín departs from a place called the *mirador* ("lookout"), a site which includes a parking lot, restrooms, an irregularly open restaurant, and several cabins. These cabins hold six people and rent for $31, or so I was told. Inquire at the restaurant. To get there, take a second class bus for Los Reyes from Uruapan and get off in Angahuan (1.5 hr). You can ask for directions to the *mirador* although you will probably be approached immediately by someone offering guide services.

Lázaro Cárdenas. The only reason to come to Lázaro Cárdenas is the Pacific coast. The city itself is ugly, modern sprawl situated around a steel mill. North of town, however, is the almost completely undeveloped coast of Michoacán.

The small town of **Playa Azul** is 26 km (15 mi) north of Lázaro Cárdenas. This is the only thing on the Michoacán coast that could be called a resort. It has a lovely and usually deserted beach. However, during the weekends, crowds from the nearby city take over this otherwise sleepy beach town. There are several cheap hotels but lodging can be a problem on weekends. To get there catch a second class bus from the Lázaro Cárdenas bus station or a *colectivo* on Av. Lázaro Cárdenas.

Another 50 km (30 mi) up the coast is **Caleta de Campos**, an even smaller and more idyllic version of Playa Azul. Located at the mouth of the Río Nexpa, this town enjoys crystal clear water and two beautiful beaches. The streets are dirt and the one good hotel almost always fills up on weekends. To get there catch a second class bus in Lázaro Cárdenas.

Train to Jalisco

West northwest of Mexico City is the state of Jalisco. It is a region of variety. The mile-high, semi-arid eastern portion of the state contrasts strikingly with the tropical lowlands of the Pacific coast, as does the traditional and very Mexican city of Guadalajara with the resort city of Puerto Vallarta.

Physiographically, the state from Guadalajara east is part of the high, rolling plateau of central Mexico. To the west and southwest the terrain is broken by ranges of the Sierra Madre Occidental. Most of the coast is mountainous except for the southern part where the coastal lowlands are covered by coconut, banana, and papaya plantations. Before the arrival of the Spanish in the 1520s most of eastern and central Jalisco was inhabited by the Chimalhuacan Indians. Almost nothing remains of this culture unless you count the name of the state, which derives from a native word meaning "sandy place."

The first stages of the Spanish conquest of this region were executed by Nuño Beltran de Guzmán. In his ambition he called the area Greater Spain and hoped to create a personal fiefdom whose power and wealth would eclipse that of New Spain. However, his greed and cruelty toward the Indians led the

Viceroy of New Spain, Antonio de Mendoza, to replace him with
Pérez de la Torre. The region was renamed New Galicia. Following Mexican Independence in 1821 New Galicia was divided
among several states, but its core became Jalisco.

Today Jalisco is a relatively prosperous state with a diversified
economy based on agriculture, cattle, tourism, industry, and
crafts. The state has fewer apparent indigenous influences than
many other areas of Mexico. In fact, it is considered a very
"Mexican" state by reason of being the birthplace of tequila,
mariachi music, the *jarabe* or Mexican hat dance, the *charros*
(rodeo), and the sombrero.

Train Services. Trains 5 and 6 ("Tapatio") connect Mexico
City with Guadalajara and provide special first class service,
second class coach, a sleeping car, and a dining car.

TAPATIO TRAIN

| Lv. | 8:30 PM | Mexico City | 8:25 AM (+1) | Ar. |
| Ar. | 8:15 AM (+1) | Guadalajara | 9:00 PM | Lv. |

RATES FROM MEXICO CITY TO GUADALAJARA	Special 1st cl. Reserved	2nd cl. Coach	(1) Rmtte	(2) Rmtte	(2) Bedrm	(4) Bedrm
	$9.68	5.13	39.35	64.94	78.71	137.74

Guadalajara

The first city of Guadalajara was established under the orders
of Nuño Beltran de Guzmán in 1531. However, the relentless
hostility of the Caxcanes Indians, who defeated and killed Pedro
de Alvarado, forced the relocation of the city three times. Finally, in 1542, Cristóbal de Oñate moved the city to its present
location.

During the colonial period Guadalajara served as the capital of
New Galicia. It was also the seat of an archbishopric as wealthy
as that of Mexico City and which stretched throughout what is
today western and northern Mexico and the southern United
States. Guadalajara was almost as powerful as Mexico City, the

Guadalajara, Jalisco

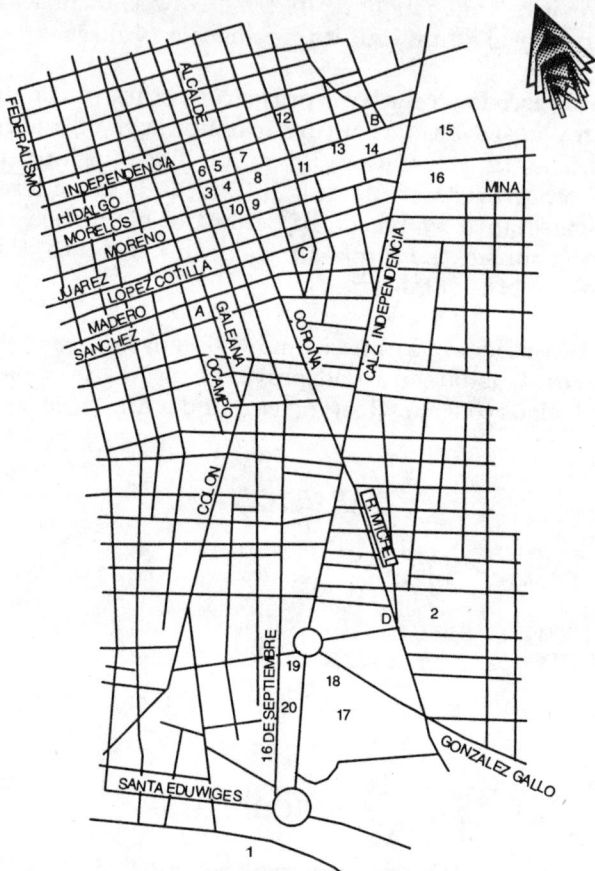

1 ~ train station
2 ~ old bus station
3 ~ Plaza de los Laureles
4 ~ Cathedral
5 ~ Illustrious Men of Jalisco Rotunda
6 ~ Palacio Municipal
7 ~ Museo Regional de Guadalajara
8 ~ Plaza de la Liberacion
9 ~ Palacio de Gobierno
10~ Plaza de Armas
11~ Teatro Degollado
12~ post office
13~ Plaza Tapatia
14~ tourist office
15~ Instituto Cultural Cabanas
16~ Mercado Libertad
17~ Parque Agua Azul
18~ Casa de la Artesanias
19~ Casa de la Cultura
20~ Museo de Arqueologia
A ~ Hotel Hamilton
B ~ Hotel Las Americas
C ~ Hotel Universo
D ~ Gran Hotel Canada

original dream of Nuño Beltran but stripped of personal ambition.

In 1810, at the beginning of the Mexican War of Independence, the city was in the hands of insurgent forces led by José Antonio Torres. In late 1810 Miguel Hidalgo arrived and remained until early 1811. During his stay he issued both an edict abolishing slavery and the Agrarian Law which ordered the return of lands to the Indians. With the achievement of independence some years later, Guadalajara became the capital of Jalisco. Today, Guadalajara is Mexico's second largest city with four million inhabitants and counting. While pollution has taken some of the bloom off the "City of the Roses," it remains an intriguing Mexican city, a mix of the traditional and modern, with many things for the visitor to do, see, and learn.

Getting Around. Guadalajara has a new **bus station** and unfortunately it is out in the middle of nowhere, specifically, on the highway to Zapotlanejo. To get there from the central area catch bus #275 going south at the intersection of 16 de Septiembre and Av. Juárez. The trip takes about 40 minutes. There are also shuttle buses which run between the old station and the new. The old station is near Parque Agua Azul on Av. R. Michel. To get between the **train station** (estación de ferrocarriles) and the historic center of town use bus #62A. It runs along Calzada Independencia Sur. The tourist office in Plaza Tapatia has good information on local bus routes.

Crafts. *Artesanía* in Guadalajara is dominated by the neighborhoods of **Tonalá** and **Tlaquepaque** and by the culture of Jalisco's **Huichol** Indians. Tonalá produces an immense variety of ceramics of various forms, styles, and colors. Tlaquepaque has traded in much of its working class garb for upscale curio stores but the neighborhood still contains several glass-blowing and wood working shops.

The Huichol Indians live in isolated, mountainous areas in western Jalisco. Having remained largely uncorrupted in their spiritual beliefs, the Huichol incorporate the still meaningful symbols of their religion into their crafts. More than that, every item of apparel or use made by them is, essentially, a prayer to their gods. In the markets of Guadalajara and the neighborhood of Zapopan, one can often find the Huicholes making and selling these crafts, principally beaded masks, bowls, bags, and necklaces and embroidered shirts, blouses, and belts. Their eye-catching colors and imagery are unmistakable.

Sights. Most of the things to see in Guadalajara are located near the historic center of the city. Here there are a series of lovely plazas filled with fountains, statuary, and park benches. On Avenida 16 de Septiembre and on the east side of **Plaza de los Laureles** is the **Cathedral**. Construction was started in 1571 but the twin 66-meter towers had to be rebuilt after the earthquake of 1818. Inside is the painting "La Inmaculada Concepción" by the Spanish painter Esteban Murillo.

Immediately north of the Cathedral is the **Illustrious Men of Jalisco Rotunda** which contains the remains of several famous men of Jalisco. West of the rotunda is the **Palacio Municipal**. Although a modern building, this structure was built in a neo-colonial style with an interior courtyard. Beside the stairway there is a five panel mural by Gabriel Flores depicting the founding of Guadalajara. On the other side of the Rotunda is the **Museo Regional de Guadalajara** (Guadalajara Regional Museum). Originally a house, this 18th Century building became a museum in 1918. It has 14 permanent exhibition rooms including: Paleontology; Contemporary Paintings; Paintings from the 17th, 18th, and 19th Centuries; Ethnography; Archeology; and the History of Jalisco. The museum is open Tues-Sun, 9 a.m. to 3 p.m. Just south of the museum is the lovely, tree-lined **Plaza de la Liberación** (also known as "Plaza de los Dos Copas") with its twin fountains and four-m statue of Miguel Hidalgo.

Opposite the Regional Museum on the other side of the plaza is the **Palacio de Gobierno** (Government Palace). This public building was begun in 1643 and finished in 1790. The chief attractions here are several murals painted by the great Mexican muralist and Jalisco native son, José Clemente Orozco. In the main stairway are three of his murals. The center one, called "Social Struggle" and containing a powerful likeness of Miguel Hidalgo, was inspired by the anxieties, tragedies, and dema-goguery of contemporary society. The mural to the right is entitled "The Contemporary Circus," while to the left is "The

Ghost of Religion in Alliance with Militarism." In the former chamber of the state congress Orozco painted murals representing the three social movements which have shaped Mexico: the Independence, the Reform, and the Revolution.

In front of the Palacio de Gobierno is the **Plaza de Armas**, a pleasant place to sit and observe. An exquisite French kiosk stands in the center of the plaza. Built in the 19th Century, the eight figures which support the roof represent different musical instruments. On Sundays and Thursdays the state band gives concerts here. At the eastern end of Plaza de la Liberación is the **Teatro Degollado** (Degollado Theater). Built between 1855 and 1866, this lovely, neo-classic building has a Corinthian-columned portico topped by a triangular facade on which is depicted in high relief an allegory of nine muses. Inside on the vaulted ceiling there is a fine oil painting by Jacobo Galvez and Gerardo Suárez representing Dante's Fourth Song in the Divine Comedy. The building is normally closed except during performances. Check at the tourist office for the theater's performance schedule.

The **post office** (Correos) is a block north of the Degollado at Independencia and V. Carranza. East of Teatro Degollado is the huge, modern **Plaza Tapatia**. Inaugurated in 1982, this nine-block pedestrian mall contains several fountains, pieces of sculpture, and tree-lined arcades. The most impressive fountain is in the middle of the plaza. This surreal work consists of five large hand-worked bronze castings and is titled "**Quetzalcóatl Immolation**."

At the corner of Morelos and G. Suárez is a building which during the colonial period served as the Holy Inquisition headquarters. Today the building houses the Jalisco **Tourism Department**. There is almost always someone who speaks English. Here you can get information on the numerous bus routes in Guadalajara as well as on cultural events in the city.

At the eastern limit of Plaza Tapatia is the **Instituto Cultural Cabañas** (Cabañas Cultural Institute). Built in the first half of the 19th Century to serve as an orphanage, this large, impressive structure now serves as a combination museum and art school. The museum includes a permanent display of work by the muralist José Clemente Orozco and other, temporary art exhibits. The Orozco collection consists of 360 pieces of his work displayed in 18 rooms, the most extensive collection of his art anywhere. However, the amazing heart and soul of the Institute are to be found in the chapel. Here, in the 1930s, Clemente Orozco covered the walls and dome of the chapel with powerful, dark murals which are masterpieces of modern art. The theme of the work is the Spanish conquest of native America and the murals eloquently express the death, destruction, and despair of this event. But there is also a bit of hope in his "Man of Fire" mural in the dome of the chapel. The Institute is open Tues-Sun, 10 a.m. to 6 p.m.

Just south of the Instituto Cultural Cabañas at the corner of Calzada Independencia Sur and Av. Javier Mina is the huge **Mercado Libertad** (Liberty Market). This is one of the largest roofed markets in Latin America. Here one can find all types of crafts, clothing, household items, fruits, vegetables, and meats. On the upper floor there is a section of small restaurants serving a wide variety of Mexican dishes. It is open from 6 a.m. to 8 p.m.

The **University of Guadalajara** is about 13 blocks west of Av. 16 de Septiembre at the intersection of Av. Juárez and Av. Tolsa (975 Juárez). Located on the south side of Av. Juárez, this 1914 French Renaissance-style building contains two more Clemente Orozco murals painted between 1936 and 1939. One is painted in the cupola of the auditorium and is entitled "The Pentaphasic Man." The second, painted on the scenery wall behind the stage, is "The People and Their Leaders." The latter mural is especially interesting. One interpretation of its meaning is that society's leaders use the law to protect their position at the expense of the masses. There are other interpretations. Right behind the building is the **Expiatorio Church**, a striking neo-Gothic structure built in 1930. To get to the university, catch any westbound bus on Av. Juárez. To return to the central area, walk three blocks north to Av. Hidalgo and catch any eastbound bus.

A little over 20 blocks south of Plaza Tapatia along Calzada Independencia Sur is a cluster of interesting sights. To get there, take bus 62A south on Calzada Independencia. Immediately after you pass the traffic circle at Constituyentes you will see on the left the first location of interest, **Parque Agua Azul** (Blue Water Park). This large park is a nice place to picnic and to get away from the city for a while. The swimming pools are usually dirty. At the north end of the park is the **Teatro Experimental** (Experimental Theater) and the **Casa de las Artesanías** (open Mon-Fri, 10 a.m. to 7 p.m., and Sat-Sun, 10 a.m. to 2 p.m.).

Across from the park at the intersection of Constituyentes and Calz. Independencia is the **Casa de la Cultura** (Culture House). This is a state government institution dedicated to increasing culture. The building contains the State Public Library where there is a fine mural by the Jalisco artist Gabriel Flores. There are four galleries which house exhibits of paintings, drawings, photographs, and/or sculpture. Films are shown in the auditorium and classes are taught in such subjects as painting, Nahuatl language, and folkloric dance. The Casa is open Mon-Sat, 8:30 a.m. to 8:30 p.m.

Just south of the Casa de la Cultura along Calz. Independencia is the **Museo de Arqueologia del Occidente de Mexico** (Archeology Museum of Western Mexico). This museum has a small but interesting collection of artifacts from the cultures that inhabited the Jalisco, Colima, and Nayarit regions. It is open Tues-Sun, 10 a.m. to 2 p.m.

Fiestas. On October 12 there is the celebration of the **Virgin of Zapopan**. During the preceding four months the holy image has visited every church in Guadalajara and on this date it is returned to its home basílica in the neighborhood of Zapopan. This pilgrimage began in 1734 when the Virgin of Zapopan was named the patron saint of Guadalajara. The image of the virgin travels from the Cathedral to Zapopan accompanied by thousands of believers along with music, dancing, singing, and praying. The **October Fiestas** begin with a big parade the first Saturday in October and end the first Sunday of November. Artisan, industrial, and commercial expositions as well as performances by various artists take place at the Benito Juárez Auditorium. During the entire month of February there are artistic and cultural events in Plaza Tapatia to celebrate the **Founding of Guadalajara.**

Classes. The American Institute for Foreign Study (AIFS) offers classes in a number of areas including Spanish language, art, literature, Latin American and Mexican studies, economics, history, and development studies. Contact:

Coll Div, AIFS
102 Greenwich Ave.
Greenwich, CT 06830

The Universidad de Guadalajara offers classes in Spanish, art, literature, economics, history, social sciences, and Latin American studies. Contact:

Adriana Ayala Rubio
Ctr de Estudios para Extranjeros
Univ. de Guadalajara
Apdo. 1-4521
Guadalajara, Jalisco 44100, Mexico

Centro Mexicano Internacional offers both university- affiliated programs in language, social sciences, and fine arts and unaffiliated intensive Spanish classes. Contact:

Mexico Programs
2626 North Mesa, Suite 355
El Paso, TX 79902
1-800-426-1349

Climate. Guadalajara's climate is semi-arid and temperate. It never freezes and the hottest months are May and June with average temperatures of 72 and 73.4°F, respectively. The lowest recorded temperature was 41.9°F in January, 1955. The rainy season is June to October.

Excursions. There are several interesting excursions from the historic center of Guadalajara. At the north end of Calzada Independencia about 10 km (6 mi) from the center is **Barranca de Oblatos** (Oblates Canyon). The Río Santiago runs at the bottom of this 630-m-deep canyon. There is an outstanding view and guides can be hired for the descent to the bottom. Here is also the Balneario Los Comachos, with a large swimming pool, picnic area, barbecue pits, and food vendors. The place gets crowded on weekends. To get there, catch bus #45 going north on Calz. Independencia and ride it to the end of the line.

On the same side of town as Barranca de Oblatos is **Barranca de Huentitan**, on the Río Lerma. There is a trail to the canyon bottom which takes an hour. Up on top and almost on the edge of the canyon is the **Guadalajara Zoo** (Tues-Sun, 10 a.m. to 6 p.m.) Nearby, at 599 Av. Flores Magón, is the city **Planetarium** (open Tues-Sun, 10 a.m. to 7 p.m.). Get bus #54 going north on Calz. Independencia and stay on until the end of the line.

The town of **Zapopan** is on the northwest outskirts of Guadalajara. This municipality is not only the greatest corn producer in Mexico, it is also one of the most important religious centers west of Mexico City. This is because the venerated Virgin of Zapopan normally resides in the town's baroque Basílica (1730). According to legend, this 25-cm-high statue was responsible for a 1531 Spanish victory over the Chimalhuacan Indians. The story goes that during the battle a friar displayed the image of the Virgin and, overcome by awe, the Indians surrendered and were baptised. During a 1734 epidemic the Virgin of Zapopan was taken to afflicted towns and villages. In each case, her appearance caused the epidemic to end. That is why today she spends four months of every year traveling to different churches in the Guadalajara area spreading health and good luck.

Next to the Basílica is the **Museo de Arte Huichol** (Museum of Huichol Art) with interesting examples of Huichol Indian art. The Huichol are among the Mexican indigenous groups least affected by Western culture. For more information on the Huichol, see the section on Tepic. The **Zapopan Tourism Office** is located at 111 Vicente Guerrero. To get to Zapopan, catch bus #275 going north at the corner of Corona and Juárez.

Only eight km (five mi) southeast from Guadalajara's central district is **San Pedro Tlaquepaque**. This town was one of the most important artisan centers in Mexico and is still famous for its blown glass. Most of the workshops, however, have become boutiques and upscale crafts and curio shops. Nowadays, Tlaquepaque is more of a shopping than a working area. The **Tlaquepaque Tourism Office** is at 80 Guillermo Prieto. **El Museo Regional de la Cerámica** (Regional Ceramics Mu-

Scene from the Tonalá market, Guadalajara

seum) is at 237 Independencia and will give you a good idea of
the quality and variety of ceramic crafts produced in Jalisco. It
is open Tues- Sat, 10 a.m. to 4 p.m. and Sun, 10 a.m. to 1 p.m.

On the eastern outskirts of Guadalajara is the community of
Tonalá whose name comes from a Nahuatl word meaning
"where the sun rises." Tonalá has been called the "Pottery
Cradle of Mexico" though, actually, a considerable variety of
crafts are produced here. Tonalá is also less flashy and less
touristy than Tlaquepaque. The **Tonalá Tourism Office** is at
180 Morelos. **Cerro de la Reina** (Queen Hill) offers a superb
view of Guadalajara and the entire Atemajac Valley. Thursday
and Sunday are the days of the *tianguis* (Indian market). On
these days the main plaza fills to overflowing with hundreds of
craftspersons showing and selling their products.

To get to both Tlaquepaque and Tonalá, take bus #275 south
from the intersection of 16 de Septiembre and Av. Juárez.

Lake Chapala is about 50 km (30 mi) south of Guadalajara and
is Mexico's largest lake. It is also, because of its setting, fine
weather, and low cost of living, the location of perhaps the

largest colony of expatriate North Americans in the world. Tens of thousands of retirees have made Lake Chapala their home. The towns of **Chapala** and **Ajijic** have suffered the greatest transformation from this influx, while the fishing village of **Jocotepec** has been less affected. If you feel the need to speak English or just want to see the beautiful lake, especially at sunrise and sunset, then take bus #275 south to the new bus station. Transportes Guadalajara-Chapala in Building 5 runs second class buses to the towns around the lake.

Finally, if you like tequila or just want to see the town where this fiery and most Mexican liquor is made, catch a bus to the town of **Tequila**. The Sauza and Cuervo distilleries have public tours so you can track the progress of the liquor from its start as the juice of thick-leaved agave plants until it becomes the inevitable free sample. Tequila is 61 km (36 mi) from Guadalajara and a major stop on the highway to Tepic and Ixtlán del Río. Any bus from the new bus station to Tepic can get you to Tequila.

Train To Manzanillo

The train from Guadalajara to Manzanillo passes through a diversity of landscapes before reaching the coast. Leaving the high, rolling plateau around Guadalajara the train is soon in the crumpled, mountainous landscape of southern Jalisco. Its only stop here is the town of Ciudad Guzmán. The train continues south of Ciudad Guzmán, offering spectacular views of the two often snow-capped volcanoes, Nevado de Colima and Volcán de Colima. Sit on the right side of the train for the best view.

About 60 km (36 mi) south of Guzmán the train enters the state of Colima, one of the smallest states in Mexico. Soon after crossing the border the train makes a second stop in the capital city, also called Colima. This town sits in a wide, well watered valley watched over by the two volcanoes to the north.

Leaving Colima city the train winds through the Sierra Madre del Sur and begins a rapid descent to the tropical coastal lowlands, eventually arriving in the city of Manzanillo. Along the way pine forests and mountain streams give way to banana plantations and sultry lagoons.

Train Services. The train "Colimense" provides second class coach service only from Guadalajara to Ciudad Guzmán, Colima, and Manzanillo.

COLIMENSE TRAIN

					2nd. cl. Coach
Lv.	9:00 AM	Guadalajara	2:07 PM	Ar.	
	12:00 PM	Ciudad Guzmán	11:05 AM		$ 1.16
	3:00 PM	Colima	8:00 AM		2.19
Ar.	6:00 PM	Manzanillo	6:20 AM	Lv.	2.97

Ciudad Guzmán

This small town is situated in a high valley only 20 km northeast of the two volcanoes, Nevado de Colima (4,240 m) and Volcán de Colima (3,820 m). Proximity to the volcanoes, and the national park that surrounds them, is Ciudad Guzmán's chief claim to fame. A somewhat less famous claim is that the great muralist José Clemente Orozco was born here.

Sights. The main attraction in the town is the **Museo Regional de las Culturas de Occidente** (Regional Museum of Western Cultures). This museum has a nice though small collection of pre-Hispanic artifacts from the cultures which inhabited western Michoacán, Jalisco, Colima, and Nayarit. There are also paintings by José Clemente Orozco.

Excursions. Unless you have access to a four-wheel drive vehicle, the hike from the village of Fresnito to the summit of Nevado de Colima takes a couple of days. Take water. There is an occasional logging truck which goes up the road to the summit but they are unpredictable. Not only is there a spectacular view from the top but there is also, usually, snow. You can get a bus to Fresnito at the Ciudad Guzmán bus station. Also, two km north of the town is a hot spring called **La Catarina**. Take the bus for Santa Catarina.

Colima

Most of the state of Colima is covered by the mountains of the Sierra Madre del Sur. The city of Colima sits in a rare, broad, inter-montane valley in the western corner of the state. The only other flat land in the state is found along the coast. Northwest of the town of Armeria the coastal lowlands are a narrow strip caught between the highlands and the Pacific, while south of that town the coastal plain broadens, extending as far as 20 km inland. The city of Colima was founded 1523, the third city established by the Spanish in New Spain. However, Colima grew very slowly during the colonial period so, despite the city's antiquity, most of the structures in the city date from the post-colonial period.

Today, Colima is a city of 160,000 people located in a fertile agricultural area. To the north are the twin volcanoes, Nevado de Colima and Volcán de Colima. The latter volcano last erupted in 1941 causing considerable loss of life. It still emits fumes occasionally. Colima is a charming and laid-back town full of friendly people. There are few tourists here.

Getting Around. The **train station** is about 12 blocks south of the Plaza Principal. There are minivans which run between the station and downtown, carry several passengers, and are very cheap. Also, for about one dollar the visitor can take a cab. Or walk. It's only 12 blocks. The **bus station** is three blocks south of the Plaza Principal on Reforma.

Sights. In downtown Colima there are three plazas in a line running northwest to southeast. The most westerly is the **Plaza Principal**. East of the plaza is the **Cathedral** which, though originally built in the 16th Century, has been rebuilt several times since, with the most recent reconstruction occurring after the 1941 earthquake.

Also east of the Plaza Principal is the **Palacio de Gobierno** which dates from the late 19th Century. Inside are murals painted by Jorge Chávez Carrillo depicting the post-Conquest history of New Spain and Mexico. One block north of the Palacio at Zaragoza and Reforma is the **Casa de las Artesanías Colima** (Colima House of Crafts). Local crafts, including clay

Colima, Colima

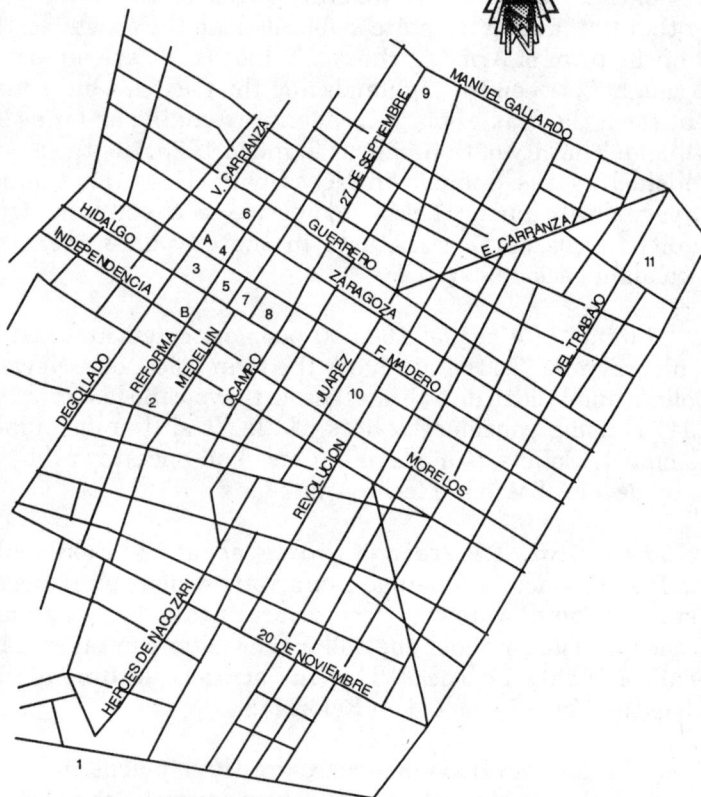

1 ~ train station
2 ~ bus station
3 ~ Plaza Principal
4 ~ Cathedral
5 ~ Palacio de Gobierno
6 ~ Casa de las Artesanias Colima
7 ~ Jardin Quintero
8 ~ tourist office
9 ~ Museo Nacional de la Mascara, la Danza, y el Arte
     Popular de Occidente
10~ Jardin Nunez
11~ Casa de la Cultura
     Museo de las Culturas de Occidente
A ~ Hotel Ceballos
B ~ Hotel San Cristobal

copies of the famous "Colima dogs" figures, are displayed and sold.

Immediately east of the Palacio is the second plaza, **Jardín Quintero**. The **tourist office** is across the street and east of the Jardín. At the corner of 27 de Septiembre and Manuel Gallardo is the **Museo Nacional de la Máscara, la Danza, y el Arte Popular de Occidente** (National Museum of Masks, Dance, and Popular Art of the West). This museum has a large display of pre-Hispanic as well as modern Indian masks, ritual clothing, and other artifacts. The museum is open Mon-Sat, 10 a.m. to 1:30 p.m.

Jardín Nuñez, the third plaza, is three blocks east of Jardín Quintero. To the northeast about 10 blocks at the corner of Paseo Independencia and Ejército Nacional is the **Casa de la Cultura** (House of Culture). This government-run complex includes exhibit halls, art schools, theaters, and the **Museo de las Culturas de Occidente** (Museum of Western Cultures). Besides art exhibits, there are dance, music, and drama recitals held at the Casa de la Cultura. The Museo de las Culturas has an outstanding collection of over 700 pre-Hispanic artifacts from this region. The exhibits include one devoted to the "Colima dog" figure which is unique to this area. There are also displays on the ethnographic history of the region. The museum is open Tues-Sun, 9 a.m. to 1 p.m. and 4 p.m. to 6 p.m.

Fiestas. The **Colima Regional Fair** is held the last week in October to promote the products of the region. Crafts, industrial, and agricultural displays take place in the historic center of town.

Climate. At 494 m above sea level and about 50 km from the coast Colima enjoys warm but not oppressively hot temperatures. Winters are mild and pleasant. The area does get about 100 cm (40 in) of rain a year, most of this in the summer.

Manzanillo

Manzanillo is Mexico's most important Pacific port and a growing industrial center. It is also a popular beach resort because of excellent conditions for fishing, boating, and swimming. Aside from the beaches, this city of 70,000 people is not a pretty place. Nor is it a cheap place. Also, bring insect repellent as the fresh water lagoons in the area are prolific mosquito hatcheries.

Getting Around. It is a short walk from the **train station** to downtown. It is also easy to get to any of the area's major beaches from here since local buses depart regularly for the beaches from the station. The **bus station** is about one km east of downtown. You can either walk the distance, catch a local bus marked "Centro," or pay a cab driver $2 to take you to *el centro*.

Sights. There is really no reason to go to Manzanillo except the beach, but there are some nice ones. The closest beach to the zócalo is **Playa San Pedrito**, about a kilometer east of the main plaza. However, this spot is too close to the industrial and commercial operations of the city to be very pleasant. Across the Bahía de Manzanillo are **Playa Las Brisas** and **Playa Azul**. This continuous stretch of fine beach contains most of the town's resort hotels. Still, the beaches are so long that they are never crowded.

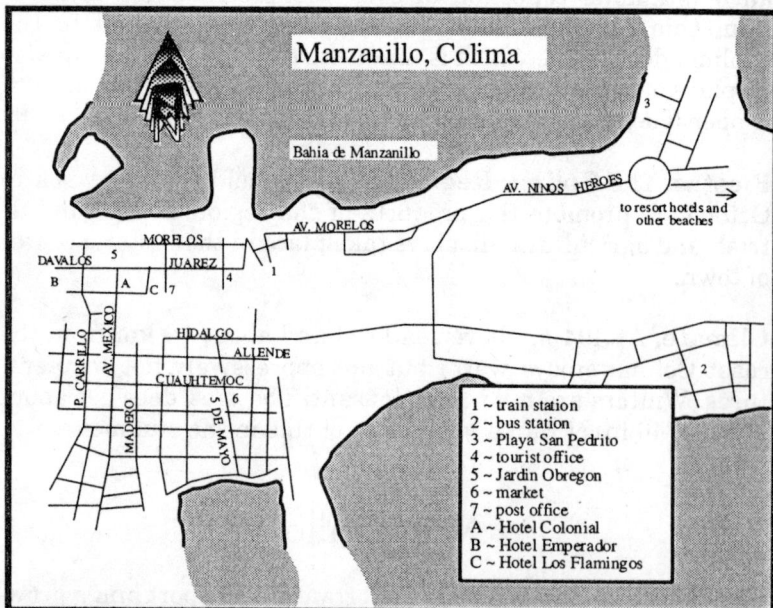

Manzanillo, Colima

Bahia de Manzanillo

AV. NIÑOS HEROES

to resort hotels and other beaches

MORELOS
AV. MORELOS
DAVALOS   5
JUAREZ
B   A   C   7
HIDALGO
ALLENDE
CUAUHTEMOC
P. CARRILLO
AV. MEXICO
MADERO
5 DE MAYO

1 ~ train station
2 ~ bus station
3 ~ Playa San Pedrito
4 ~ tourist office
5 ~ Jardin Obregon
6 ~ market
7 ~ post office
A ~ Hotel Colonial
B ~ Hotel Emperador
C ~ Hotel Los Flamingos

Continuing west along the curving coastline leads to the Bahía de Santiago and the four best beaches in the area: **La Audiencia**, **Olas Altas**, **Santiago**, and **Miramar**. Surf boards can be rented at Miramar. To get to Las Brisas or Playa Azul, take any bus marked "Las Brisas" from the train station. To get to the beaches in the Bahía de Santiago, grab any bus marked "Miramar." It will stop at each beach.

Manzanillo is also well-known as a sports fishing center with people coming here to fish for yellowtail, sailfish, marlin, and shark among others. The best fishing is from November through May. Boats, gear, and guides can be rented.

Climate. Not surprisingly, Manzanillo is hot and humid. Massive storms occasionally come ashore, especially during August and September.

Train Along The West Coast

Leaving the city of Guadalajara, the train winds its way westward across the northern part of the state of Jalisco and through the foothills of the Sierra Madre Occidental. After about 70 km (42 mi) the train enters the small coastal state of Nayarit. Here the mountains continue but the vegetation takes a distinct turn toward the tropical. Just past the Ceboruco volcano the railroad angles northwestward and soon arrives at the capital of the state, Tepic.

Nayarit borders the states of Sinaloa and Durango to the north, Jalisco to the east and south, and the Pacific Ocean to the west. Its name comes from a Coran Indian word meaning "god of battles." The eastern part of the state is dominated by the almost impenetrable Sierra Madre Occidental. These mountains protect the lands and cultures of the Cora and Huichol Indians. The only way in is either by long hike or airplane.

The central area of the state consists of broad valleys broken by a northwest-trending series of volcanos. Notable among these are the volcanos Ceboruco, Tepeltitic, and Sanguanguey. This latter overlooks the city of Tepic.

Nayarit's coastline is beautiful, tropical, and largely uncommer-
cialized, the exception being the town of San Blas. The state also
boasts the longest beach in the entire country, Novillero, which
measures at 72 km (45 mi).

Before the arrival of the Spanish most of the state was occupied
by nomadic Indian groups whose cultures left few lasting records. However, in the southern part of the state at Ixtlán del
Río is an important though poorly restored archeological site.
Here evidence of Toltec culture establishes this as the western-
most site of that central Mexican civilization. Today, the indigenous groups which have survived in Nayarit are found in the
mountains. The Tepehuanos live in the sierras of the northwestern corner of the state and extend into southern Durango. The
villages of the Cora Indians are located deep in the Sierra
Madres in the eastern part of the state. The similarly inaccessible Huichol communities are found south of the Cora and extend
into northern Jalisco.

After leaving Tepic the train quickly descends to the broad
coastal plain of northwestern Nayarit and crosses into Sinaloa
state. This is a good time for a nap, cards, or some reading as
the scenery changes very little until you approach Mazatlán.
Within about 80 km (48 mi) of that city the railway begins to
skirt the eastern margin of a series of freshwater lagoons and
marshes. If you are sitting on the left side of the car you have
an excellent chance of spotting a variety of waterfowl such as
great blue heron, reddish egret, cattle egret, Mexican tiger-bit-
tern, Jabiru stork, and white-faced ibis.

The long, thin state of Sinaloa is sandwiched between the
rugged Sierra Madre Occidental to the east and the Gulf of
California and Pacific Ocean to the west. It is bordered to the
north by the states of Sonora and Chihuahua, to the east by
Durango, and to the south by Nayarit. The sierras are so formi-
dable here that only one road manages to cross them, the
Mazatlán-Durango highway. It is a spectacular and scary road
across the rocky spine of the mountains. Be sure to smell the
breath of any bus driver offering to take you across.

Stretching northwest along the coast, Sinaloa is a series of
fertile valleys and coastal lowlands well-watered by the rivers

and streams which tumble off the western flanks of the Sierra Madres. The major agricultural products include sugar cane, tomatos, cotton, wheat, and rice. Mining, fishing, and tourism follow in importance to the state's economy.

At the time of the arrival of the Spanish Sinaloa was inhabited by Nahua Indian tribes which survived by hunting and fishing. Among the indigenous groups living in the region were the Chimalhuacanos, Tepehuanos, Mayos, and Gusanes. Today there is virtually no indigenous influence left in the state. Both Mazatlán and Culiacán, the capital of Sinaloa, were founded by Nuño Beltran de Guzmán in 1531. The hostility of the Indians and the remoteness of the region, however, prevented these towns from being anything more than tiny Spanish outposts for 250 years.

North of Mazatlán the railroad hugs the coast for about 100 km (60 mi) and then angles inland toward the capital city of Culiacán. The countryside here consists of vast irrigated fields disappearing into the distance.

From Culiacán to the border of Sonora 200 km (120 mi) away the scenery varies from farmland to rangeland to wasteland so it may once again be time for the knitting or that 600-page novel. But if you are open to it, there is no stretch of track that doesn't offer startling glimpses into Mexican life and culture: an old man riding horseback with a guitar slung over his shoulder; women washing clothes in the waters of a brown river and drying them on lava-rock boulders under a desert sky; eight year-old boys herding goats in a land so sparse that even grasshoppers ignore and fly past it. These scenes are the stuff of life in rural Mexico.

Sonora is the second largest state in the country and were it not for dams and irrigation projects this state would be essentially one big desert. The ranges of the Sierra Madre Occidental, which occupy the eastern half of the state, capture some rainfall. The rivers which then sneak out of the highlands are dammed to provide water for huge agricultural projects in the south around Ciudad Obregón and Navojoa. The northern part of the state remains desert. Several hundred years ago this region was occupied by a variety of different indigenous groups,

notably the Pima, Papago, Yaqui, Mayo, Opato, and Seri. When
the Spaniards first arrived they found settled, agricultural
native tribes living in the fertile river valleys of southern Sonora. Chief among these tribes were the Yaqui and Mayo people.
The Indians repulsed the first Spanish military efforts and for
the next 300 years their only real contact with the Europeans
was in the form of Catholic missionaries. By the 1880s the
Indians' land was being eyed greedily by wealthy Mexican
businessmen. Technocrats of the Porfirio Díaz dictatorship declared that the indigenes were not using the land efficiently and
that in the hands of capitalists the land could yield important
agricultural exports. So the government seized the Yaqui and
Mayo farms and turned the land over to *criollo* businessmen.
The Yaqui responded by forming a guerrilla army which raided
the Mexican operations and retreated into the rugged Sierra
Madres when necessary. Under the leadership of Cajeme, an
ally of Benito Juárez in the War of the Reform, the Yaqui troops
defeated every military force sent after them. But they could not
defeat hunger. Without land to grow food, the Yaqui were forced
by starvation to surrender.

To make the area safe for profitmaking, the governor of Sonora,
Ramón Corral, had Cajeme shot and ordered the rest of the
recalcitrant Yaqui sold to the henequen plantation owners of
distant Yucatán. Corral grew rich from the sale of human beings
and the Yaqui rebellion was crushed. Today, there are still
Yaqui and Mayo in Sonora. But with little access to water or the
best land, most of them work as low-wage laborers on huge
corporate farms, on the land that was once theirs.

The first sustained Spanish presence in the region began in the
mid-17th Century when gold was discovered in southern Sonora
and a string of missions was built in northern Sonora. While the
gold led to the founding and rapid growth of the town of Alamos,
the missions produced a slower but steady growth of agricultural towns in the north.

Today Sonora is one of the wealthiest states in Mexico largely
because of the bounty of its irrigated croplands. This state
produces more wheat than any other as well as 30 percent of
Mexico's annual cotton production. Other important products
are soybeans, alfalfa, and cattle. Mining is important to the

state's economy as well. However, the most dynamic sector of the economy is manufacturing. *Maquiladora* plants are springing up right and left in Hermosillo and manufacturing for export to the United States everything from camping gear to automobile engines.

After passing through the cities of Navojoa and Ciudad Obregón in the southern agricultural heartland of the state, the railroad slowly curves west and intersects the coastline at Empalme. The port of Guaymas is 10 km (6 mi) to the west. From here the train turns northward and after 150 km (90 mi) arrives at the capital city of Hermosillo. Past the city the track continues north through a flat arid landscape inhabited by saguaro, cholla, and ocotillo cacti. To the east one can see the hazy blue outlier ranges of the Sierra Madres.

At Benjamín Hill the train divides with one segment continuing north to the border town of Nogales. The remainder of the train travels west northwest to the city of Mexicali in Baja California. During the daytime in the summer this part of the state is a furnace.

Train Services. Trains 1 and 2 ("Pacífico") provide special first class service between Guadalajara and several cities in northwestern Mexico. In order of increasing distance from Guadalajara these cities are: Tepic, Mazatlán, Culiacán, Sufragio, Navojoa, Ciudad Obregón, Empalme, Hermosillo, Benjamín Hill, and Nogales. At Benjamín Hill a line branches off the main track and provides service to Mexicali in Baja California. Second class coach service between Guadalajara, Nogales, Mexicali, and points in between is provided by Trains 3 and 4.

PACÍFICO TRAIN

Train 2		Guadalajara	Train 1		Reserved Seat
Lv.	9:30 AM	Guadalajara	7:00 PM	Ar.	
	1:35 PM	Tepic	1:30 PM		$ 7.97
	6:30 PM	Mazatlán	8:15 AM		17.13
	9:44 PM	Culiacán	5:26 AM		23.52
	0:45 AM(+1)	Sufragio	2:15 AM		29.61
	2:45 AM	Navojoa	12:36 AM	(+1)	33.68
	3:57 AM	Ciudad Obregón	11:24 PM		35.71
	5:40 AM	Empalme	9:55 PM		39.19

7:45 AM	Hermosillo	7:45 PM		43.26
9:25 AM	Benjamín Hill	5:44 PM		47.03
Ar. 11:50 AM	Nogales	3:30 PM	Lv.	51.10

| Lv. 9:25 AM | Benjamín Hill | 5:10 PM | Ar. | |
| Ar. 5:55 PM | Mexicali | 9:00 AM | Lv. | 62.42 |

				2nd. Class
Train 3		Train 4		Coach
Lv. 12:00 PM	Guadalajara	5:55 PM	Ar.	
4:45 PM	Tepic	10:25 AM		$ 2.32
10:55 PM	Mazatlán	4:35 AM		4.94
2:40 AM(+1)	Culiacán	0:30 AM(+1)		6.81
7:10 AM	Sufragio	8:15 PM		8.55
5:56 PM	Benjamín Hill	9:30 AM		13.58
Ar. 9:00 PM	Nogales	7:00 AM	Lv.	14.77

| Lv. 9:20 PM | Benjamín Hill | 7:30 AM(+1) | Ar. | |
| Ar. 6:15 AM(+1) | Mexicali | 9:50 PM | Lv. | 18.03 |

Tepic

Tepic was officially founded in 1531 by Nuño Beltran de Guzmán on the flank of the extinct Volcán Sanguanguey. Its name derives from a Nahuatl word meaning "place among hills." Despite the early date of its founding, Tepic languished for hundreds of years. Only after the construction of the railroad did the town begin to grow, serving as a commercial center for the rich agricultural region surrounding it. With a current population of around 150,000 inhabitants, Tepic is the capital of Nayarit state.

Getting Around. The **train station** is an easy walk from the zócalo, about 10 blocks to the west on Av. Allende. Likewise the **bus station** is close to the center of town near the intersection of Insurgentes and P. Sanchez.

Sights. Tepic is a fairly dull town. There are really only two good reasons to stop here: the **Museo Regional de Antropología e Historia** (the Regional Museum of Anthropology and History) and several interesting excursions which can be made into the surrounding countryside. The Regional Museum is two blocks north of the zócalo at the corner of Av. Mexico and

Tepic, Nayarit

1 ~ train station
2 ~ bus station
3 ~ Plaza Principal
4 ~ Museo Regional de Antropologia e Historia
5 ~ Cathedral
6 ~ post office
7 ~ tourist office
A ~ Hotel Sierra de Alicia/Hotel Imperial

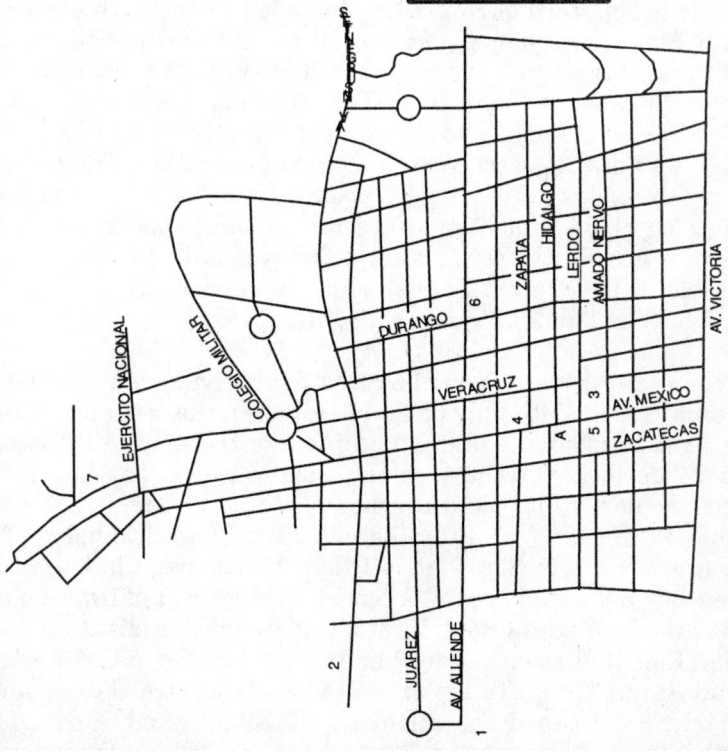

Zapata. Occupying the 18th Century former house of the Count
of Miravalle, the museum contains an outstanding collection of
ceramic artifacts found in Nayarit. These pieces range from the
classic period (400-600 AD) to the post-classic (900-1100 AD)
with many of these latter having been collected at Ixtlán del Río.
Unfortunately, the collections are poorly organized and inade-
quately labelled. Despite this it is the best collection of its type
in Mexico. The museum also contains displays on Coran and
Huichol ethnography. The museum is open Tues-Sun, 9 a.m. to
1 p.m. and 5 p.m. to 7 p.m.

There are several shops on the main plaza which sell crafts
produced by the Cora and Huichol Indians. And that's about all
there is to do in Tepic.

Excursions. On the Pacific coast 69 km (43 mi) northeast of
Tepic is the town of **San Blas**. Founded in the 17th Century,
San Blas was a major port during the colonial period. In the
18th Century Spain made a determined effort to explore and
colonize what is today Baja California and the west coast of
North America as far as Alaska. During this flurry of Spanish
activity San Blas served as the base of operation. The priests,
Fray Junípero Serra and Francisco Kino, departed from San
Blas on their expeditions to establish missions in the Cali-
fornias and northwest Mexico. A fort was built in the 1760s to
protect the port from English and Dutch buccaneers. Its ruins
can be found on a hill just east of town.

Today, San Blas is a combination fishing village and low-key
beach resort. With only 6,000 inhabitants, the town has a very
relaxed atmosphere and is nothing like the more famous and
more developed resorts on the Pacific coast. The setting is
spectacular: white sand beaches bordered on one side by the
blue Pacific and on the other by lush jungle canopies. The
nearest beach to San Blas is **Playa El Borrega** but the best
beaches are found several kilometers southeast of town on the
Bahía de Matanchén. In order of increasing distance from
San Blas these beaches are **Las Islitas**, **Los Cocos**, **Miramar**,
and **Santa Cruz**. To get out to these idyllic stretches of sand,
catch a bus at the bus station at Calle Sinaloa and Canalizo for
the village of Santa Cruz. This 25-km trip follows the curve of
the Bahía de Matanchén passing each beach in turn. Simply

take your pick of paradises by shouting "Baja" to the bus driver.

But sea air is not all that San Blas offers. Boats leaving from the dock at the San Cristóbal bridge (on the road into town) take passengers to the fresh water springs of **La Tovara**. The half-hour cruise up river passes through lush jungle and deposits visitors at a lovely pool fed by a crystalline spring. Take your swimsuit and insect repellent. There is a small restaurant at La Tovara but there are no overnight facilities. The price of the cruise is fixed by the tourist office and a maximum of six people can fit in the launch.

To get to San Blas, catch a 2nd class Norte de Sonora bus at the

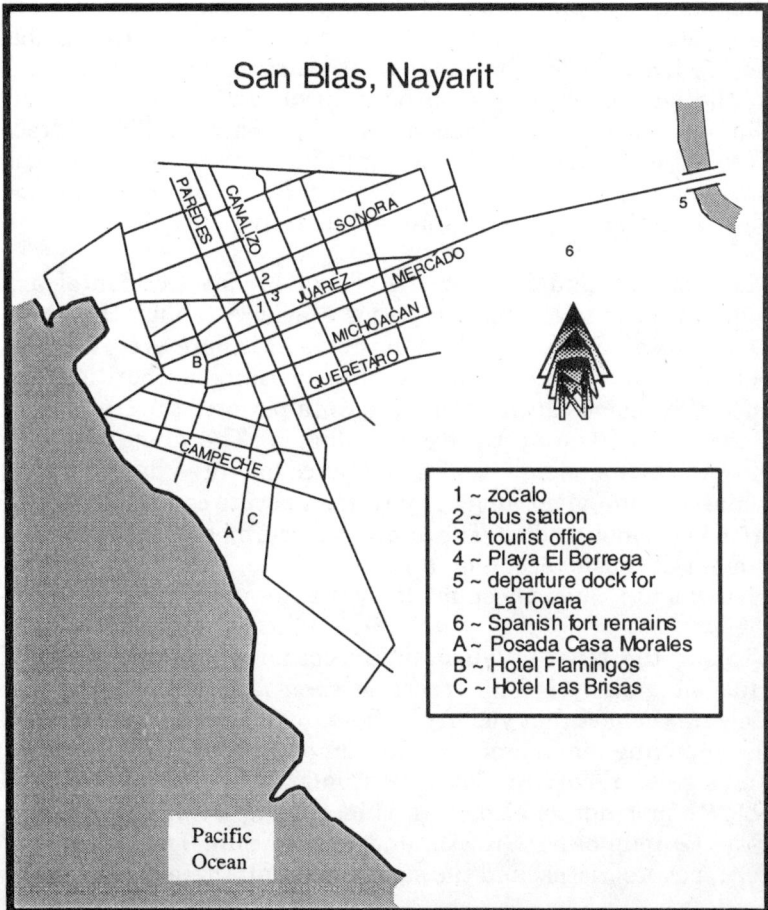

San Blas, Nayarit

1 ~ zocalo
2 ~ bus station
3 ~ tourist office
4 ~ Playa El Borrega
5 ~ departure dock for La Tovara
6 ~ Spanish fort remains
A ~ Posada Casa Morales
B ~ Hotel Flamingos
C ~ Hotel Las Brisas

Pacific Ocean

station in Tepic. There are several a day and the trip takes about one and a half hours. One final word of warning: the heat and the bugs are two reasons that the paradisiacal San Blas hasn't blossomed into a mega-tourist center. So take your sunscreen and heavy duty insect repellent and you will have a more pleasant stay.

Hidden in the mountains of eastern Nayarit are the communities of the **Cora** and **Huichol** Indians. It is possible to visit these areas but it is not easy. Nor should it be. As with all the indigenous people of Mexico, these people have suffered from their encounter with European/Western culture. The inaccessibility of their mountain fastness has saved them from the worst effects but the pressure to change, though less violent now, is relentless. Both the Cora and Huichol survive by farming and raising livestock on what small plots of arable land they can find in the sierras. Both people have incorporated only minimal Christian dogma and ceremony into their native religious practices. The Huichol especially continue to practice an almost unchanged pre-Conquest spirituality. Both cultures also employ the hallucinogenic peyote cactus in their rituals.

The Cora communities in the Sierra Madre Occidental are centered around the town of Jesús María. Although this town has a mix of *mestizo* and Indian people, it is here every December 31 that the Cora elect their governing authorities. On special occasions such as this the Cora perform the traditional *Danza de la Urraca* (Dance of the Magpie). The young men who perform this ancient ritual must dance for three days nonstop while consuming nothing but peyote. A peyote concoction is also rubbed on their bodies. The dance is performed to the accompaniment of music played on a violin, a flute, and drums—all the instruments having been made by the Coran children.

Visiting the town of Guadalupe Ocotlán in the heartland of Huichol country is like traveling even farther back in time. Despite the fact that you arrive here by plane, there seem to be fewer jarring reminders of the contemporaneous scientific world and a greater, encompassing spirituality. The Huichol still worship their traditional deities, chief among them Grandfather Fire, Grandmother Growth, and Father Sun. They also deify corn, peyote cactus, and the sacred deer, all three being considered manifestations of the same god. Their most important ceremonial rituals are associated with the planting and harvesting seasons. The Huichol are very creative people and not shy about incorporating modern materials, such as glass beads and acrylic yarn, into their art. While they may use contemporary materials, the content uncompromisingly reflects their religious symbols and myths. Unlike Western cultures, the Huichol do not separate their lives from their art. Everything in nature has spiritual meaning and this includes their actions and crafts.

If you are prepared to leave camera, videocam, and ethnocentrism at home, then you might be allowed to visit either one or both regions. The tourist office in Tepic knows the procedures necessary and will help you through the process.

Mazatlán

Mazatlán clusters along 25 km (15 mi) of curvaceous Pacific coast which alternates between fine sandy beaches and rocky promontories. This city of 275,000 people is really two cities: the northern resort area, the **Zona Dorada** (Golden Zone), where modern, high-rise hotels crowd the beach, and the southern **Old Mazatlán** which is the historic center of the city.

The first settlement here was founded in 1531 but it remained tiny, often virtually disappearing, until the 1800s. By the early 19th Century the growth of exports from the newly independent Mexico led to the rapid development of the port of Mazatlán. But the town still faced problems. In 1847, as one of the theaters of the U.S.-Mexican War, Mazatlán was occupied by U.S. troops. Then, in 1864, it was the turn of the French military, which occupied the port as part of Napoleon III's effort to install the puppet-emperor Maximillian on the Mexican "throne." The remainder of the 19th Century allowed for more normal growth of the port. The city's fishing industry began to grow rapidly in the early 20th Century and Mazatlán's tourism industry began to take off in the post-war boom years of the 1950s. It is the original Mexican resort town, the "Pearl of the Pacific."

Today, Mazatlán remains a popular resort destination for both Mexicans and North Americans. It is not as glitzy as the newer

Mazatlan, Sinaloa

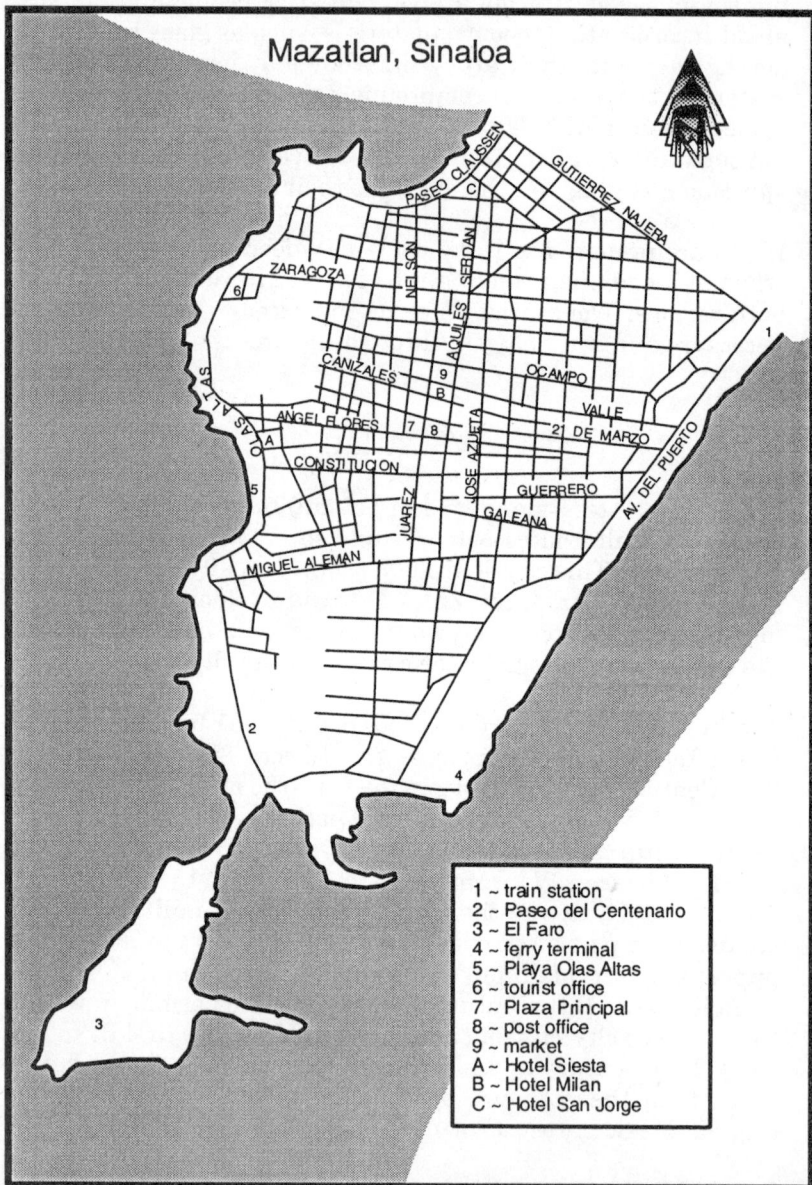

1 ~ train station
2 ~ Paseo del Centenario
3 ~ El Faro
4 ~ ferry terminal
5 ~ Playa Olas Altas
6 ~ tourist office
7 ~ Plaza Principal
8 ~ post office
9 ~ market
A ~ Hotel Siesta
B ~ Hotel Milan
C ~ Hotel San Jorge

resort areas but compensates for this by being cheaper than places like Ixtapa or Cancún. Mazatlán also compensates by remaining a truly Mexican town. Old Mazatlán is remarkably independent of the resort area to the north and effectively counterbalances the Zona Dorada with its own solidly Mexican atmosphere. Many people return to Mazatlán precisely because it is not simply an enclave of corporate North America.

Getting Around. As far as local transportation goes, if the bus system is frustrating you take a *pulmonia*. These three-wheeled golf carts pass for taxis in Mazatlán. They are ubiquitous, especially along the always popular Malecón, and they are cheap. The **train station** is about five km northwest from the center of Old Mazatlán on Gabriel Leyva. The "Insurgentes" bus travels between downtown and the train station. The **bus station** is just west of the intersection of Río Tamazula and Av. Ejército Mexicano. "Playa Sur," "Playa Azul," and "Villa Galaxia" buses run along Ejército Mexicano to the center of Old Mazatlán, though the "Villa Galaxia" bus only goes as far as the market.

Sights. Dichotomous Mazatlán is strung together by a seaside promenade which, because this is Mexico, changes its name several times along its length. At its rocky southern extreme this coast-hugging road is **Paseo del Centenario**. The cliffs to which it clings offer nice walkways and lookouts over the Pacific. But the finest observation point over both the sea and city is off the southern tip of the Paseo where on top of a rocky spit of land is **El Faro**, at 157 m the highest lighthouse in the Western Hemisphere and, after Gibraltar, the second highest in the world. The 40-minute climb to the summit of the hill starts out on a dirt road but the last 30 meters are via a dirt path. The view from the top is well worth the effort but take something to drink. Just east of El Faro at the mouth of the Bahía Dársena is the **ferry terminal**. There are daily ferry departures for the town of La Paz in Baja California Sur. (For more information see the "Excursion" section.) Northeast of the ferry offices in the Bahía Dársena are the commercial docks where most of the fishing fleet sits when not at sea.

To the north, Paseo del Centenario becomes **Calzada Olas Altas**. Its namesake, **Playa Olas Altas**, is a well-worn, second class beach which is still a lovely place for a stroll. Just north of the beach the road and coast are forced to bulge westward by the hill, Cerro de la Neveria. Just west of Neveria on Olas Altas is one of two **tourist offices** in Mazatlán. The other is in the Zona Dorada. On the southern flank of Cerro de la Neveria Av. Angel Flores intersects Calz. Olas Altas. Ten blocks east of this intersection is the historic center of the city, the heart of Old Mazatlán. While there are not many sights here in the center, it is where most of the cheap hotels and public services are found.

The **Plaza Principal** or zócalo is at Juárez and 21 de Marzo. The plaza is small but quite lush and, especially in the evenings, festive. To the north is the uninteresting **Cathedral** and just east of the zócalo is the **post** and **telegraph office**. Two blocks north of the plaza on Av. Juárez is the **market**.

Getting around from the center of Old Mazatlán is easy. The "Playa Sur" bus runs south on Av. Aquiles Serdán to the ferry terminal, the base of El Faro, and along Playa Olas Altas before returning to the downtown area. The bus "Sábalo" travels between Old Mazatlán and the Zona Dorada. You can catch it on Av. Juárez next to the market.

After it curves around Cerro de la Neveria, Calz. Olas Altas becomes **Paseo Claussen** briefly and then, as the beach front promenade begins the long curve around Bahía Puerto Viejo and toward the northern resort area, it changes one last time to **Av. del Mar. Playa Norte** is a nice, uncrowded beach halfway between the old and new parts of the city. **Playa las Gaviotas** is at the northern terminus of Av. del Mar and is considered the beginning of the Zona Dorada. Just beyond las Gaviotas is **Playa Sábalo** which is always full of red-skinned tourists. The beaches continue for 10 km (six mi) past Sábalo, becoming less crowded as their distance from the Zona Dorada increases.

If you get tired of the mainland you can make arrangements at Hotel El Cid in the Zona Dorada for excursions to the islands which are just off the coast. The islands **Venados**, **Chivas**, and **Pájaros** offer excellent diving and snorkeling, birdwatching, and empty beaches. But take your own food, water, and sun protection as there are no services on the islands.

Fiestas. The festival for which Mazatlán is famous is **Carnival.** This week-long pre-Lenten celebration takes place primarily along the Calzada Olas Altas although there are outbreaks of festivities all over town. Tens of thousands of Mazatlecos and tourists, both Mexican and foreign, shed their inhibitions and their sobriety. The festivities include parades, costume balls, formal balls, fireworks displays, and plenty of singing, dancing, and drinking. The hotels fill up at Carnival time so book a hotel room well in advance.

Classes. Back in Mazatlán, Centro de Idiomas offers Spanish conversation classes at all levels with a maximum of six students per class. Contact:

Centro de Idiomas, S.A.
Belisario Dominguez 1908
Mazatlán, Sinaloa, MEXICO

Climate. Summers are very hot and humid. Most of the rainfall is in the summer and there are occasional, destructive Pacific storms (hurricanes) which can come ashore in late summer or early fall. Winters are drier, temperate, but only very rarely cool. The visitor should take precautions to protect eyes and skin from bright sun.

Excursions. Feel like something different? How about a low-budget cruise? The city of **La Paz** in Baja California Sur is only a 16-hour overnight ferry ride away from Mazatlán. The ferries depart daily and offer three classes of accommodation: salon class where you sit in a non-reclining chair for the duration; tourist class where you share a dorm-like room with up to four beds and a wash stand; and cabin class with two single beds and a bathroom. The ferries have facilities such as cafeteria, video room, restaurant/bar, store, and medical and security services. Children under 12 travel half-price, those under two are free, and pregnant women are not allowed to travel. Passengers disembark at the Pichilingue docks which are 17 km north of La Paz. There are cabs and buses waiting to transport travelers into town.

Located on a delightful bay and surrounded by the austere Bajan desert, La Paz is a wonderful mix of energy and tranquil-

La Paz, Baja California Sur

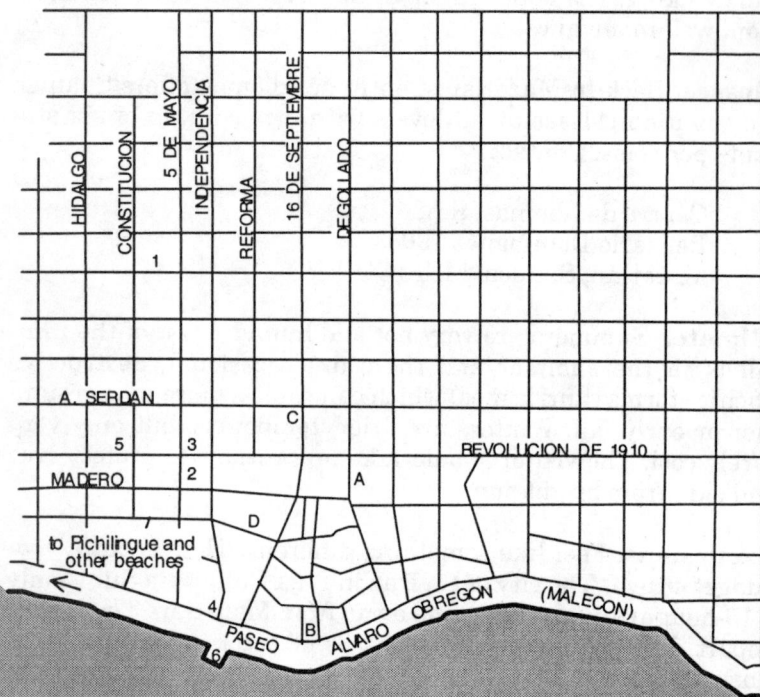

HIDALGO

CONSTITUCION

5 DE MAYO

INDEPENDENCIA

REFORMA

16 DE SEPTIEMBRE

DEGOLADO

1

A. SERDAN

C

5   3

REVOLUCION DE 1910

MADERO   2

A

to Pichilingue and
other beaches

D

4

B   ALVARO OBREGON   (MALECON)

PASEO

6

1 ~ Museo de Antropologia
2 ~ Plaza Constitucion
3 ~ Mision de Nuestra Senora
   de la Paz
4 ~ Autotransportes Aguila
5 ~ post office

6 ~ tourist office
A ~ Pension California
B ~ Hotel La Perla
C ~ Hotel Purisima
D ~ Posada San Miguel

ity. The palm-lined *malecón* along the waterfront is perfect for strolling and provides a great vantage point for watching the legendary La Paz sunsets. The **Museo de Antropología** (Anthropology Museum) at Altamirano and 5 de Mayo has displays on the geology and ethnology of southern Baja and on the colonial and modern history of the area.

The main plaza is **Plaza Constitución**. The old buildings around the plaza have been gracefully taken over by bookshops, restaurants, and theaters. Beside the plaza is the **Misión de Nuestra Señora de La Paz**. Although the church is modern, the site is that of La Paz's first mission which was built in 1720 by the Jesuits.

A series of excellent beaches are north of the city. All offer superb diving and snorkeling opportunities. Equipment can be rented at either of two dive shops in La Paz. These shops also arrange diving and snorkeling excursions. If you are not going on a package excursion, you can either take a taxi or public transportation to the beaches. "Autotransportes Aguila" runs buses from La Paz (the bus station is at Independencia and Alvaro Obregón) to the ferry docks at Pichilingue. About 100 m beyond the docks is **Pichilingue Beach**. There are a couple of restaurants and bathrooms here. Although there are beaches and a dirt road beyond Pichilingue there is no public transport. On the way to the docks, the bus passes the beaches of **Palmira**, **Corumuel**, and **Tesoro**. All have at least a restaurant and some shade. When you see a beach that looks good just shout "*Baja!*" and the driver will stop the bus to let you off. To get a bus back into town stand out on the road and flag one down. They really will stop.

Culiacán

There's really no reason to stop here unless you're interested in irrigated agriculture. The town is also a regional center for drug smuggling operations.

Sufragio

Sufragio is at the intersection of the "Pacífico" and the "Chihuahua-Pacífico" train routes. Unless you're making connections here to go to Los Mochis (please don't) or on the Copper Canyon train (please do), there is no reason to stop.

Navojoa

Navojoa is notable only as the gateway to the colonial town of Alamos. Buses run hourly from Navojoa to Alamos. The **bus station** is located near the main plaza on Av. Guerrero. The **train station** is three blocks due east of the plaza.

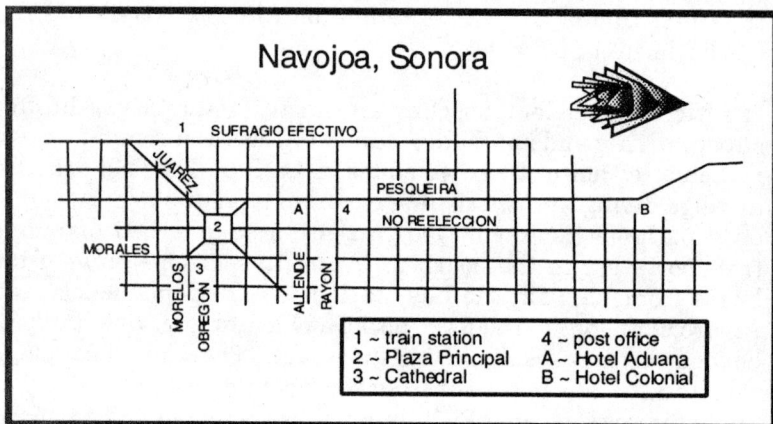

Navojoa, Sonora

1 ~ train station   4 ~ post office
2 ~ Plaza Principal   A ~ Hotel Aduana
3 ~ Cathedral   B ~ Hotel Colonial

Excursions. Alamos and its 5,000 inhabitants are cradled by the foothills of the Sierra Madre Occidental. In the 18th Century this mining town grew to 30,000 people and was one of the richest cities in Mexico. Gold and silver millionaires built elegant mansions and spent money on other luxuries as though the boom would go on forever. But the boom didn't. The exhaustion of the precious metal deposits, droughts, Indian raids, and, finally, the Mexican Revolution took their toll on Alamos so that by 1920 the town was largely abandoned.

Then, in the 1940s, North Americans discovered this deserted town with its decaying colonial mansions. U.S. retirees, artists, and investors began to move to Alamos and to buy and restore these colonial gems. The town is now beautifully restored and is the finest example of colonial Mexican architecture on the northwest coast. The population of Alamos is an easygoing mix

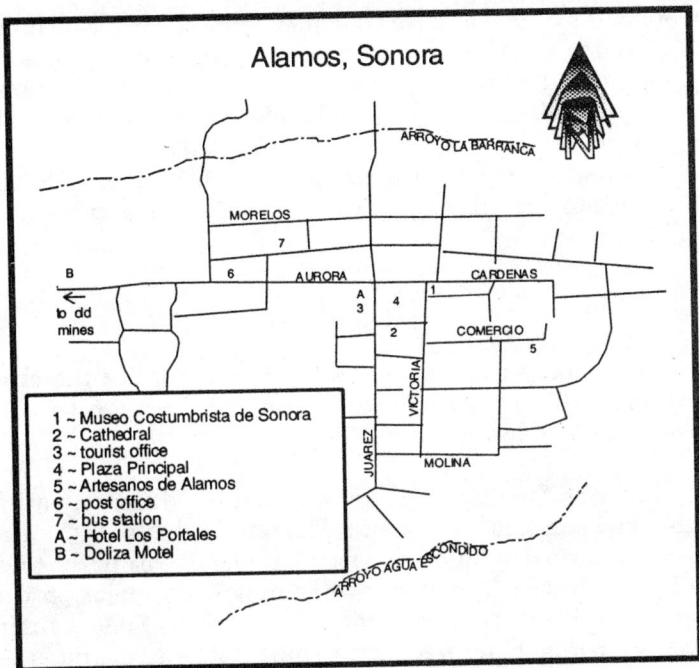

Alamos, Sonora

1 ~ Museo Costumbrista de Sonora
2 ~ Cathedral
3 ~ tourist office
4 ~ Plaza Principal
5 ~ Artesanos de Alamos
6 ~ post office
7 ~ bus station
A ~ Hotel Los Portales
B ~ Doliza Motel

of both Mexicans and North Americans although most of the Americans leave town during the severe Sonoran summer.

El Museo Costumbrista de Sonora (Museum of Sonoran Customs) contains displays of household items, clothes, mining equipment, and old photographs, all designed to show what life was like in this area back in the 19th Century. The museum is on the east side of the main plaza. The **Cathedral**, which is just south of the plaza, dates from the late 18th Century. The **tourist office** is located in the Hotel Los Portales which is immediately west of the plaza. If you are interested, ask here about excursions to the old mines and to the Indian villages in the hills. Arts and crafts from the region around Alamos can be viewed and purchased at the non-profit **Artesanos de Alamos** on Calle Comercio one block east of the plaza. The **bus station** is on Calle Morelos opposite the Plaza Alameda.

Ciudad Obregón

Ciudad Obregón sits in the middle of the fertile Yaqui Valley surrounded by thousands of irrigated acres of corn, wheat, rice, cotton, and vegetables. The wealth and productivity of the area is palpable and most of it is owned or controlled by foreigners. The Yaqui Indians have been relegated to the nearby, water-poor towns of **Cocorit**, **Bacum**, **Torin**, **Vicam**, and **Potam**. The only reason to visit this city is to fix this image of fertility and wealth in one's mind and then to visit the Yaqui towns.

Empalme

Empalme is only noteworthy as the train stop for the city of **Guaymas**, 10 km (six mi) to the west. Buses run regularly between the two towns.

Guaymas was founded in 1701 when Father Juan Salvatierra established a mission at the site. The town didn't really begin to grow until the early 1800s, when expanding trade put the town's fine harbor to use. Today Guaymas remains a major port and most of the silver, gold, and copper produced by Sonora's mines is shipped through here. A large fishing fleet also operates from the harbor and seafood processing is a growing industry in the town. Guaymas is a dynamic working-class town and generally holds little interest for the traveler.

Two exceptions to this observation are **Bahía San Carlos** and the **ferry terminal**. San Carlos is an area of lovely beaches curving between a deep blue bay and the rugged pink mountains of the Sonoran desert. Unfortunately, San Carlos has been taken over by gringos. There are two large marinas, an 18-hole golf course, motorhomes crowded into trailer parks, upscale hotels and restaurants, and myriad sail and power boats bobbing on the bright waters of Bahía San Carlos. If this appeals to you, then there are frequent buses traveling the 16 km (10 mi) between Guaymas and San Carlos.

Another reason for stopping at Guaymas is that ferry service connects this town with that of Santa Rosalia in Baja California Sur. The ferry departs Guaymas at 10 a.m. on Sunday, Tuesday, Friday, and Saturday. The trip takes eight hours. On the Guaymas side it is easy to get a ticket the day before you want to leave. In Santa Rosalia, however, it is sometimes more difficult.

Hermosillo

Hermosillo is a modern, friendly, and growing city. Founded in 1700, today it has over half a million inhabitants and is one of the fastest growing cities in Mexico. The basis for this rapid

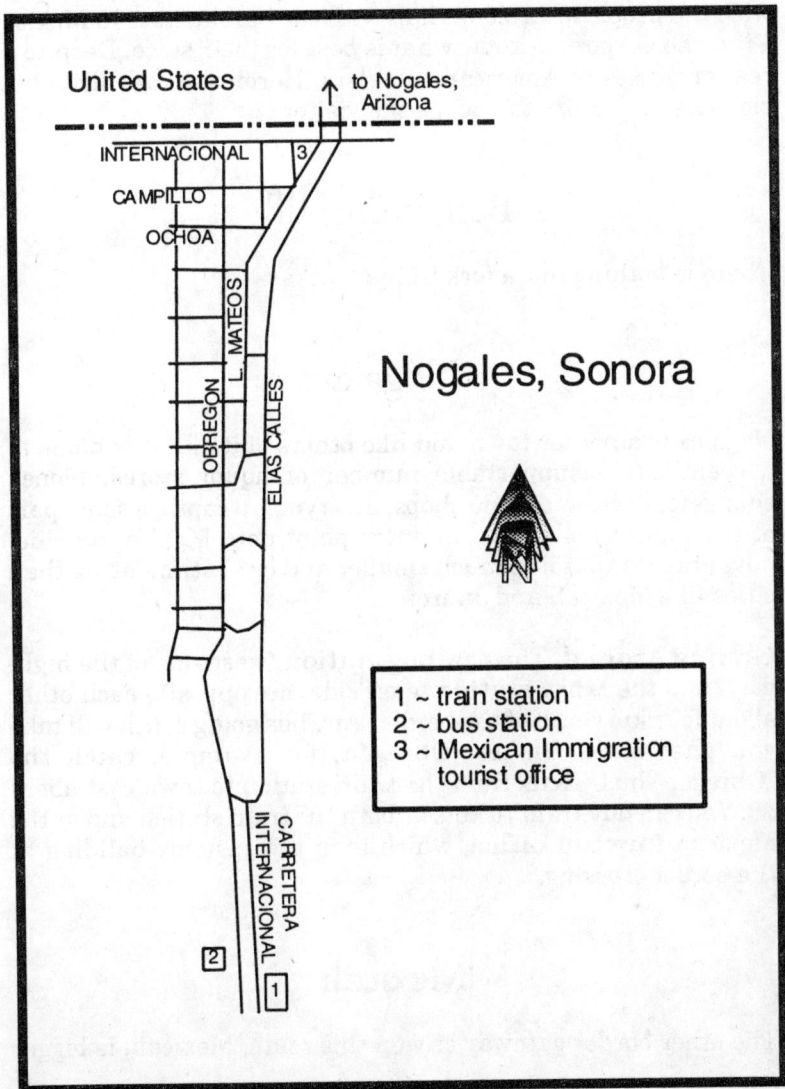

United States

to Nogales,
Arizona

INTERNACIONAL

3

CAMPILLO

OCHOA

L. MATEOS

OBREGON

ELIAS CALLES

Nogales, Sonora

1 ~ train station
2 ~ bus station
3 ~ Mexican Immigration
     tourist office

CARRETERA
INTERNACIONAL

2

1

growth is a dynamic manufacturing-for-export sector. U.S.-made components are assembled into finished products, which are then exported for sale to the United States.

It's not just the economy, however, that has a close association with things U.S. Many of the people here have traveled in the southwest U.S. and are openly admiring of American culture. These urban Sonorans often feel that they have more in common with the people of Arizona than with the bureaucrats in Mexico City who purport to know what is best for their state. Despite a real openness to American travelers, Hermosillo has little besides its modernity to engage the visitor.

Benjamín Hill

There is nothing but a fork in the tracks.

Nogales

Nogales is a border town and like others of its ilk it is home to a seemingly insupportable number of liquor stores, money changers, bars, and curio shops, all trying to capture some part of the tourist dollar. As an entry point onto Mexico, its chief advantage is that it is much smaller and less intimidating than cities like Mexicali and Juárez.

Getting Around. The new **bus station** (west side of the highway) and the **train station** (east side) are opposite each other about four km south of the border. Any bus going south will take you past both. On Av. Obregón, for example, catch the "Obregón" bus. Taxis from the train station to town cost about $3. You can buy train tickets at both the train station and at the Mexican **tourism office**, which is in the customs building at the border crossing.

Mexicali

The other border gateway city on this route, Mexicali, is bigger than Nogales and therefore has fewer saving graces. Don't spend any more time here than it takes to pick up that bottle of rum you promised Uncle Tony.

Getting Around. The **train station** is near the intersection of Calzada López Mateos and Calle Ulises Irigoyen, about four km south of the border. The **bus station** is near the train station at Calz. López Mateos and Calz. Independencia. From the border, the "Centro Cívico" bus goes to the train station and the "Central Camionera" to the bus station.

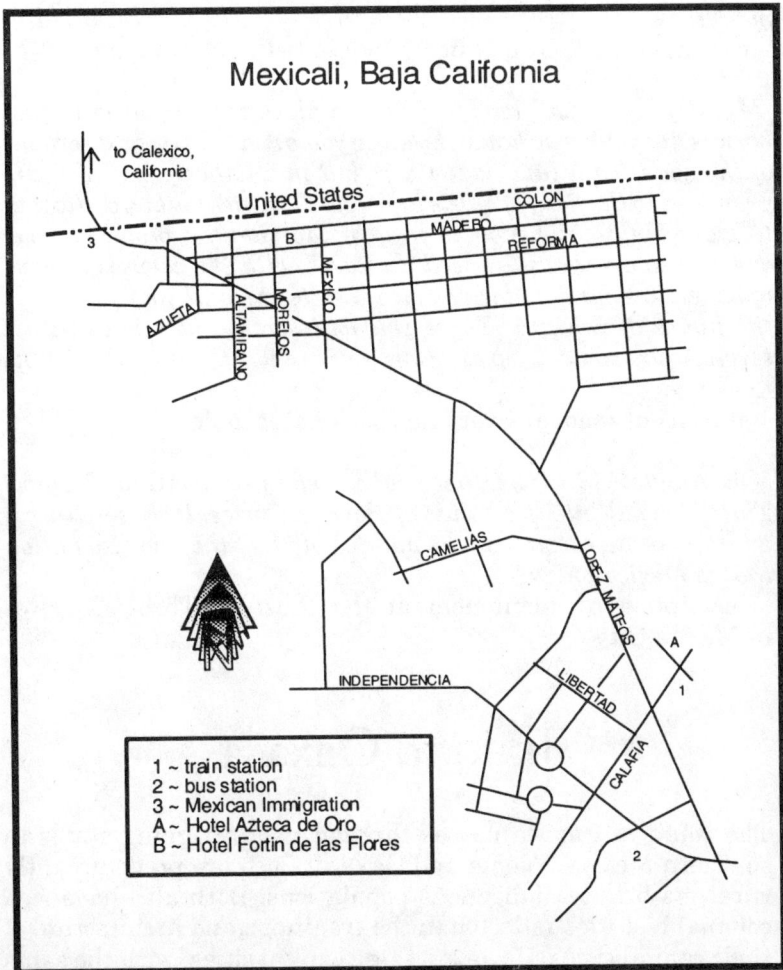

Mexicali, Baja California

Chapter 4
Routes South & East of Mexico City

"If Christians pray to the saints that are made by carpenters, why should not the Huichol pray to the sun which is so much better made?"
—-comment made by a Huichol Indian to Carl Lumholtz

"My very loved and tender son: this place where you were just born is not your true house, because you are a soldier and servant of the gods. Your land is not here but in another place. You are promised to the field of battle and your faculties will be dedicated to war. Your obligation is to give the sun the blood of your enemies to drink and to feed the earth with the corpses of your opponents. Your own land, your inheritance, and your fortune is the house of the sun. There you will serve and rejoice in his service if by some happy fortune you are worthy of dying by the flowery death."
—-statement made to every newborn Aztec male

"On August 13, 1521, heroically defended by Cuauhtémoc, Tlatelolco fell into the hands of Hernán Cortés. It was neither a triumph or defeat: it was the painful birth of the mestizo *nation that is Mexico today."*
—-inscription on monument at the Plaza of Three Cultures in Mexico City

Train to Oaxaca

The route to Oaxaca passes through two intriguing states in southern Mexico, Puebla and Oaxaca. Both are predominantly rural, with large indigenous populations. Both also have rich colonial histories reflected in the traditions and architecture of their capital cities. However, these capital cities, with the same

Rail Routes South, Southeast, and East of Mexico City

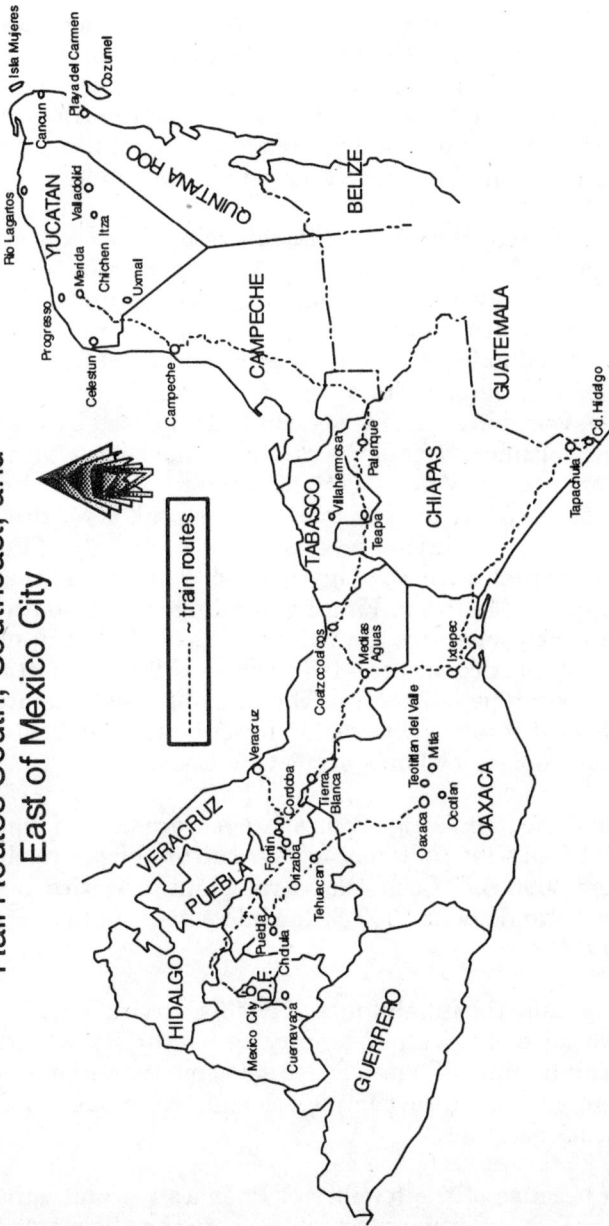

~ train routes

names as their surrounding states, wear these traditions to a very different effect. Puebla is like an old-money aristocrat who has discovered the lucrative pleasure of modern commercial activities and now shows both its colonial treasures and its industrial enterprises with equal pride. Oaxaca, on the other hand, is the aristocrat who failed to make the transition to the modern world and now, with reserve and gentility, parades its decaying colonial masterpieces before the public.

The long, irregular state of Puebla is bordered to the south by the states of Guerrero and Oaxaca, to the east by Veracruz, and to the west by Hidalgo, Tlaxcala, Mexico, and Morelos. The semi-arid southern third of the state is a confused, crumpled landscape dominated by the Sierra Madre del Sur. The middle part of Puebla consists of broad, high altitude valleys full of fertile, volcanic soil. This section is dominated by the presence of four volcanos. East of the capital on the border with the state of Veracruz is Volcán Citlaltépetl or, as it is also known, Orizaba. At 5,747 m, this snow-capped peak is Mexico's highest mountain. A few kilometers northeast of the city of Puebla and on the border with the tiny state of Tlaxcala is the 4,461-m volcano, La Malinche. Finally, in a huge north-south trending ridge which separates the Valley of Puebla from the smog-filled Valley of Mexico, are the twin volcanos Iztaccíhuatl (5,230 m) and Popocatépetl (5,465 m). The remainder of the state extends northward into the Sierra Madre Oriental and eastward into the subtropical lowlands of the Gulf Coast.

Arcaeological investigations in caves around Tehuacán have established that rudimentary agriculture began in this region around 7000 B.C. Corn, the sacred plant of Mexico, began to be domesticated about 5000 B.C. while pottery didn't appear until 2000 B.C.

By this time the inhabitants of Puebla, having killed off most of the larger game, were sedentary agriculturists settled in farming and fishing villages. These settlements stimulated the development of more complex social, religious, and artistic institutions.

Both because of the fertility of Puebla's volcanic soils and because of its intermediate position between the coastal lowland

and the central highland cultures, Puebla became a veritable highway along which different people passed and some settled. In the late pre-Classic the mysterious Olmec culture left its mark, as did the later Teotihuacán civilization (0-600 A.D.). During the later years of the Teotihuacán empire, the classic Veracruz culture dominated northern Puebla and influenced the major city-state of Cholula. Beginning around the 9th Century, successive waves of Chichimec tribes from arid northcentral Mexico entered the margins of central Mexico. As cities and civilizations fell to these "barbarians," refugees were produced, many of whom fled to the city of Cholula and other areas of Puebla. When, in the 12th Century, the Toltec empire fell to another surge of Chichimec warriors, Cholula was again the destination for many of the Toltec survivors. By the end of the 15th Century, the militaristic Aztecs had conquered most of Puebla and had incorporated it into their loose-knit empire.

In 1519, during his march from the Gulf Coast to the Aztec capital of Tenochtitlán, Cortés traveled through central Puebla. After slaughtering 6,000 people in Cholula, be and his troops climbed the volcanic ridge formed by Iztaccíhuatl and Popocatépetl, crossed between the two peaks at the Paso de Cortés, and continued on to meet Moctezuma and destiny.

Today, with the exception of the cities of Puebla and Tehuacán, this state is a collection of hundreds of small Indian villages hidden along dilapidated roads which wind through endless mountains. Scattered throughout the state in these isolated villages are 400,000 Nahua Indians. The Nahua are Mexico's largest indigenous group and are of the same cultural-linguistic family as the Aztecs. In addition to the Nahua, there are an estimated 100,000 other Indians in Puebla, with the majority of these being Totonacs in the north (60,000) and Mixtecs in the south (20,000). This large indigenous population makes Puebla one of the premier crafts regions in Mexico.

South of Puebla is the state of Oaxaca. This large, mountainous state is bordered to the west by Guerrero, to the north by Puebla and Veracruz, to the east by Chiapas, and to the south by the Pacific Ocean. The Oaxacan landscape is an almost unrelieved expanse of mountains with flat land being found only in a narrow strip along the Pacific coast, in the Central Valley where the city of Oaxaca is located, and in the eastern part of the state where Oaxaca meets the Isthmus of Tehuantepec.

Several thousand years ago, the Central Valley of Oaxaca had a wetter climate than it does today. There were lakes, forests, and fertile soils. These conditions prompted human habitation of the valley as early as 8000 B.C. and by 2000 B.C. there were permanent settlements. With a benign climate, abundant resources, and security provided by endless mountain ranges, these people developed several dynamic and creative cultures. The first culture of which there is an archaeological record, and a nameless one, appeared around 800 B.C. at Monte Albán and other sites in the valley. Though influenced by the Olmecs, this culture exhibited significant differences, being more advanced than the Olmecs in the areas of writing, the calendar, and mathematics. The oldest structures at Monte Albán demonstrate that this unknown people had the most sophisticated architecture in all of contemporaneous Mesoamerica.

The Zapotecs, who had been in the Central Valley since 250 B.C., probably occupied Monte Albán around 100 B.C. and remained there until that spectacular center was abandoned around 750 A.D. The Zapotecs were magnificent architects and builders as any visitor to Monte Albán can attest. Their civilization reached its zenith between 250 A.D. and 750 A.D. and was significantly influenced by the contemporaneous Teotihuacán culture.

Despite their abandonment of Monte Albán in 750 A.D., the Zapotecs continued to occupy other important centers in the Valley of Oaxaca such as Zaachila and Yagul. But for unknown reasons their civilization was in decline. So when the Mixtecs began moving into the valley in the 12th Century, there was little the Zapotecs could do in the face of this more dynamic culture. From this point on both people occupied the central valley with the Mixtec apparently assuming the role of ruling elite in most of the valley's population centers. Animosity between these two intermingled Oaxacan cultures facilitated the Aztec conquest of the valley by the early 16th Century. However, the Aztecs could not overcome stiffened Mixtec and Zapotec resistance and were unable to advance into southern Oaxaca.

After the Spanish arrived and overthrew Tenochtitlán, the Oaxacans were indisposed to trade one empire for another. Cortés had to send four expeditions into the area between 1520 and 1526 before it was safe enough to establish the city of Oaxaca in 1529. Sporadic Indian uprisings in Oaxaca continued throughout the colonial period.

Today Oaxaca has about three million people, of which a third are Indian. There are over 15 different indigenous groups in Oaxaca, each with its own language and customs. These demographics have produced a highly disorganized state and a situation where the majority of the rural, traditional population is not only outside the Mexican mainstream, but is ignorant of that mainstream's very existence. The practical impact of this lack of social cohesion has been a lack of political and economic power for the peasants and Indians of Oaxaca. This region is the second poorest state in Mexico. Since modernity and economic growth have passed by Oaxaca, the state remains pretty much as it has for thousands of years: a region of small Indian villages which survive by tilling unproductive soil and by making crafts. Oaxaca, along with Chiapas, is the most indigenous area in Mexico. A million people here speak an Indian dialect as their first language and Spanish, if they speak it at all, only as a second. There is some comfort in this for the visitor who also speaks Spanish, if at all, only as a distant second language.

There are other comforts for the visitor to Oaxaca. Zapotec and Mixtec artisans produce some of the finest textiles and pottery in Mexico. Also, archaeological sites in the Valley of Oaxaca are numerous and are more convenient and better preserved than those in central Mexico. Fiestas and celebrations here have a strong Indian flavor to them. Finally, as a Mexican backwater, Oaxaca embraces the traveled-out traveler with its unhurried spirit as if to say, "I have been here thousands of years. There is no reason to hurry to tomorrow."

Train Services. Trains 111 and 112 ("Oaxaqueño") provide special first class reserved and second class coach service between Mexico City and Puebla, Tehuacán, and Oaxaca.

OAXAQUEÑO TRAIN

Train 111		Train 112		1st.cl. Reserved	2nd.cl. Coach
Lv. 7:00 PM	Mexico City	9:20 AM	Ar.		
11:50 PM	Puebla	4:05 AM		$7.00	1.81
2:35 AM(+1)	Tehuacán	1:35 AM(+1)		11.06	2.84
Ar. 9:25 AM	Oaxaca	7:00 PM	Lv.	18.90	4.87

Puebla

Puebla, along with several other cities in Mexico, has a rich collection of colonial architectural masterpieces, over 1,000 in the downtown area alone. However, there is no other town in the country which seems, simultaneously, so European in its style. Puebla is a very Spanish city with its baroque churches, colorful, hand painted tiles, and narrow, cobbled streets. There is also a healthy dose of French neoclassic which was thrown in during the early Independence period when France was the chic culture emulated by this town's very aristocratic elite.

The town was originally founded by the Spanish in 1531 as Ciudad de los Angeles and laid out along a strict grid pattern centered on the zócalo. Several years later it became Puebla de los Angeles. The town's intermediate position on the road between Mexico City and the port of Veracruz was the basis for its early growth and it remained Mexico's second largest city until the late 19th Century when it was surpassed by Guadalajara. But Puebla did not rely solely on commerce to fuel its economic growth. It has a strong manufacturing tradition, beginning with pottery and tile in the 16th Century and later expanding into the production of glass and textiles.

Puebla is also the point of origin of one of the most popular Hispanic holidays, one celebrated from Mexico to Chicago, **Cinco de Mayo**. On May 5, 1862, 2,000 Mexican troops under General Ignacio de Zaragoza defeated an invasion force of 6,000 French troops at Puebla. Although the French took the city the following year and held it until 1867, May 5 is celebrated world-wide by people of Mexican descent because, after all, Mexico doesn't have that many military victories.

Today Puebla is Mexico's fourth largest city with 1.2 million

The plaza, Puebla

people and with a growing industrial base. It is also a very conservative and Catholic town with a traditional and proud elite. To highlight their city's charms, the Pueblan leaders have taken significant steps to beautify Puebla by renovating colonial and 19th Century downtown structures and by closing streets to vehicular traffic and creating pedestrian malls. These efforts have not been wasted because, while Puebla's outskirts exhibit the hectic confusion of any large, growing city, the downtown area exudes a slower-paced continental charm.

Getting Around. The **train station** is at the north end of Calle 7 Norte. "Estación Nueva" buses travel between downtown and the station but it is better to take a cab. The **bus station** is northwest of the city's center. Colectivos marked "CAPU" or "Ruta 48" run along Calle 11 Norte to the bus station. You have gone too far if you pass under a pedestrian walkway.

Crafts. One of the things that the visitor to Puebla notices immediately is the vividly colorful **Talavera tile** which is used in buildings throughout the city. This hand-painted tile was introduced to Puebla by settlers from Talavera de la Reina, Spain, in the 17th Century and it is still produced and sold in

1 ~ Plaza de Armas
2 ~ Cathedral
3 ~ Casa de la Cultura
    Palafox Library
    tourist office
4 ~ post office
5 ~ Museo Amparo
6 ~ Callejon del Sapo
7 ~ Puebla University
    La Compania
8 ~ San Cristobal Church
    Museo de la Revolucion
9 ~ Teatro Principal
10~ Casa del Alfenique
    Museo del Estado
11~ Barrio del Artista

12~ El Parian
13~ San Francisco Church
    Centro Artesanal
14~ Casa de los Munecos
    Museo de la Universidad
15~ Church of Santo Domingo
    Mercado Victoria
16~ Exconvento Santa Monica
17~ Exconvento de Santa Rosa
    Museo de Artesanias del
    Estado de Puebla
18~ Museo Bello
19~ Centro Civico 5 de Mayo
A ~ Hostal de Halconeros
B ~ Hotel Teresita
C ~ Hotel Colonial

9 PTE.
7 PTE.
5 PTE.
3 PTE.
2 PTE.
4 PTE.
6 PTE.

5 SUR
3 SUR
16 DE SEPTIEMBRE
2 SUR
4 SUR

B
18
A
4
3
2
1
5
C
15
14
8
5 OTE.
7 OTE.
9 OTE.
3 OTE.
6
7
10
11
12
9

HEROES DEL 5 DE MAYO
REFORMA

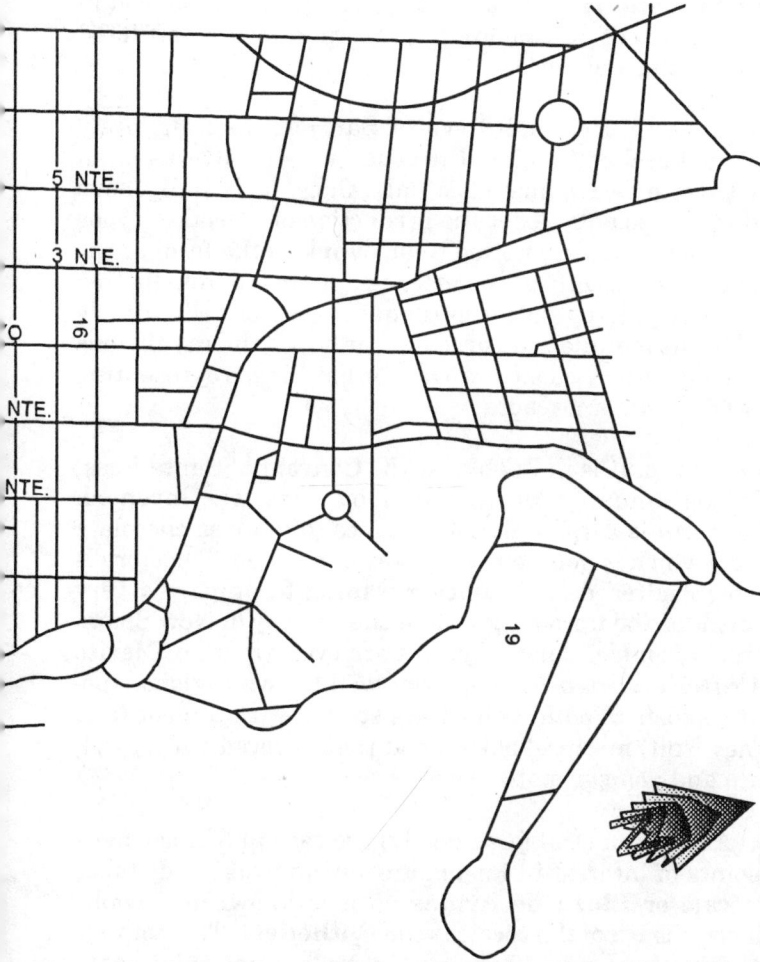

Puebla, Puebla

Puebla. Beautiful **Talavera pottery**, as well as other styles of pottery, is also produced in Puebla. One can also find elaborate **ceramic candelabra** in Puebla. These crafts are produced in the town of Izúcar de Matamoros and incorporate hand-sculpted flowers, animals, and birds.

Otomí Indians in the small town of San Pablito craft lovely cross-stitched and embroidered **textiles** whose patterns often reflect native, pre-Hispanic spiritual values. This indigenous community is also notable for the production of two other types of crafts. One is intricate netted **bead work** in the form of hat bands and belts. The other is *amate*, a paper made from fig tree bark whose origins predate the conquest. Historically, *amate* was used in the manufacture of codices or books and in religious rituals. Today, it is used as a canvas for paintings representing village scenes and landscapes.

Comida Tipica. It is in Puebla, at the Convent of Santa Rosa, that what is arguably Mexico's national dish was invented. *Mole Poblano* is a spicy chocolate sauce (often less chocolate than spicy) which is poured over turkey or chicken. The story is that Sister Andrea de la Asunción wanted to prepare a very special dish for the upcoming visit of the Viceroy of New Spain. The result was *mole*. Variations of it are everywhere in Mexico today. *Chiles en nogada* is another well known regional specialty. It consists of *chiles* which are stuffed with a meat (and sometimes fruit) mixture, baked, and then covered with a walnut sauce and pomegranate seeds.

Sights. As is often (and fortuitously) the case in Mexico, most of the points of interest in Puebla are within walking distance of the zócalo or **Plaza de Armas** as it is known in Puebla. Immediately south of the zócalo is the **Cathedral**. This impressive structure has twin 70-m bell towers, a dome inlaid with beautiful glazed tile, and marble floors. The main altar was designed by Manuel Tolsá and carved from onyx, as is the pulpit. There are paintings in the sacristy by Baltasar de Echave y Rioja. Construction on the Cathedral was begun in the mid-1500s and was completed in 1649.

Behind the Cathedral is the **Casa de la Cultura**. This cultural center is in a fine colonial building that was the Archbishop's

Palace but now houses a concert hall, lecture room, cafeteria, and, most important, the **Palafox Library**. In 1646 Bishop Juan de Palafox y Mendoza founded the library by contributing his collection of 5,000 books. Today the library contains close to 50,000 books, most of them hundreds of years old and many of them priceless. The bookcases are handcarved cedar and the reading tables are inlaid with onyx. The Casa de la Cultura frequently shows U.S. and other foreign films.

The **tourist office** is beside the Casa de Cultura at Av. 5 Oriente #3. It is open Mon-Fri, 8 a.m. to 8 p.m., and Sat-Sun, 9 a.m. to 2 p.m. Just around the corner on 16 de Septiembre is the **post office**. Opposite the post office on 16 de Septiembre is **Telefonos de Mexico** and a long distance phone booth.

Two blocks south of the Casa de la Cultura at the intersection of Av. 9 Oriente and Calle 2 Sur is the **Museo Amparo**, Puebla's newest museum and one of the finest in all of Mexico. Housed in a lovely colonial (1534) building, this collection of pre-Hispanic art is not the largest in Mexico but its layout is superbly designed and uses a high tech information system. Visitors rent headsets at the entrance and can then plug in to interactive compact disc monitors in each display area. After choosing one of four languages–Spanish, English, French, or Japanese–the visitor listens to information relevant to the particular display while viewing explanatory images on the monitor. You can also search an extensive menu of artifacts and select any for elaboration. The museum is open daily, except Tues, 10 a.m. to 6 p.m.

Two blocks east of the Casa de Cultura is **Callejón del Sapo**. This alleyway is a wonderful place to browse as it is full of little shops and vendors selling antiques, books, records, and junk. East of the zócalo on Calle 4 Sur is a lovely 16th Century building which contains **Puebla University**. Check out the flowery, sunny courtyards and the stucco ceilings in the Salón Melchor de Covarrubias. The formerly Jesuit church of **La Compañía** is next door and is now part of the university. North of the university at Av. 6 Oriente and Calle 4 Norte is **San Cristóbal Church** which has a beautiful 17th Century baroque facade. Half a block west of the church is the **Museo de la Revolución** (Museum of the Revolution), which is also the

Casa de los Serdán (Serdán House). The Serdán family, brothers Aquiles and Maximo and sisters Carmen and Natalia, were revolutionaries who opposed the dictator Porfirio Díaz. On November 18, 1910, on orders from Díaz, the Serdán house was surrounded by 500 troops and police. After a 14-hour gun battle, the house was taken. Along with almost everyone else, Aquiles Serdán was killed and became one of the first martyrs of the Mexican Revolution. Today the house contains some Mexican Revolution exhibits and the original bullet holes from the government's 1910 assault.

East of the museum on Calle 6 Norte is the **Teatro Principal**. This theater was built in 1756, burned in 1902, and rebuilt in the 1930s. One block south at the corner of Calle 6 Norte and Av. 4 Oriente is the **Casa del Alfeñique** (Tues-Sun, 10 a.m. to 5 p.m.). Formerly a residence for visiting dignitaries, this building now houses the **Museo del Estado** (State Museum). While the state museum with its displays of 17th, 18th, and 19th Century artifacts is interesting, the exterior of the building itself is the real draw. Done in glazed blue and white tile against a background of red, this facade is an unexcelled example of Pueblan baroque.

Just east of the Alfeñique on Calle 8 Norte is the **Barrio del Artista**, which is a collection of artisans' and artists' workshops. Immediately south of the Barrio is **El Parián**, a market specializing in Pueblan crafts of generally inferior quality–but cheap. On the other side of Blvd. Héroes del 5 de Mayo from the Teatro Principal is the **San Francisco Church**. Considered the oldest church in the city, it was established in 1535 but the present structure was completed in 1667. The church has a strikingly colorful tiled facade and inside, in a small chapel near the main altar, are the well preserved remains of Sebastián de Aparicio. Sebastián came to New Spain in the early 1530s and designed many of the country's roads. He later became a Franciscan priest and several years after his death he was beatified by the Catholic church. In one of the church buildings is the **Centro Artesanal** which sells crafts from around the state. It is closed Monday.

East of the zócalo on Calle 2 Norte is the **Casa de los Muñecos** (House of the Figurines). This building is another landmark of

Ornate interior, Santo Domingo Church, Puebla

Puebla style. The facade is inlaid with figurine tiles grotesquely representing the enemies of the builder. The Casa was built in the 18th Century and today houses the **Museo de la Universidad**.

The church of **Santo Domingo** is two blocks north of the zócalo at Av. 4 Poniente and 5 de Mayo. This is the most richly decorated church in Puebla. Inside the church the **Capilla del Rosario** (Rosary Chapel) assaults the senses with its gilded figures, polychromed ceramics, carved stone and cast plaster. No inch of space is left unadorned in this most baroque chapel. Hundreds of flickering candles add the final touches to the atmosphere. Santo Domingo was built in the early 17th Century while the Capilla del Rosario was added in the latter part of that century.

Behind the Church of Santo Domingo is the **Mercado Victoria**. While this used to be the city's main market, the beautification and renovation campaign is transforming this striking 1912 structure into something like a mall. North of the Mercado Victoria on 5 de Mayo is the **Exconvento de Santa Monica**. The anti-clerical laws of 1857 abolished monasteries and convents. Legend has it, however, that this convent continued to function secretly until it was discovered in 1934. Hidden doorways, secret passages, and the complicity of Puebla's very religious elite allowed this ruse to succeed for 80 years. Some recent investigators question the veracity of this story. Regardless, today's visitor to the exconvent can tour the museum's exhibits of religious art and of convent artifacts such as self-flagellation devices. The museum is closed on Monday.

Behind the convent is a Talavera **tile factory**. Here you can buy, window shop, or just watch as these artisans ply their craft.

Scene in the plaza, Puebla

buy, window shop, or just watch as these artisans ply their craft.
On Calle 3 Norte a couple of blocks south of Santa Monica is the
Exconvento de Santa Rosa. Built in the 17th Century, this
building now houses the **Museo de Artesanías del Estado de
Puebla** which has a truly excellent collection of crafts from
around the state. There are displays of pottery, textiles, clothing, and carved stone but for many the highlight of the museum
is the superbly restored colonial kitchen with inlaid glazed tile
and cooking paraphernalia from the 18th Century. There are
tours in Spanish.

West of the zócalo on Calle 3 Sur is the **Museo Bello** which
contains the amazing and eclectic fine arts collection of the 19th
Century industrialist José Luis Bello. The pieces in the collection come from all over the world and include watches, clothing,
porcelain, furniture, musical instruments, paintings, and much
more. There are tours in both Spanish and English of this
intriguing museum.

A couple of kilometers north of the zócalo is the **Centro Cívico
Cinco de Mayo** (5th of May Civic Center). This park extends
east from Calle 2 Norte and includes the site of the May 5, 1862

Mexican victory over the French as well as several museums and science centers. The **Museo de la Intervención** is located in the west end of the park in a fort used by the Mexican troops. It contains documents and displays covering the French occupation of Mexico. In the park there are also a planetarium with shows in the afternoon daily (closed Monday like everything else), the **Museo de Historia Natural** (Natural History Museum), and the **Museo de Antropología e Historia** (Anthropology and History Museum). To get to the park, take the bus "Fuertes" from downtown on Calle 2 Norte.

Classes. Summer classes in Spanish, crafts, culinary arts, history, and Mexican studies are offered in the small town of Zacatlan near Puebla. Contact:

> Francisco Gaytan, Dir.
> Centro Zacatlan
> PO Box 11891
> Milwaukee, WI 53211

Climate. At an altitude of 2,162 m, Puebla has a cool, temperate climate, though temperatures never drop below freezing. The coldest month is January, with an average daily temperature of 12°C (54°F) while the warmest is May at 19°C (66°F). Virtually all of Puebla's 84 cm (33 in) of annual rainfall comes in June through September.

Excursions. The town of **Cholula** is 12 km (7 mi) west of Puebla. This site has been continuously occupied by human beings for almost 2,500 years. The initial settlement was around 400 B.C. and by 200 A.D. the town was a major trading center. Cholula has also been influenced or conquered by just about every civilization that has come down the pike in central Mexico. Its earliest pottery shows a distinct Olmec influence. The city flourished contemporaneously with Teotihuacán (0-600 A.D.) and was strongly influenced by that other city-state. From the land of the Maya, the Olmeca-Xicallanca arrived and dominated the city beginning around 600 A.D. Later, around 1000 A.D., the Toltecs conquered the city and the descendents of their occupation were overrun by the Aztec military in 1400 A.D. In the pre-Hispanic period, it was the Indian custom of both the conqueror and the conquered to assimilate the gods of the other

Cholula, Puebla

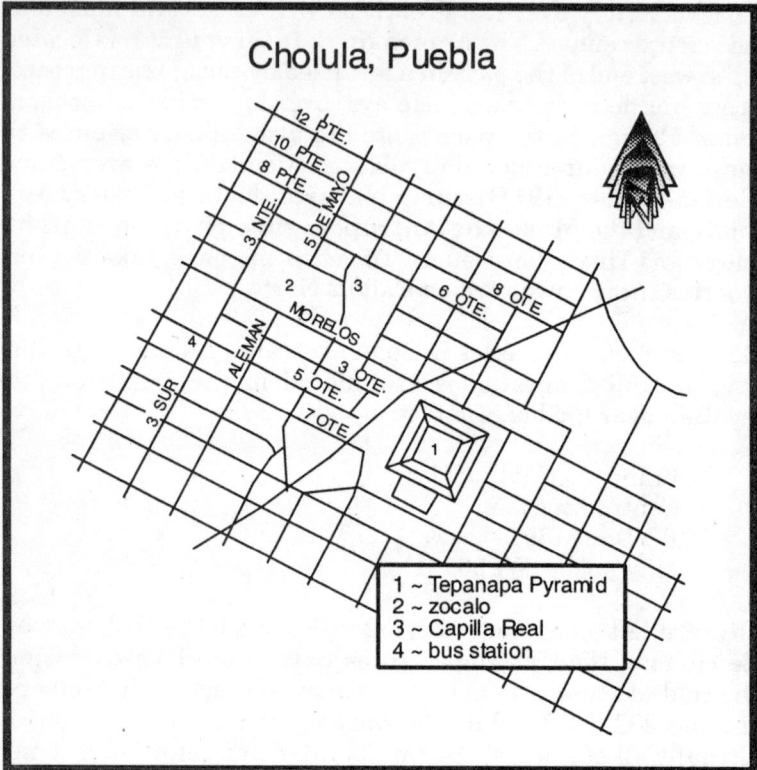

1 ~ Tepanapa Pyramid
2 ~ zocalo
3 ~ Capilla Real
4 ~ bus station

because one didn't want to run the risk of offending an unknown but powerful god. Consequently, Cholula, having been the meeting point of several cultures, assimilated quite a few gods. By the time Cortés arrived on his way to meet Moctezuma, Cholula was something of a holy city with hundreds of temples for dozens of gods.

In 1519 Cortés found a city of 100,000 people. He had been asked by Moctezuma to travel to Tenochtitlán by way of Cholula. At first Cortés was well received by the Cholulans, but then something happened and accounts differ as to what it was. Cortés was informed that the Cholulans, on orders from the Aztec leader, were planning an ambush. Some say that this was the real plan, others say that this story was concocted by the hated Doña Marina (La Malinche). But the Spaniards responded by attacking. Several thousand Cholulans were massacred and then the city was looted by Cortés' Indian allies.

Today Cholula is a quiet town of 20,000 people. Its most outstanding feature is the **Tepanapa Pyramid**. Coming into town on the bus from Puebla you see it and it doesn't look that remarkable. In fact, it looks like a big dirt hill with a church on top. That "hill" is the crumbling ruin of the largest pyramid in the Americas and one that is volumetrically larger than Egypt's Pyramid of Cheops. The pyramid is a couple of blocks southeast of Cholula's zócalo. Tepanapa is actually a series of five pyramids superimposed one upon the other. An 8 km long labyrinth of tunnels has been cut into the structure in the search for its secrets. Some of these tunnels are lighted and open to the public. The entrance is on the northeast side of Tepanapa. Guides are available.

Opposite the entrance is a small museum with displays of artifacts found in the area. On the south side of the pyramid is the Great Plaza where excavations have revealed the main approach to Tepanapa. A path leads to the top of the mound where there is a church and nice view of the surrounding town. The archeological site is open Tues-Sun, 9 a.m. to 5 p.m.

Interior of the Church of Santa Maria, Tonantzintla

The other point of interest in Cholula is the **Capilla Real** (Royal Chapel). This 16th Century Franciscan church is built in an unusual Arabic style with seven naves and 49 domes. To get to Cholula, go to the Puebla-Cholula bus station at Av. 8 Poniente and Calle 7 Norte in Puebla. Catch a bus marked "Cholula."

Four kilometers from Cholula is the village of **Tonantzintla** with its remarkable **Iglesia de Santa María**. The facade is pretty, with colorful tiles inlaid in yellow stucco. Blue bells swing in the bell towers. But the outside of the church is austere in comparison with the inside. A riot of plaster bas-relief figures covers the walls, ceilings, and domes of this church. Every square centimeter of the interior is decorated with fruits, vines, faces, cherubs, angels, and saints painted in bright colors and clearly crafted by indigenous artisans. It is easily one of the most "pagan" Catholic churches in Mexico. Above the altar is an image of the Virgin of Guadalupe surrounded by a blue neon light. *Puro México.*

To get to Tonantzintla, catch the bus labelled "Tonantzintla, Acatepec" on Av. 8 Poniente just west of Calle 11 Norte. The trip takes about 25 minutes and deposits you two blocks from the church.

Tehuacán

Springs near the town are the source of most of the bottled mineral water consumed in Mexico. The best reason to stop in Tehuacán, a town of 70,000, is the **Museo del Valle de Tehuacán** (Museum of the Valley of Tehuacán). These archeological, anthropological, and botanical exhibits document the extensive research which has been done on the human presence in the Tehuacán Valley.

Oaxaca

You feel it right away in Oaxaca: this is a place with history. Not linear history, not day by day, year by year, century by century history, not history on a time line where each important event has a year assigned to it. Oaxaca is a place of living history, a rich, multicultural mosaic which breathes life into the past, the present, and, most of all, the future. It is a history of the future.

Most Mexican indigenous cultures conceived of time as a circular rather than linear phenomenon. For the Indian, to know the past was to know the future. Calm, yet vibrant, Oaxaca embodies this sense of time. You can see the proof of this in the European travelers sipping chocolate around Mexico's finest zócalo; you can see it in the colonial churches which endure in this land of earthquakes; but mostly you see the proof in the

Oaxaca, Oaxaca

CALZ. NIÑOS HEROES DE CHAPULTEPEC

P. DIAZ
REFORMA
PINO SUAREZ
ESCALERA
ALLENDE
BRAVO
MATAMOROS
GARCIA VIGIL
M. ALCALA
ABASOLO
MURGUIA
CRESPO
MORELOS
INDEPENDENCIA
HIDALGO
TRUJANO
LAS CASAS
GUERRERO
CALZ MADERO
ORIENTE
PERIFERICO
20 DE NOVIEMBRE
GALEANA
BUSTAMANTE
LOPEZ

1 ~ train station
2 ~ 2nd class bus station
3 ~ 1st class bus station
4 ~ Plaza Principal
5 ~ Palacio de Gobierno
6 ~ Juarez Market
7 ~ Teatro Macedonio Alcala
8 ~ Cathedral
9 ~ Alameda
10~ post office
11~ tourist office
12~ Museo Rufino Tamayo
13~ Museo de Oaxaca

14~ Church of Santo Domingo
     Museo Regional de Oaxaca
15~ Plazuela del Carmen Alto
16~ Museo Casa de Juarez
17~ Cerro del Fortin
18~ Guelaguetza Auditorium
19~ Church of La Soledad
20~ Central de Abastos
21~ Autobuses Turisticos station
A ~ Hotel Reforma
B ~ Meson del Rey
C ~ Hotel Principal
D ~ Hotel Colon

determination of the indigenous people here to maintain their culture. The future is the past.

This city of 180,000 people is located in the subtropical Central Valley at 1,550 m (5,040 ft). Surrounding the city are the ranges of the Sierra Madre del Sur. The present town was laid out by the Spanish in 1529. Oaxaca quickly became the primary administrative and commercial center in southern Mexico. It was an island of Spanish colonialism in a sea of hostile and diverse Indian tribes.

Today the city is still a colonial masterpiece despite the best efforts of this seismically active area to topple its structures. And, while these Spanish buildings are old, far older still are the cultures of the people who come to the city to trade: Zapotecs, Mixtecs, and other indigenous people, dressed in distinctive and colorful costumes, are found in the markets and at the zócalo selling their wares, grudging victims of camera-totting tourists.

Getting Around. The **train station** is two km west of the zócalo on Calz. Madero, which is the extension of Av. Independencia. To get there catch the "Estación" bus on Av. Hidalgo.

The **1st class bus station** is located on Calz. Niños Héroes de Chapultepec two km north of the plaza. This bus station is generally for journeys beyond the Central Valley of Oaxaca. It is not easy to get here directly by city bus so a taxi is the best option. The **2nd class bus station** is beside the Central de Abastos and here you can get buses to the villages in the Valley. Vans and buses marked "Abastos" run on Av. Hidalgo between downtown and the station.

A very useful city bus is the "Circular" or "Circular Panteón" which travels between the zócalo, 2nd class bus station, the train station, and the 1st class bus station. It can be a long trip, however.

Crafts. Oaxaca is a city filled with *artesanía*. This is largely because both the Zapotecs and, especially, the Mixtecs excelled at intricate and detailed work. Perhaps Oaxaca is most famous for the **black pottery** produced in the village of San Bartolo Coyotepec. The artisans in Atzompa make **green-glazed ce-**

ramics in a variety of forms while the weavers in Teotitlán del Valle fashion the finest **wool blankets and sarapes** in Mexico. Some of these wool weavings employ traditional designs and colors, but the tourist trade has inspired a move toward garish, artificial dyes and contemporary design themes.

Oaxaca City itself is well-known for its **gold filigree** and **silver jewelry**. Other types of **metal work** are also popular here. *Machetes* are locally manufactured and etched with colorful, often enigmatic, mottoes. Thin sheets of tin are cut, painted, and shaped into a variety of decorative forms. Mitla and San Antonino are famous for **embroidered blouses** and **dresses** while several villages in the sierras produce wonderfully detailed indigenous clothing such as *huipiles*. Finally, imaginative, colorful, and often fantastical **wooden animals** are carved in the towns of San Martín Tilcajete, Arrazola Xoxo, and Cuilapan.

While you can visit all these villages and observe the artisans at work in their workshops and stores, it is also possible to see much of the best work from the surrounding area in the galleries, shops, and markets of Oaxaca City. With the exception of the most exclusive shops (where the quality is correspondingly higher), prices are not significantly greater. Some of the shops which sell crafts from the region are the government-run Fonart store at García Vigil and Bravo, Yalalag at Alcalá 104, Aripo at García Vigil 809, and Cicijo at García Vigil 212. There are many others. Most can arrange shipping for you.

Comida Tipica. *Mole Oaxaqueño* is a variation on a theme of *mole Poblano*. It is notable for being sweeter than the Pueblan variety due to the inclusion of bananas among the ingredients and is usually served over tamales or chicken.

Sights. Oaxaca's **Plaza Principal** or zócalo is, I think, the finest in Mexico—not so much for its physical beauty as for its wonderful gaiety and activity. Bands seem to play every night from the Porfirian-era kiosk at the center of the plaza. Most evenings see the plaza full of strolling parents with kids in tow, vendors hawking toys, balloons, and snacks, indigenes selling anything from blankets to colored tin Christmas tree ornaments, and foreigners mesmerized by the sights, sounds, and smells of another world. Open-air cafes and restaurants line the perimeter of the plaza.

On the south side of the plaza is the **Palacio de Gobierno** (Government Palace). Built in the late 19th Century, this building contains a mural representing Oaxaca's history and the personalities that created that history. The **Juárez Market**, which contains mostly food products, is a block south of the Palacio at Av. Las Casas and Cabrera. This is an amazing place even if you are not planning to buy food. There are endless and unknown varieties of beans, *chiles*, and tropical fruits while the fragrances of *chile*, coffee, and chocolate perfume the air. However, the meat section might make you a vegetarian.

East of the plaza at the corner of Independencia and 5 de Mayo is the **Teatro Macedonio Alcalá**. Completed in the last days of the Porfiriato, this French-style theater is replete with marble and has five balconies in the auditorium. To inquire about performances, ask at the tourist office.

Immediately north of the plaza is the **Cathedral**. This structure was begun in 1553 but earthquake damage forced its rebuilding several times. It has a baroque facade but a somber interior. Fronting the cathedral is the **Alameda** and on the other side of the Alameda is the **post office**. North of the Alameda at the corner of García Vigil and Independencia is one of two **tourist offices** in the city. The other is at Morelos and 5 de Mayo. These offices are generally both excellent and will have information on cultural events in the city and on excursions to other places in the Valley of Oaxaca.

North of the tourist office on Morelos between Díaz and Tinoco y Palacios is the **Museo Rufino Tamayo**. This fine collection of pre-Hispanic sculpture was donated by the Oaxacan painter Rufino Tamayo and includes pieces from the Aztec, Teotihuacán, Maya, Huastec, and Colima cultures. The museum is beautifully designed and is open Sun, 10 a.m. to 3 p.m., every other day, 10 a.m. to 2 p.m. and 4 p.m. to 7 p.m., but is closed Tues. Three blocks east of Museo Rufino Tamayo on Macedonio Alcalá is the **Museo de Oaxaca**. This museum features temporary exhibits of paintings by mostly young Oaxacan artists. There is one permanent display devoted to the Oaxacan artist

Miguel Cabrera (1695-1768). It is open Tues-Sun, 10 a.m. to 2 p.m. and 5 p.m. to 8 p.m.

Three blocks north of the Museo de Oaxaca on Macedonio Alcalá is the **Church of Santo Domingo**. Construction of this church was begun by the Dominicans in 1572 and it was put into service in the early 1600s. However, work continued on the interior of the church for another 200 years and if you go inside you will see why. The domes, walls, and columns of the interior are totally covered with an explosion of polychromed plaster and gilded reliefs. It is one of the finest baroque interiors in Mexico.

Next to the church in what used to be a monastery is the **Museo Regional de Oaxaca**. This two-story 16th Century building contains ethnographical and archeological exhibits covering the history and cultures of Oaxaca. But the preeminent display is the collection of artifacts from Tomb 7 at Monte Albán. This tomb was constructed by the Zapotecs and presumably held a Zapotec personage. However, some time after the Zapotecs abandoned Monte Albán, the Mixtecs began emptying Zapotec tombs and interring their own dead in them. Tomb 7 was one such tomb. It was discovered by Alfonso Caso in 1932 and, along with human remains, contained a treasure of finely worked gold, silver, jade, alabaster, turquoise, bone, onyx, and crystal. This treasure is now exhibited in a special section of the Museo Regional. The museum is open Tues-Sun, 10 a.m. to 6 p.m.

Almost directly across from the museum is the **Plazuela del Carmen Alto**. Here Triqui Indian women weave and sell their work. One block north of the Plazuela on García Vigil is the **Museo Casa de Juárez** (Juárez House Museum). This house was actually owned by Antonio Salanueva but it was here in 1818 that 12 year-old Benito Juárez found a job. Salanueva paid for the young Indian boy's education and the rest is history. Today the house contains Salanueva's bookbindery as well as furniture, portraits and other memorabilia from the period or relevant to Juárez's life. It is open Tues-Sun, 10 a.m. to 2 p.m. and 4 p.m. to 7 p.m.

About one km northwest of the plaza is **Cerro del Fortín** (Small Fort Hill). On the south end of the hill is the **Guelaguetza Auditorium** where the annual festival of the same name is held. On the western flank of the hill is the planetarium, which has two or three shows a night after 6 p.m. It is open Tues-Sun. Just north of the planetarium is the observatory which is also open to the public and which was donated to Oaxaca by the city of Palo Alto, California.

The **Church of La Soledad** is five blocks west of the zócalo on Independencia. The interior of this 17th Century church is lavishly decorated with gold leaf. Also inside is a stone statue of La Virgen de la Soledad. Legend has it that centuries ago this image miraculously appeared on this spot and for that reason a church was built. Today, La Virgen stands by the altar and wears a 2.5-kg gold crown encrusted with hundreds of pearls.

About one km west of the zócalo near the 2nd class bus terminal is the **Central de Abastos**, Oaxaca's main market. Multiply the sights, sounds, and smells of the Juárez Market by three and you have a good approximation of the Central. To visit it is a sublime yet harrowing experience. The market is open every day but Saturday is the *tianguis* or Indian market day and it is then that the market really hops.

Fiestas. The premier celebration in Oaxaca is the **Guelaguetza**. The centerpiece of the Guelaguetza is a series of folkloric dances which represent the seven regions of Oaxaca and which are performed the last two Mondays in July in the open-air auditorium on Cerro del Fortín. However, there are also a number of other events going on in town during these two weeks and many of these are free. Contact the tourist office for a schedule. On December 18 is the festival of **La Virgen de la Soledad**, the city's patron saint. Most of the festivities take place at La Soledad church and consist of fireworks, processions, and dances.

Classes. The Instituto Cultural Oaxaca offers classes in the Spanish, Zapotec, and Mixtec languages. There are also classes in dance, ceramics, and weaving. Contact:

> Instituto Cultural Oaxaca
> Av. Juárez 909
> Oaxaca, Oaxaca MEXICO
> tel. 5-34-04

Climate. Oaxaca's climate is very much like Puebla's except that it is slightly warmer. Almost all of Oaxaca's rain falls in summer afternoon cloudbursts which, when they are done, make way for warm, sunny weather.

Excursions. There are so many interesting destinations near Oaxaca City that the traveler afoot might want to consider a tour group. There are a number of such operators in Oaxaca and the tourist office has current tour information. Despite this, I'll tell you how to reach each destination by public transportation (okay, and maybe a little walking).

Monte Albán is Mexico's most spectacular archeological site and one of the most important. These ruins sit on an artificially flattened mountain 10 km southwest of Oaxaca City. From the clouds, Monte Albán guards the Valley of Oaxaca. The site was first occupied between 800 and 400 B.C. by a people strongly influenced, though probably not identical with, the Olmecs of the Gulf Coast. They were responsible for constructing the inner Danzante Building on the west side of the Monte Albán complex. These people also carved the bas-relief Danzante figures which seem to represent dead or dying captives. These figures, which were carved as early as 700 B.C., include calendrical and language glyphs, which makes Monte Albán the site of the earliest writing in Mexico.

By 100 B.C. the Zapotecs were installed at Monte Albán and they continued the process of developing the center and building monumental structures. The golden age of the site occurred between 250 A.D. and 750 A.D., during which period most of the structures visible today were built. The population on the arid flanks and summit of the mountain probably exceeded 25,000 people and Monte Albán was the politico-religious center for hundreds of Zapotec communities in the Valley of Oaxaca. For some unknown reason around 750 A.D. Monte Albán was abandoned though it was still used for religious and burial ceremonies. With the collapse of Monte Albán, the Zapotec political system became decentralized throughout the Oaxaca Valley.

When the Mixtec began moving into the Valley in the 12th Century Monte Albán was a decaying necropolis, inhabited only by the dead in hundreds of Zapotec tombs. The Mixtec, who

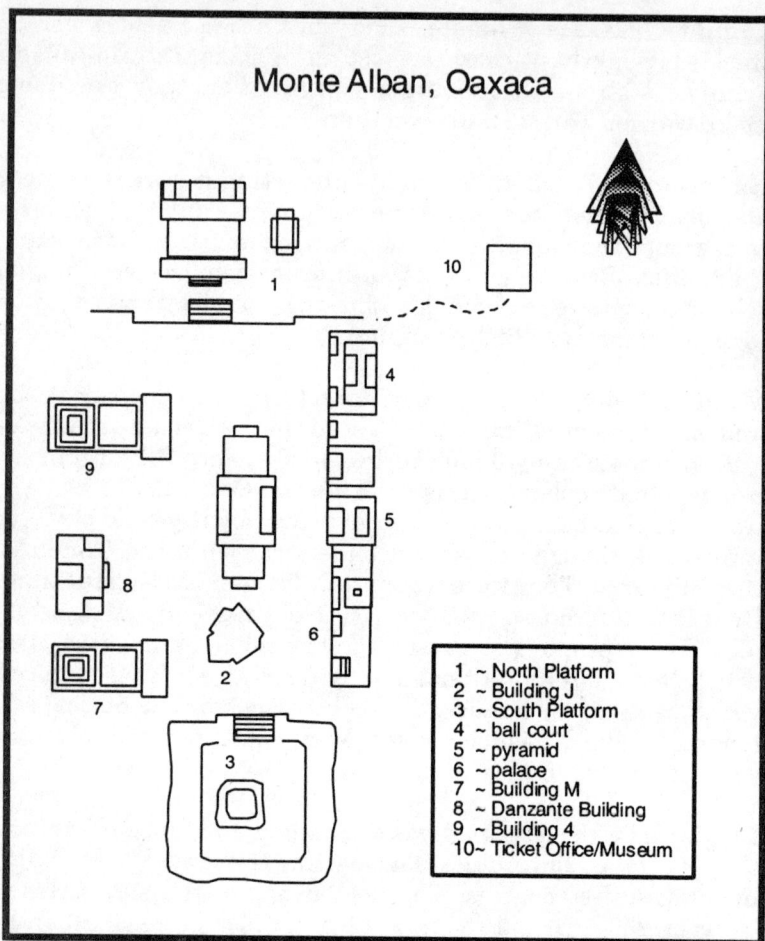

Monte Alban, Oaxaca

1 ~ North Platform
2 ~ Building J
3 ~ South Platform
4 ~ ball court
5 ~ pyramid
6 ~ palace
7 ~ Building M
8 ~ Danzante Building
9 ~ Building 4
10~ Ticket Office/Museum

apparently never occupied the site, began removing the Zapotec remains from these tombs and interring their own dead therein. Tomb 7, because of the treasure found there, is the most famous of these recycled crypts.

After the Conquest, the Spanish excavated intermittently at Monte Albán searching for treasure. In the 1930s and 1940s the first scientific excavations and reconstructions at the site were undertaken by Alfonso Caso. Today the site is organized around the **Great Plaza** which is aligned north-south and which measures 300 m by 200 m. At one end of the plaza is the imposing **North Platform**. At the top of the broad staircase are the remains of 12 masonry columns indicating that this was once a roofed platform. North of the columns is a sunken patio with an altar and beyond this are unexcavated mounds on the platform's superstructure. Built during Monte Albán's classic period (250 A.D. to 750 A.D.), this platform was constructed on top of structures dating back to the earliest period of occupation at the site.

In the middle of the Great Plaza are a series of structures, the most interesting of which is the southern one, **Building J**. This arrow-head-shaped building points away from the axis of the plaza at an angle of about 45 degrees and is widely thought to have been an observatory. This is also one of the oldest structures on the site, dating to around 250 B.C. Glyphs and figures on the building's panels depict military victories.

At the southern end of the plaza is the largely unexcavated **South Platform**. This is the tallest structure at the site and by ascending the steep, broad stairway you can gain an excellent perspective on Monte Albán as well as on the valleys that fall away to the sides of this archeological aerie.

Along the eastern perimeter of the Great Plaza is a line of structures. The first and northernmost is a **ball court** constructed in the shape of an I. The next structure is the **pyramid**. A tunnel runs from the south side of this building to the cluster of structures in the center of the plaza. A jade bat-god mask was found on the altar in front of the pyramid. It is now in the Museum of Anthropology in Mexico City. The final building in this row is the **palace** which appears to have been a dwelling for someone of importance.

On the west side of the plaza there is a set of three non-contiguous structures. The southernmost, near the South Platform, is **Building M**. It has a broad central stairway leading to the summit of the structure. Here are the remains of four columns which once supported a roof over what must have been a temple. In front of the stairway is an enclosed patio.

Next in line on the west side is the **Danzante Building**, so-called after the danzante bas-relief carvings on it. These figures portray enemies slain either in combat or sacrifice. The glyphs with the figures represent Mexico's oldest writing system. The core of this building, including the danzantes, dates from Monte Albán's earliest period of occupation, perhaps as early as 700 B.C. Later modifications were made to the building in the 3rd or 4th Century A.D. The final building on the west side is **Building 4**. It is a close duplicate of Building M.

Several of the tombs at the site are open and can be examined by visitors. **Tomb 105** is across the road from the parking lot and near an unexcavated ball court. The murals inside show a distinct Teotihuacán influence and are thought to represent the nine gods of Death and their female companions.

Tomb 7 is just off the northwest corner of the parking lot. The burial chamber is located under what may have been a temple. This, of course, is the Zapotec tomb which was later appropriated by the Mixtecs for their dead and filled with the funeral treasure now located in the Oaxaca Regional Museum. **Tomb 104** and **Tomb 172** are in the same mound behind the North Platform. Tomb 104 is a beautifully designed crypt. Its elaborate facade is graced by a funeral urn representing a seated figure wearing a headdress likeness of the rain god, Cocijo. The stone slab which originally covered the tomb entrance is covered with glyphs. The interior of the burial chamber is covered with murals representing, among other things, the god of renewal, Xipe Totec, and possibly Quetzalcóatl. Tomb 172 is at the base of the same mound. The human remains and funerary offerings were left in place.

Monte Albán is open daily from 8 a.m. to 5 p.m. There is a small museum near the parking lot to help you get your archeological bearings. Also, a flashlight comes in handy for the tombs. Buses go to Monte Albán from the Autobuses Turísticos station at the Hotel Mesón del Angel on Av. Mina between Díaz and Mier y Terán. Departures are every two hours from 9:30 a.m. to 3:30 p.m. The last bus returning to Oaxaca leaves Monte Albán at 5:30 p.m.

Excursions along the road to Mitla. All of the following places, with the exception of Teotitlán del Valle, are served by the Transportes Oaxaca-Istmo buses operating out of the 2nd class bus station.

At 14 km from Oaxaca is the town of **El Tule**. Here, in the churchyard, is a giant ahuehuete tree (a type of cypress) which is over 2,000 years old and whose trunk has a basal perimeter of 42 m. If you're in a hurry, you can see the tree in passing if you sit on the left side of the bus going to Mitla.

At 24 km there is a turn off to the right which leads, after one km, to the Zapotec archeological site, **Dainzú**. Although very incompletely excavated, this site is quite interesting. Dainzú was settled before 300 B.C. and apparently abandoned sometime after 1000 A.D. Its most significant feature so far is a set of figures carved, bas-relief fashion, on irregularly shaped stone slabs. These slabs are incorporated into the facade of the platform on the left as you approach the site. These incised figures mostly represent ball players in very active positions and are executed in the same style as the Danzante figures at Monte Albán. Dainzú and Monte Albán are the only archeological sites in Oaxaca where such "Olmecoid" carvings have been found. There are similar figures carved in the rock at the top of the hill above the platform. The platform dates from about 300 B.C.

Down the hill from the platform are the remains of other structures. There is a partially restored ball court dating to about 1000 A.D. There are also several tombs, one of which has a jaguar's head for its lintel and stone lintel supports carved in the form of the jaguar's two front legs.

At 27 km from Oaxaca there is a turn off to the left and four km down this road is the village of **Teotitlán del Valle**. This is one of Mexico's most famous traditional weaving villages and its hundreds of artisans produce an estimated 75 per cent of Oaxaca's rugs and wall hangings. Here weavings of all styles are sold in literally hundreds of places: houses, workshops, stores, and, most often, combinations of all three. While the prices here are not much cheaper than in the city, the selection is simply huge. There are also opportunities to watch the weavers at work. Transportation to Teotitlán is via Autotransportes Valle del Norte which operates out of the 2nd class bus station in Oaxaca.

The village of **Tlacolula** is 33 km from Oaxaca. Its Sunday *tianguis* is one of the finest Indian markets in the entire valley and has a dominating indigenous quality which reminds the

Yagul, Oaxaca

PATH TO FORTRESS

1 ~ Patio of the Triple Tomb
2 ~ ball court
3 ~ Patio 1
4 ~ Council Hall
5 ~ Palace of the Six Patios
6 ~ Patio 3

5

6

4

3

2

1

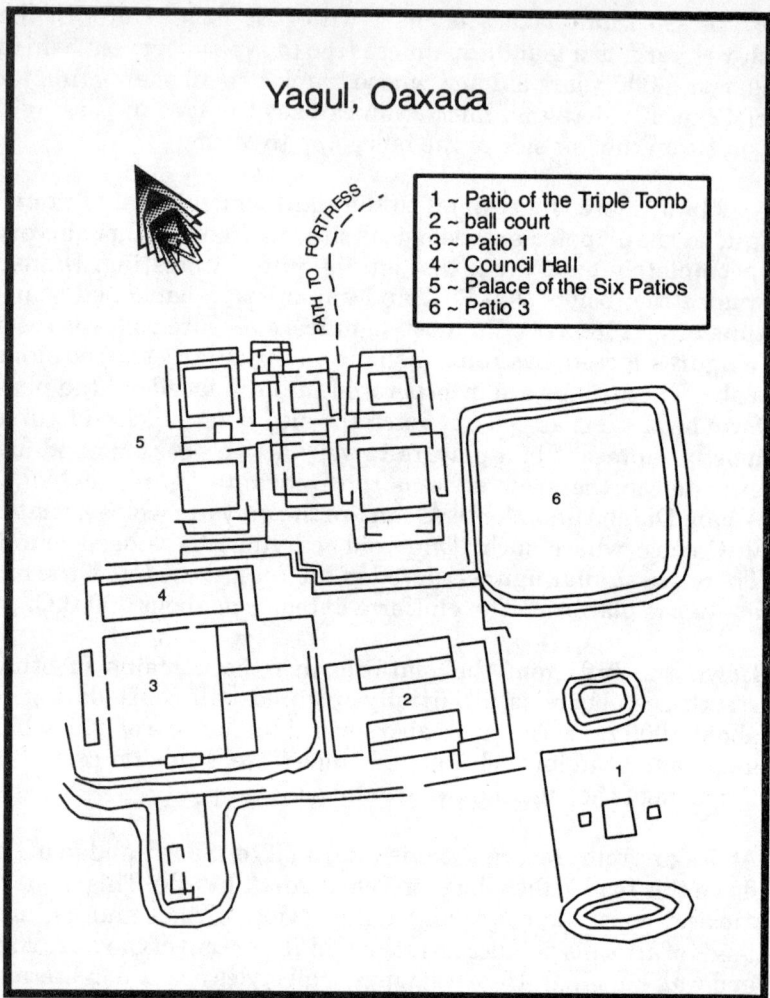

doing this same thing. Go early.

At 35 km is a paved road to the left which leads 1.5 km to the archeological site of **Yagul**. This well excavated and nicely restored site is on a rocky hilltop of stark beauty. Although this location was first occupied as early as 400 B.C., all the structures now restored date from the Mixtec occupation of the city, that is, after 1100 A.D.

A path leads north from the parking lot to the Great Fortress located on the craggy rock spire which overlooks the site. There are ruins here as well as a wonderful, panoramic view of Yagul below. Tomb 28 is on this hill and can be entered if you get the key from the attendant. As you approach the main complex of structures from the parking lot, the Patio of the Triple Tomb is down on the left. On the west side of the patio is the entrance to a chamber containing three crypts off a small hall. The main crypt has a facade decorated with two carved human heads. The door of the tomb is incised with Mixtec glyphs. Just west of the Patio of the Triple Tomb is the fully restored Ball Court. Continuing west is the Patio 1 complex, on the northern side of which is an enormous room, the Council Chamber. This room was once decorated with stone mosaics, presumably like the structures at Mitla. North of the Ball Court and Patio 1 is the Palace of the Six Patios. This complex, maze-like structure was built by the Mixtecs on top of earlier Zapotec buildings and was likely a ruler's residence.

The next stop along the route is the village of **Mitla** with its famed archeological zone. For most of its long history Mitla was occupied and controlled by the Zapotecs and it grew considerably after the abandonment of Monte Albán. Sometime after 1100 A.D. the city was under the political control of the Mixtecs and probably remained so until the arrival of the Aztec armies in the late 15th Century. At the time of the Conquest, Mitla was a functioning Zapotec center. However, by the end of the 16th Century, slavery and disease had decimated the native population and little remained of the former city.

The buildings at the site today with their distinctive cut-stone mosaics are generally believed to have been built during the Mixtec era. Although the extent of the excavated structures is small, Mitla at one time was a very large city as indicated by the remains of houses, graves, forts, and temples over several square kilometers. There are several groups of structures at Mitla. However, there are really only two of interest to most people: the Church Group and the Column Group. The Church Group is the northernmost complex and consists of palace-like structures which are partially covered by a 16th Century Catholic church. There are two patios, the smaller of which still has faint traces of a mural. High walls enclose both patios. The horizontal upper panels consist of mortarless, cut-stone mosaics

Mitla, Oaxaca

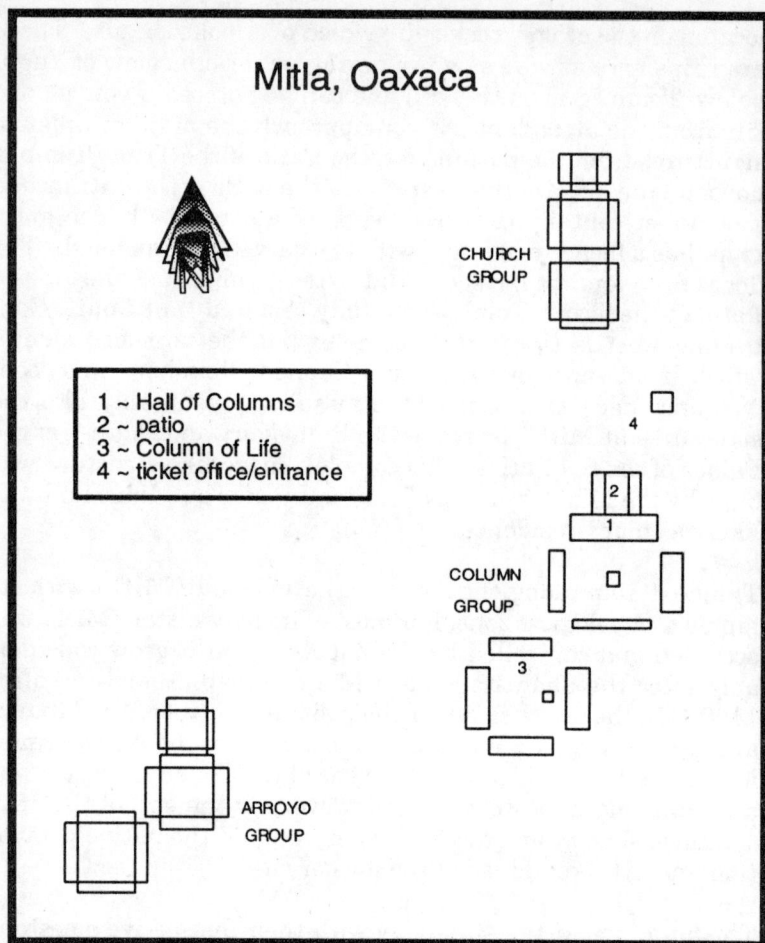

CHURCH
GROUP

1 ~ Hall of Columns
2 ~ patio
3 ~ Column of Life
4 ~ ticket office/entrance

4

2
1

COLUMN

GROUP

3

ARROYO
GROUP

in a variety of geometric patterns.

The Column Group is just south of the Church Group and has the best preserved buildings in the entire site. The Column Group consists of two large, sunken quadrangles surrounded by long structures. On the north side of the northern quadrangle is the Hall of Columns. This hall is 38 m long and 7 m wide and contains six monolithic, conical columns which at one time supported a roof. A low, narrow passage in the north wall of the Hall of Columns leads to a patio with four small chambers around it. These chambers are heavily decorated with stone mosaics in a variety of patterns. However, most of these mosaics are badly deteriorated.

Like its northern neighbor, the southern quadrangle is surrounded by four long galleries. In the eastern gallery, a stairway leads to a cruciform burial chamber beneath the quadrangle floor. There is another cross-shaped tomb in the north gallery whose roof is partially supported by a massive column. This support is known as the "Column of Life" and legend has it that if you embrace this column you will know how many years you have left to live.

There is something of a museum (Frissell Museum) located near the town's plaza in the Posada La Sorpresa. Both the museum and the archeological site are open daily, 9 a.m. to 6 p.m.

Excursions on the road to Ocotlán. All of the following destinations are served by the Estrella del Valle buses operating out of the 2nd class bus station in Oaxaca.

San Bartolo Coyotepec is 12 km south of Oaxaca on Hwy 175 and is world famous as the source of the polished, black pottery so prominent in Oaxaca's markets and shops. The woman who discovered how to give the normally dull black pottery its now distinctive shine, Rosa Valente Nieto Real, is now dead but her family continues to produce high-quality pottery. There are signs to "Doña Rosa Alfareria."

At 33 km from Oaxaca is the village of **Ocotlán** which is the site of a wonderfully exuberant, exotic, and crowded *tianguis* every Friday. Again, it is best to go early in the day.

Train to Veracruz

In several ways, Veracruz is a rich state: rich in history, rich in resources, and rich in cultural heterogeneity. In terms of history, Veracruz is the site of the Olmec culture, the oldest indigenous civilization in Mexico and considered by many to be the "mother culture" of all subsequent Mesoamerican civilizations.

Later, it was on the Veracruz coast that Cortés landed in 1519, destined to change the face of indigenous Mexico. The port of Veracruz has been invaded by pirates, the British, French, Spanish, and the United States and served briefly as the capital of Mexico for Benito Juárez and Venustiano Carranza.

In terms of resources, the state's rich soils are watered by over 40 rivers which rise on the eastern flanks of the Sierra Madre Oriental and flow through Veracruz to the Gulf of Mexico. The cooler mountain slopes produce coffee and citrus while the tropical lowlands yield sugarcane, cotton, and tobacco. Since early in this century, rock formations deep beneath Veracruz have yielded oil and natural gas and today much of Mexico's petrochemical industry is located here.

Finally, in terms of culture, this state still contains vital elements of indigenous belief-systems, values, and ceremonies. Almost half a million Indians reside in Veracruz out of a total population of seven million. The Spanish influence remains in such colonial cities as Jalapa, Córdoba, and Orizaba. And in the port of Veracruz, Caribbean influences can be found in music and dance.

This north-south trending state is about 600 km long and, though very irregular, averages 100 km wide. The erratic western border dips and climbs among the pine-covered peaks of the Sierra Madre Oriental but from these cool heights the landscape quickly descends to the lush, hot coastal plain. On its western border with Puebla, Veracruz shares Mexico's highest mountain, the snow-covered Citlaltépetl (the Indian name), called Pico de Orizaba by the Spanish. This mountain, at 5,747 m elevation, is also the third highest in North America.

The Olmec civilization began here in Veracruz. Little is really known about the Olmecs. It is known that this was the first civilization in Mesoamerica and that it laid the foundation for all that were to follow. What is not known is where these people were from, what language they spoke, or where they went. The Olmec heartland was the Gulf Coast, specifically, southern Veracruz and eastern Tabasco. One of the mysteries left us by these people is why their culture would find such fertile ground in this hot, humid, swampy, and generally inhospitable part of

Mexico. Despite this evidence of poor planning their civilization spanned the middle to late Formative Period, 1200 B.C. to perhaps as late as 100 A.D. The earliest major Olmec site is San Lorenzo in Veracruz. It was occupied from around 1200 to 900 B.C. at which time it was violently destroyed. The Olmecs apparently then moved their ceremonial center to La Venta in Tabasco. This unusual site consists of an island of dry land, about five square kilometers, surrounded by swamp. This site was also violently destroyed around 400 B.C. The last major Olmec center was Tres Zapotes which may have endured until around 100 A.D.

This culture is most famous for the huge, carved basalt heads and delicately incised jade and serpentine ceremonial axes found at several sites. The most common design motif, and one that was obviously important in the Olmec religion, was the were-jaguar, an image that was part jaguar, part human and usually either an infant or child. It is known that the Olmec worshipped a number of gods. It is also thought that the Olmec may have invented the Long Count calendar which was later employed by the Maya. Olmec influence extended over much of central and southern Mexico. Olmec figurines, murals, and carvings are found from the Valley of Mexico, to Guerrero and Oaxaca, and as far south as Guatemala. It is suspected that the culture was spread by either missionaries or traders rather than armies but that is one of many uncertainties concerning this elusive culture.

The next great civilization in Veracruz developed in the central and northern part of the state and is known simply as "Classic Veracruz." El Tajín, near Papantla in northern Veracruz, was one of this culture's great cities and it flourished from 600 A.D. to 900 A.D. Other main centers are Las Higueras and El Zapotal but El Tajín is the only site to be thoroughly excavated and explored. Despite this, little is known about this culture.

Although the Classic Veracruz civilization had begun to decline much earlier, the destruction of El Tajín by Chichimec Indians was the final nail in the coffin. Even before the fall of El Tajín, the Totonac Indians had begun constructing their cultural centers of Zempoala and Isla de los Sacrificios. But there was little time for their culture to develop because much of Veracruz came under the military control of, first, the Toltecs and next, the Aztecs.

When Hernán Cortés arrived on the coast of Veracruz he found the Totonac Indians living unhappily under the harsh rule of the Aztecs. At this point, Cortés made two fortuitous discoveries. First, he learned that the Aztec's bitter subjects could be convinced to ally with the Europeans against the Aztecs. One of the important keys to the Conquest is the support the Spanish received from Indian allies like the Totonacs and Tlaxcalans. Second, he found that one of the women he had been given knew the major central Mexican dialects, as well as Mayan. Used in conjunction with the Spaniard, Gerónimo de Aguilar, who also knew Mayan, she would prove invaluable in the political and military struggle ahead. This woman, called Doña Marina by the Spaniards, became known as La Malinche and this pejorative phrase today symbolizes the rape and betrayal of Mexico.

During the colonial period the city of Veracruz became New Spain's most important port. But heat, humidity, diseases, and pirates kept it small. Other towns were established in the cooler, healthier western highlands of Veracruz: Orizaba to protect trade along the Veracruz-Mexico City road, Jalapa, and Córdoba.

New diseases brought by the Europeans did not respect the assistance given the Spaniards by the Totonacs. The native people of Veracruz were decimated by plagues of smallpox and measles. To provide a workforce to replace the rapidly disappearing Indians, the Spanish began to import African slaves. These newest casualties of the Conquest arrived at and were sold in the port of Veracruz. Some remained in this area working on plantations while other were taken to the mines of central Mexico. Some of these slaves escaped and found freedom in the rain forests of the sierras. They joined together with runaway Indians, intermarried, and formed hidden, desperate communities. Today you can see the legacy of these Africans in the physical features of the people of Veracruz. You also find this legacy in their nickname. The people of this state call themselves "Jarochos," which is an archaic Spanish term signifying a person of mixed Negro and Indian blood.

During the 19th Century Veracruz was the main gateway into Mexico for invading armies. The United States army came through here on its way to Mexico City in 1847. Then, in 1861, the French arrived and began a six-year struggle to make Mexico part of the French empire.

In the early 1900s, textile workers in Orizaba and Córdoba began to form unions. Demands for better working conditions and pay led to strikes and then to bloody repression of the movement by the government of Porfirio Díaz. This was the beginning of the collapse of the Porfiriato.

Today, despite its resources, Veracruz is not a wealthy state. A large percentage of its people are still employed in agriculture. While oil production has created many jobs, it has also created one of the most polluted cities in the world, Minatitlán in southern Veracruz. Meanwhile, energy of another sort has created controversy and fear with the fitful start-up of the nuclear power plant at Laguna Verde on the Veracruz coast.

Train Services. The "Jarocho" provides special first class reserved and second class coach service between Mexico City and Orizaba, Fortín de las Flores, Córdoba, and Veracruz. There is a sleeping car. Second class coach service on this route is provided by trains 51 and 52. This is a very scenic trip. The train passes from the austere central plateau to the pine forests of the cloud-draped sierras where the central highlands begin their spectacular collapse to the Gulf Coast. Magnificent, snow-covered Citlaltépetl watches as the train winds through forested canyons decked out in rivers and orchids. Unfortunately, the "Jarocho" traverses this route at night. However, the regular coach train runs during daylight hours so the more intrepid may want to consider second class coach travel.

JAROCHO TRAIN

Lv.	9:15 PM	Mexico City	7:40 AM	Ar.
	4:00 AM(+1)	Orizaba	0:30 AM(+1)	
	4:33 AM	Fortín	0:08 AM	
	4:45 AM	Córdoba	11:35 PM	
Ar.	7:10 AM	Veracruz	9:30 PM	Lv.

RATES FROM MEXICO CITY TO:	Special 1st cl. Reserved	2nd cl. Coach	Rmtte (1)	Rmtte (2)	Bedrm (2)	Bedrm (4)
Orizaba	$ 9.16	2.55	19.68	32.45	39.35	68.87
Fortín	9.74	2.71	20.97	34.58	41.94	73.34
Córdoba	9.90	2.77	21.29	35.13	42.58	74.52
Veracruz	13.06	3.65	28.06	46.29	56.13	98.23

	Train 51			Train 52		2nd.cl. Coach
Lv.	7:45 AM	Mexico City		6:55 PM	Ar.	
	3:55 PM	Fortín		10:50 AM		$ 2.71
	4:10 PM	Córdoba		10:35 AM		2.77
Ar.	6:50 PM	Veracruz		8:00 AM	Lv.	3.65

Orizaba

Located in a naturally defensive position on the road between the Gulf Coast and the Valley of Mexico, Orizaba was the site of both Aztec and Spanish garrisons. Today the city is an industrial and commercial center with little to recommend it to the traveler.

Fortín de las Flores

Its name, meaning "little fort of the flowers," gives a hint as to the chief attraction here. Fortín is a much smaller and more pleasant town to hang out in than is Orizaba. In the spring the neighborhoods and plazas in the town explode in a technicolor carnival of blossoms. If you're looking for a quiet, lovely place to stop, then Fortín may be it. Fortín is between Córdoba and Orizaba, seven km from the former and 11 km from the latter.

Getting Around. Fortín is a small town with everything of interest (actually, everything period) within walking distance of the main plaza or, as it's called in Fortín, the **Parque Central**. The **train station** is on Calle 1 Norte two blocks north of the plaza. The **bus station** with service to Veracruz and Mexico City is on Avenida 1 three blocks west of the plaza. Buses for the short trip to Córdoba or Orizaba are found one block east of the plaza on Avenida 1.

Córdoba

This colonial town is a commercial and food processing center for the rich agricultural region which surrounds it. It is about the size of Orizaba but lacks that city's congestion. Córdoba shares with Fortín an abundance of camellias, azaleas, bougainvilla, orchids, and gardenias. Spring is lovely here as well. Córdoba's chief claim to fame dates back to the War for Independence. It was here in 1821 that the Treaty of Córdoba was signed by General Agustín Iturbide, representing Mexico, and Viceroy Juan O'Donojú, representing Spain. This document established the independence of Mexico.

Getting Around. The **train station** is on the south side of town at Avenida 11 and Calle 33. The **1st class bus station** is west of the plaza at Avenida 3 and Calle 4.

Sights. Córdoba is not awash with places to go and things to do. It does have a few more than Fortín while retaining a relaxed charm and beauty. The large **Plaza de Armas** is arcaded on three sides with appealing sidewalk cafes and a lot of greenery. It is a pleasant place to watch people and has music on weekend evenings. At the southeast end of the plaza is **La Parroquia de la Inmaculada Concepción**. This 17th Century parish church has a 24-carat gold altar. A **tourist office** with maps and brochures is at 308 Calle 5 off the south corner of the plaza. Skip the very poor **Museo Municipal** at 303 Calle 3 south of the square. The **post office** is on Avenida 3 northwest of the plaza.

Climate. This description applies to all three towns: Córdoba, Fortín, and Orizaba. This area gets a lot of rain, ranging from 214 cm (84 in) per year in Orizaba to 230 cm (91 in) in Córdoba. About 80 percent of this falls in June through October with September being the wettest month. Combining this moisture with warm summer temperatures makes these towns quite uncomfortable during the rainy season. Winter and spring are cool, rarely cold, with only a fraction of the rain.

Veracruz, Veracruz

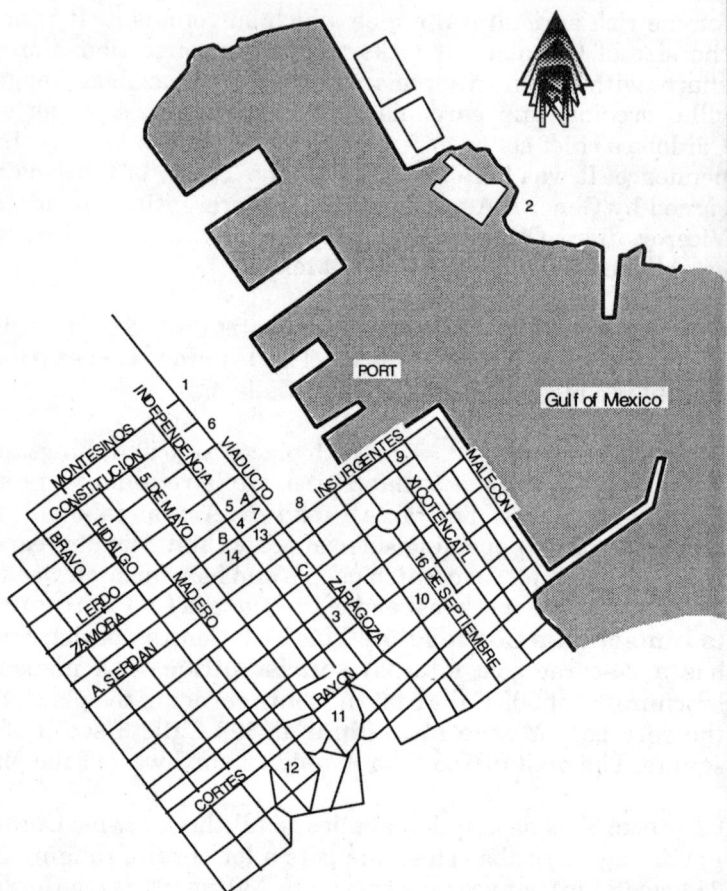

PORT

Gulf of Mexico

INDEPENDENCIA

MONTESINOS

CONSTITUCION

BRAVO

HIDALGO

5 DE MAYO

VIADUCTO

LERDO

ZAMORA

A. SERDAN

MADERO

INSURGENTES

XICOTENCATL

MALECON

C. ZARAGOZA

16 DE SEPTIEMBRE

BAYON

CORTES

1 ~ train station	10 ~ Baluarte de Santiago
2 ~ Castillo de San Juan de Ulua	Museo Historico
3 ~ Museo Cultural de la Ciudad	11 ~ Parque Zamora
4 ~ Plaza de la Constitucion	12 ~ Mercado Hidalgo
5 ~ Los Portales	13 ~ Cathedral
6 ~ post office	14 ~ Gran Cafe de la Parroquia
7 ~ Palacio Municipal	A ~ Hotel Imperial
tourist office	Hotel Rias
8 ~ Mercado de Artesanias	B ~ Gran Hotel Diligencias
9 ~ Faro Venustiano Carranza	C ~ Hotel Santillana

Veracruz

Veracruz was the first Spanish settlement in Mexico. In 1519, Hernán Cortés, before marching inland to meet Moctezuma, founded the town of Villa Rica de la Vera Cruz at what is now La Antigua on the coast between modern Veracruz and Zempoala. The town was moved to its present location in 1598. Despite being New Spain's only legal port, Veracruz grey slowly and sometimes not at all. Heat, disease, and pirates made it uncomfortable, unhealthy, and unsafe. The port was a prime target of French and English buccaneers and their attacks often resulted in considerable loss of life and property. Ironically, Veracruz was not only the first Spanish settlement in Mexico, it was also the last stronghold of Spanish royalist forces during the War of Independence. In 1822, besieged Spanish troops were finally removed from the fort at San Juan de Ulúa.

Veracruz was also where the royalist pretensions of Agustín Iturbide were critically injured. Antonio López de Santa Anna, commander of the Mexican forces opposing the Spanish troops in San Juan de Ulúa, turned against Emperor Agustín I, joined forces with other republican independence leaders, and proclaimed a Mexican republic. Soon after, Iturbide went into exile.

During the 19th Century, Veracruz was destined to suffer at the hands of more foreign troops. In the 1838 Pastry War, Santa Anna was again the hero and drove French troops from the port. Then again in 1847 U.S. forces bombarded the city causing over a thousand, mostly civilian, deaths. Finally, in 1861, French, Spanish, and British troops showed up to collect money owed them by Mexico. Spain and Britain planned to capture the Mexican customs house to recoup the principal on their loans. France's ambition ran deeper. Napoleon III wanted to add Mexico to his empire and so began his unsuccessful six-year attempt to foist Maximillian and Carlota on the unwilling Mexican people.

In 1914 during the Mexican Revolution U.S. troops returned to Veracruz. President Woodrow Wilson was informed that the Mexican dictator Victoriano Huerta was about to receive a shipload of weapons. Wilson ordered U.S. forces to prevent this and the troops did so, but with many Mexican casualties. Even

Huerta's opponents reacted angrily to this affront to Mexico's sovereignty.

Fortunately, the rest of the 20th Century has been kinder to Veracruz. The city remains an active port though its position as Mexico's main shipping port has been eclipsed by newer, more modern facilities. But it remains a very cosmopolitan place, unafraid of the non-traditional. Its people, influenced by the Caribbean and places beyond, are independent and fun-loving, eager to dance or play music at the slightest encouragement. Run-down and past its prime, Veracruz still retains a wonderful charm and character. It is a truly unique Mexican town.

Getting Around. The **train station** is within walking distance of the center on the north end of the Plaza de la República.

The **1st and 2nd class bus stations** are back- to-back on Díaz Miron three km south of the zócalo. To get there, take a taxi.

Comida Tipica. Veracruz is well known for its *salsa* (sauce) *Veracruzana* made from tomatoes, onions, garlic, olives, peppers, and spices and served over seafood dishes. It's also fair to compliment Veracruz on its strong, rich **coffee**, as most of the rest of Mexico drinks instant Nescafe.

Sights. At the center of the action in Veracruz is the **Plaza de la Constitución** or zócalo. In and of itself it is pretty with cast iron lamp posts, a fountain, and many palm trees. But, and as with the zócalo in Oaxaca, it is what goes on there that is truly fascinating. At any time of the day one might see vendors selling hand crafted toys made improbably from bottle caps and plastic orange juice bottles, foreign sailors negotiating in broken Spanish with prostitutes, bands and musicians strolling the tree shaded walkways and playing tunes designed to make people get up and dance. Almost every evening there is music in the zócalo and it often continues until late in the evening.

Opposite the north side of the plaza are the *portales*, an area of hotels and sidewalk restaurants perfect for sipping drinks, watching people, and listening to the sounds emanating from the zócalo. The **post office** is two blocks north of the plaza on Av. de la República. Just east of the Plaza de la Constitución is the 17th Century **Palacio Municipal** with its beautiful court-yard. Inside is the helpful **tourist office**.

Two blocks east of the zócalo and near the docks is the **Mercado de Artesanías** which, while interesting, doesn't have the variety of crafts markets in other parts of Mexico. Also east of the plaza, the **Paseo de Malecón** is comprised of two intersecting waterfront streets: Insurgentes which runs along the southeast edge of the main port area and Blvd. Avila Camacho which runs along the waterfront just east of the main port. On Insurgentes near its intersection with Xicotencatl is the **Faro Venustiano Carranza** (Venustiano Carranza Lighthouse) which is today a museum dedicated to the former president and revolutionary leader. There are three exhibit rooms containing some personal effects of Carranza's as well as documents relating to the Mexican Revolution. After his government had been forced out of Mexico City by the armies of Pancho Villa and Emiliano Zapata, Carranza established his government in Veracruz for a brief time. The museum is open Tues-Fri, 9 a.m. to 1 p.m. and 4 p.m. to 6 p.m., Sat-Sun, 10 a.m. to 2 p.m. and 5 p.m. to 7 p.m.

Four blocks south of the zócalo at Morales and Zaragoza is the **Museo Cultural de la Ciudad** (City Cultural Museum). The exhibits here cover the history of the region and include statuary from the Olmec, Totonac, and Huastec pre-Hispanic civilizations, ethnographical displays on contemporary Indian cultures, and some information on the 19th Century post-independence struggles. The museum is open Tues-Sun, 10 a.m. to 2 p.m. and 4 p.m. to 6 p.m.

Three blocks east of the museum at Canal and 16 de Septiembre is the **Baluarte de Santiago** (Santiago Fortress) and inside is the **Museo Histórico**. Built in 1526, this fort was once part of a defensive wall which surrounded the port. The museum contains exhibits of weapons from the 16th through 18th Centuries as well as photographs and drawings related to the history of the port. The fort is open daily from 10 a.m. to 5 p.m.

Parque Zamora is three blocks south of the Museo Cultural on Independencia and two blocks west of the park is **Mercado Hidalgo**, one of the city's main markets. On the south side of the Plaza de la Constitución is the unremarkable 18th Century

cathedral. Opposite the cathedral on Independencia is the **Gran Cafe de la Parroquia.** Famous throughout Mexico, this is the place to sit and watch people while sipping on a glass of *cafe con leche.*

The **Castillo de San Juan de Ulúa** is on what used to be an island east of the main port facility. Today a road connects it to the mainland and buses marked "San Juan de Ulúa" go there from a bus stop on Landero y Coss just east of the zócalo. Construction of this fort was begun in 1528 and modifications continued until the early 18th Century. It was the last strong-hold in Mexico of royalist Spanish troops during the War of Independence and later served as a prison for political prisoners of the Porfirio Díaz regime. It is open for visitors Tues-Sun, 10 a.m. to 5 p.m.

Fiestas. Carnival is the premier celebration in these parts and Veracruz claims to have the finest north of Rio and south of New Orleans. The nine days before Ash Wednesday are full of dancing, music, costume parties, parades with floats, and very little work. The city fills up with visitors for this party so make your reservations far ahead of time.

Climate. Warm winters and hot, humid summers with thunderstorms pretty much describe the situation here.

Excursions. While the beaches of Veracruz are not impressive, they can provide a decent respite from the heat. The best in the immediate area is the beach at **Mocambo** with shade and public swimming pools. Catch the bus marked "Boca del Río-Mocambo" on Serdán between Zaragoza and Landero y Coss.

The archeological site of **Zempoala** (also spelled Cempoala) is about 40 km (24 mi) north of Veracruz and beside the village of the same name. This is the best preserved of the Totonac cities and, along with El Tajín, the most interesting pre-Hispanic site in Veracruz. Zempoala was first occupied by the Totonacs sometime around 900 A.D. and reached the zenith of its power about 1200 A.D. In the 15th Century the city was brought into the Aztec empire. When Cortés arrived in the spring of 1519 Zempoala had a population of 30,000 and was unhappily laboring under Aztec tribute demands. In order to demonstrate Spanish power, Cortés choreographed a terrifying display of charging cavalry and discharging cannon. Having no knowledge of either horses or gunpowder, the Totonacs were awestruck and frightened. They agreed to help the Spanish against the Aztecs. Despite their agreement, Cortés ordered that the Totonac idols be destroyed.

In 1520, a second Spanish expedition arrived at Zempoala under the leadership of Pánfilo de Narváez and with orders to arrest Cortés. Cortés returned to the Totonac city with some of his own troops and defeated Narváez. This battle, subsequent diseases, and Indian slavery took their toll on Zempoala. By the early 17th Century, this city which had once boasted 30,000 souls had been reduced to eight families and soon after was abandoned to the forest. The present village was founded in the early 19th Century.

The platforms and pyramids built by the Totonacs contained a core of adobe, sand, or soil covered with ovoid, water-worn river stones in a cement matrix. Plaster was then applied to the stone facing, smoothed, and painted in red and yellow colors. The plaster is long gone so the exterior of the structures consists of the river stone layer. A defensive wall surrounds the platforms, which have been excavated. At the extreme north end of the quadrangle is the **Templo Mayor** (Main Temple). This impressive pyramid is 11 m high and has a 27-m-wide staircase on its front face. On top are the remains of a three-room structure with what was probably an altar in the largest of the rooms.

East of and adjacent to the Templo Mayor is **Las Chimeneas** (The Chimneys). In 1519, Cortés and his men were housed in a long-gone wooden structure on top of this pyramid. On the west side of the compound is the **Temple to the Wind God**. This temple is partially circular in plan view and is similar to a style which shows up in both Toltec and Aztec structures. The Temple is fronted on the east side by a rectangular platform with a broad stairway. Beside the Temple of the Wind God is the **Great Pyramid**. Facing east, this pyramid has three platforms accessed by two stairways. The site is open daily from 8 a.m. to 6 p.m. There is a small museum near the entrance. To get there, catch an ADO bus at the 1st class bus station in Veracruz. Several buses daily make the one-hour trip to Zempoala.

Train to Guatemala

This is not an easy trip nor an intrinsically interesting one. It should only be attempted by those travelers determined to go on to Guatemala. According to the schedule this journey takes about 24 hours but expect it to take at least 32 hours and possibly more. The only service on this route is second class coach.

The route begins in the city of Veracruz and travels south east through the hot, humid lowlands of southern Veracruz. As the state eases into the Isthmus of Tehuantepec, the train turns south and soon after enters the state of Oaxaca. The Isthmus is the narrowest section of Mexico, measuring about 200 km (120 mi) from the Gulf of Mexico on the north to the Pacific Ocean on the south. Numerous rivers meander through rain forests and swamps in the flat, northern half of the isthmus. The southern portion is more arid and is covered by tropical spiny forests and brush land. It is also covered by low mountains, though a narrow valley bisects the highlands and extends all the way to the southern coast. Because of the northern flatlands and this southern valley, the Isthmus of Tehuantepec was at one time considered as the site for a transoceanic canal. The construction of the Panama Canal put an end to those considerations.

After reaching the Pacific coast of Oaxaca, the route bends east, hugging the narrow coastal plain of first Oaxaca and then Chiapas. In Chiapas, the train passes through banana and palm plantations as it approaches the city of Tapachula. This is the richest agricultural area in Chiapas, this coastal strip known as the Soconusco. The earliest sign of humanity in Chiapas was found at the Santa Marta rock shelter near Ocozocoautla in the central part of the state where several burials date back to about 6700 B.C. By 1500 B.C. there were farming villages in this same area of Chiapas producing sophisticated pottery at Chiapa de Corzo. Between 1000 B.C. and 400 B.C. the Olmecs extended their influence to several sites along the Pacific coast. Then, between 200 B.C. and 200 A.D. the city-state of Izapa flourished near the present day town of Tapachula. This large, important site is widely believed to have been a link between the Olmec and the Mayan cultures. The culture of Chiapas achieved its greatest expression in the classic Maya centers of Palenque and Yaxchilán which flourished between 600 A.D. and 800 A.D. The abandonment of these great cities left a political and cultural vacuum in the area until the Aztecs conquered the fertile coastal plain.

The Spanish conquered the most hospitable areas of the state by the 1530s and administered the region out of the town of Villa Real de Chiapa (today San Cristóbal de las Casas). Spanish laws designed to protect the Indian from abuse and excessive exploitation had little effect in Chiapas. Distant from the main centers of Spanish colonial authority, Chiapan Indians suffered greatly at the hands of Spanish and *criollo* landowners.

Following the independence of Mexico, Chiapas waffled between being a part of the Central American states and being part of Mexico. In 1824 a referendum decided the issue in favor of Mexico.

Throughout the 19th Century conditions continued to be bad for Native Americans. Landowners, through legal manipulations and illegal violence, forced Indians from their traditional lands and, through debt-slavery, guaranteed themselves sufficient Indian workers for their haciendas. Several Indian uprisings failed to alter this political power imbalance. Today, conditions for the peasants and indigenous people remain desperate. Agriculture dominates the Chiapan economy but most of the best land is owned by a few rich people or companies. Most of the rural population either has no land or has an amount of land insufficient for family survival. Gunmen hired by landowners have killed hundreds of peasants in Chiapas over the last 20 years and have frustrated efforts for a more equitable distribution of farm land. Chiapas is the poorest state in Mexico.

Train Services. Trains 101 and 102 provide second class coach service from Veracruz to Tierra Blanca, Medias Aguas, Ixtepec, and Tapachula. Trains 221 and 222 offer the same class of service between Tapachula and Ciudad Hidalgo on the border with Guatemala. There is little to recommend this route except the spirit of travel and Guatemala.

	Train 102		Train 101		2nd.cl. coach
Lv.	9:00 PM	Veracruz	6:00 AM	Ar.	
	11:20 PM	Tierra Blanca	3:15 AM(+1)		$ 0.42
	4:35 AM(+1)	Medias Aguas	9:55 PM		2.61
	8:50 AM	Ixtepec	5:40 PM		3.94
Ar.	7:25 PM	Tapachula	7:30 AM	Lv.	7.45

	Train 222		Train 221		2nd.cl. coach
Lv.	1:15 PM	Tapachula	9:50 AM	Ar.	
Ar.	2:35 PM	Ciudad Hidalgo	8:30 AM	Lv.	$ 0.42

Tierra Blanca, Medias Aguas, and Ixtepec

There is no obvious reason to stop in any of these three towns.

Tapachula

With 120,000 people, Tapachula is an important commercial center for the rich agricultural region surrounding it and for Guatemalans who cross the nearby border for shopping and business purposes.

Getting Around. The **train station** is about 10 blocks south of the zócalo at the intersection of Calle 14 and Avenida Central Sur. The **1st class bus station** is at Calle 17 Oriente and Avenida 3 Norte northeast of the zócalo. There are several **2nd class bus stations**. Check with the tourist office to see which one meets your destination needs.

Sights. If you find yourself in Tapachula on your way to Guatemala or if you're really into archeology, there are a couple of things to do here. The small **Museo Regional del Soconusco** (Soconusco Regional Museum) is located in the **Palacio Municipal** on the west side of the zócalo. The **tourist office** is also in this building. There is also an interesting archeological site in the area. See the "Excursions" section below.

Climate. Tapachula ranges from hot in the winter to hot and humid in the summer. Between June and October the area receives heavy rainfall.

Excursions. The pre-Hispanic ruins at **Izapa** are among the most significant in Mexico as well as being some of the least visited due to their location. Their significance lies in the fact that the people who built this city seem to have been a link between the Olmec culture and the early Maya centers in Guatemala and eastern Chiapas.

People were settled at Izapa by 1000 B.C. and the city apparently reached its zenith between 200 B.C. and 200 A.D. The bas-relief carvings on stone monuments, or stelae, show a recognizable Olmec style but contain important differences, especially the employ of complex baroque designs and representations of groups of people. Izapan stelae are found down the Guatemalan coast and in some areas of the Guatemalan highlands. Early Maya stelae in the interior lowland centers, which postdate Izapa by a couple centuries, show clear Izapan stylistic influences.

Izapa is a large site and is divided into north and south sections by the highway. The north section is the better excavated of the two and here one can find a ball court, several platforms, and a number of stelae. The south section, which is a little hard to find, has seen little excavation to date. Despite this, there are a number of stelae and other sculptures scattered around intriguing mounds and plazas.

Second class buses marked "Unión" and "Progresso" go to Izapa. The buses leave from Calle 9 Poniente in Tapachula.

Train to the Yucatán

This is another trip which should only be attempted by those hardy in mind and body. The trip officially takes 27 hours but usually lasts a third again as long. Also, the only train service available is second class coach. And finally, just when you thought it couldn't get worse, there are reports of bandits who sometimes board the train and rob the passengers. While I have never been robbed on this route, it does happen. But let's look at the bright side. This train provides cheap access to one of the most distinctive regions of Mexico. The Yucatán and Palenque in northern Chiapas are the heart of Mexico's Mayaland. The culture, the people, the food are all different here. So is the terrain. And Yucatán also boasts the best beaches in Mexico along its Caribbean coast.

The route begins in Córdoba. From here it runs southeast and travels through the tropical interior lowlands of Veracruz. After it reaches the southern town of Medias Aguas, the route angles approximately eastward and enters the state of Tabasco. This small state hugs the Gulf Coast of Mexico. Fertile soil, heavy rainfall, and a tropical climate make the region a prodigious agricultural producer, with bananas, coconuts, pineapples, cocoa, corn, and cattle leading the way. In the eastern half of Tabasco, the combination of abundant rainfall and flat lowlands has produced a situation where fully half the surface area of this part of the state is covered by freshwater lakes, swamps, and rivers. The only significant hills in the state are at some spots along its southern border with Chiapas. In the 1970s oil was discovered in western Tabasco. Income from petroleum has significantly augmented that generated by agriculture.

Just north of where the train crosses into western Tabasco from Veracruz is the pre-Hispanic site of La Venta. Inhabited since at least 1500 B.C., La Venta became the center of Olmec culture after the destruction of San Lorenzo in Veracruz. La Venta itself was abandoned by around 400 B.C.

In 1519 Cortés landed on the Tabasco coast and, in a battle, seriously defeated the Mayan locals, killing over 200 Indians with the loss of only two Spaniards. As a peace offering, the Indians gave Cortés a gift of 20 women, one of whom was the woman known to Mexicans as La Malinche or Doña Marina.

During the colonial period Tabasco was essentially a backwater. There were no silver or gold mines and the climate was almost unbearable. Hence, few Spanish bureaucrats were interested in it and even fewer visited the area. In the late 19th Century exports of tropical produce began to be important to Mexico's economy so Tabasco became an increasingly valuable region. With the discovery of oil in the 1970s Tabasco's importance to the national economy shot up again.

The train route goes east through Tabasco, occasionally cutting across pieces of the state of Chiapas which protrude northward. In the easternmost part of Tabasco the route abruptly turns northeastward, passes into the state of Campeche, and reaches the coastal town of Campeche after about 250 km (150 mi). From Campeche the route continues roughly northeastward, enters the state of Yucatán, and terminates at the city of Mérida.

After this deviation northward from Tabasco the train passes through an unremitting expanse of flat terrain covered with thorny scrub forest and brush. This is the Yucatán Peninsula, a flat, limestone shelf with very little surface water. The reason for this lack of surface water is that the porous limestones of the peninsula quickly channel rainfall at the surface down to the water table. When the roof of a limestone cavern collapses it often creates a large pit with a lake at the bottom. These pits, called *cenotes*, can be found throughout the Yucatán Peninsula and, in this land without rivers, were vitally important to the Indian settlers of the area.

The history of the Yucatán Peninsula is dominated by the culture of the Maya. The history of the Maya began in the middle Preclassic period in the region bounded by the Yucatán Peninsula to the north and what is today Honduras to the south. The scattered agricultural villages in this area were politically distinct but linguistically united. There were two languages, Yucatec and Chontal, but these were similar enough to facilitate the exchange of goods and ideas throughout the region.

During the middle and late Preclassic the Olmec culture was flourishing west of Mayaland along Mexico's Gulf Coast. Olmec influence, carried by traders and, perhaps, by missionaries, spread throughout the Maya region. Although the depth of this influence is unclear, it is certain that the introduction of Olmec concepts of religion and politics was the seed of the classic Maya civilization. The cities of Tikal in Guatemala and Copán in Honduras were founded between 1000 and 500 B.C. but the majority of Classic Maya centers were not established until the very late Preclassic, between 0 and 200 A.D. Some were established much later. Dynastic rule apparently began in Yaxchilán in Chiapas and Uaxactún in Guatemala around 200 A.D. while Palenque began its growth as a powerful regional center around 400 A.D.

At any one moment during the Classic period there were dozens of Maya city-states whose individual political, economic, and military powers waxed and waned over time. Some centers became powerful and held sway over large areas but none, as far as can be determined, ever achieved the status of empire. Throughout the Classic period Mayaland remained an amalgam of culturally connected but politically distinct regional centers.

Nevertheless, the accomplishments of this dispersed culture were remarkable. In a terrain of thin, poor soils and almost nonexistent surface water, Mayan agriculture was able to feed a population of millions as well as maintain a nonproductive religious, political, and, probably, military elite. Mayan mathematical and astronomical sciences had also advanced beyond Europe's of the same period. The Maya were the most literate of the pre-Hispanic Mesoamerican cultures with a written glyphic language capable of great subtlety and expression. Over hundreds of years the Maya filled thousands of books with information on their dynasties, ceremonies, sciences, and history. Almost none of these texts survived the Spaniards' Catholicism and the forest's humidity. The Maya also excelled in their public art and architecture, which for them were part of the rituals of religious and political power and for us are the primary tools for unlocking the many mysteries of their history.

Between 600 and 800 A.D. the frequency of war among the Mayan cities increased. Dynasties came and went, cities rose and fell. Agriculture, always a balancing act between the harsh constraints of the natural environment and growing social needs, suffered as farmers were conscripted for military service and resources appropriated by victorious armies.

One by one the classic Maya cities in Honduras, Guatemala, Belize, and Chiapas were abandoned because of war, economic collapse, or both. New groups of Maya-speaking people from the Gulf Coast moved into the classic Maya area. Known as the Putún, these were traders and only semi-civilized, though they tried to ape the cultures of the cities they conquered.

The collapse of the southern Maya kingdoms did not extend to the northern Yucatán Peninsula. Here Mayan centers continued to flourish though most of these northern cities did not display the same degree of literacy as their southern relatives. This is almost certainly the result of foreign migrations over the centuries into the Yucatán. Some of these immigrants were Maya- speaking, semi-civilized people such as the Putún Maya and the Itzá while others may have included the Toltecs and other peoples from central Mexico. Whatever their origins, these immigrants invigorated and altered the Post-Classic Maya culture of the northern Yucatán.

The chief centers of the late Classic in the Yucatán were Cobá, Chichén Itzá, and Uxmal. Cobá was a huge city-state in the eastern part of the peninsula with a traditional Maya culture while Uxmal, located in the western Puuc Hills, was strongly influenced by the Putún Maya from Tabasco. Chichén was founded in the 9th Century by a group of seafaring, warrior merchants known as the Itzá. After years of war Chichén came to dominate all of northern Yucatán. Between about 850 A.D. and 1200 A.D. Chichén Itzá was the most powerful Mayan city-state in all the Yucatán. War with the neighboring city of Izamal led to the abandonment of Chichén in about 1200 A.D. Fifty years later the city of Mayapán was founded southwest of Chichén and was ruled by a confederation of powerful Maya families. Although Mayapán was the most powerful Maya city of its time, its culture was only a derivative, shadowy likeness of classic Maya achievements seen at sites such as Palenque and Tikal. Interclan rivalries resulted in the destruction of the city in 1450. When the Spanish arrived in the early 16th Century they found the Yucatán Maya living in politically separate villages and in a state of cultural degeneracy.

Train Services. Trains 49 and 50 provide second class coach service between Córdoba and Tierra Blanca, Medias Aguas, Coatzacoalco, Teapa, Palenque, Campeche, and Mérida. This trip takes about 27 hours, and that's when everything is going smoothly. Expect your trip to take longer. Also, there have been reports of well organized bandits victimizing passengers on this route, especially between Palenque and Mérida.

Train 49		Train 50		2nd.cl. coach
Lv. 6:30 AM	Córdoba	9:05 PM Ar.		
8:50 AM	Tierra Blanca	6:35 PM		$ 0.81
1:30 PM	Medias Aguas	1:50 PM		2.52
3:40 PM	Coatzacoalco	11:30 AM		3.32
8:05 PM	Teapa	7:35 AM		5.03
10:49 PM	Palenque	5:02 AM(+1)		5.87
5:45 AM(+1)	Campeche	9:40 PM		9.32
Ar. 9:35 AM	Mérida	6:15 PM Lv.		10.81

Tierra Blanca, Medias Aguas & Coatzacoalco

Just keep going. Coatzacoalco is an ugly town made semi-prosperous by oil.

Teapa

Teapa is an ordinary town in a rather pleasant setting. It is also the stop on this route which is closest to the city of Villahermosa. Teapa is in the rain-forest-covered hills of southern Tabasco very near the Chiapas border. Southwest of town is the small volcano El Chichonal (1,260 m) which erupted in spring of 1982. Among other destructive effects of the blast, the stone sculpture at Palenque was damaged by the acidic ash fall from the eruption.

Getting Around. With only 20,000 people, Teapa is easily navigated afoot.

Sights. As there are really no "sights" in Teapa proper, what follows in this section are actually short excursions from the town. **El Azufre spa** is five km west of the plaza and has two large pools, one with sulfur water and the other with fresh. There is also a reasonable and clean hotel here. To get there, take a taxi.

You can also swim at the **Río Puyacatengo** bridge about four km east of town. Situated in a lush, natural setting, this cool swimming hole is a perfect antidote to Teapa's tropical heat. To get there, catch the bus to Tacotalpa on the zócalo and ask the driver to let you off at the bridge ("*el puente del Río Puyacatengo*").

Las Grutas de Coconá (Coconá Caves) are a little over three km east of town and have some nice formations and an underground stream. There is also a restaurant and campground. The cave has electric lights but if you have a flashlight, take it. The caves are open daily except Monday and there are tours at 11 a.m., 1 p.m., and 3 p.m. To get there, catch the second class bus to Tacotalpa on the zócalo.

Climate. Teapa is hot and humid, with rain occurring all year long. It is in one of the wettest regions of Mexico.

Excursions. The only excursion from Teapa is to the city of **Villahermosa**, 58 km north on Hwy 195. Villahermosa began as a sleepy inland port town on the Río Grijalva. It was only in the 1950s when a highway was built connecting this part of Mexico with the capital that the city began to grow as a commercial center. Then, when oil was discovered, the boom accelerated. Today, Villahermosa is a modern city of 180,000 people and contains several interesting sights.

Parque La Venta is actually an open air museum and is one of the finest museums in the country. The original La Venta is an Olmec archeological site in far western Tabasco 129 km (77 mi) from Villahermosa. La Venta was a major center of Olmec culture from 1500 B.C. to 400 B.C., when it was destroyed. In the 1950s oil exploration activities threatened to obliterate the site. Carlos Pellicer, a local combination poet/archeologist of some renown, initiated a campaign to save the artifacts of La Venta and to find them a new home. Thus was conceived and born Parque La Venta. The park contains 30 pieces of Olmec statuary and bas-reliefs arranged in a wonderfully lush, forested setting, connected by winding trails. Animals, some free-roaming (deer, armadillos, coatimundis, and monkeys) and some caged (jaguars and crocodiles) also occupy the park.

The most impressive artifacts in the park are three huge carved stone heads, the largest of which weighs 24 tons. The basalt for these monumental sculptures was quarried in the Tuxtla Mountains, 100 km (60 mi) distant from La Venta, and was worked without benefit of metal tools. Other Olmec artifacts in the park include four bas-relief stelae and seven altars. Parque La Venta is open daily 8 a.m. to 4:30 p.m., and is located on Blvd. Grijalva, three km northwest of the main plaza. To get there, catch a bus marked "Tabasco 2000" or "Parque Linda Vista" at the zócalo. You might want to ask the bus driver if he goes to the park ("*Va al Parque La Venta?*"). The answer should be, "*Sí.*"

The **tourist office** is close to Parque La Venta at the intersection of Paseo Grijalva and Paseo Tabasco. The **Plaza de Armas** or zócalo is located on the west shore of the Río Grijalva and two blocks west of the plaza on 27 de Febrero is the **Casa de la Cultura** with local crafts on display and for sale. It is open Mon-Fri, 9 a.m. to 2 p.m. and 5 p.m. to 8 p.m. At the intersection of 27 de Febrero and Juárez is the **Museo de Arte Popular** which houses exhibits of contemporary Tabascan costumes and household artifacts. The Museo is open Tues-Sun, 9 a.m. to 2 p.m. and 5 p.m. to 8 p.m.

About six blocks south of the plaza along the Río Grijalva is the **Centro de Investigaciones de las Culturas Olmeca y Maya (CICOM)**. This complex contains the **Casa de Artes** which offers fine arts classes, the **Teatro de Estado** (State Theater) which showcases performance arts, and the **Museo Regional de Antropología** (Regional Anthropology Museum) which houses a fine collection of artifacts and materials on various pre-Hispanic cultures, but focusing on the Olmec and Maya. The Museo is open Tues-Sun, 9 a.m. to 8 p.m. To get there, catch the bus marked "CICOM" which runs along the river near the plaza. Several first and second class buses run from Teapa to Villahermosa daily. The trip takes a little over an hour.

Palenque

Palenque is both a town of 25,000 people and, several kilometers away, a Mayan archeological site. The town exists primarily to serve the thousands of visitors who come every year to see the wonderful ruins. A word of warning is in order here. The countryside around Palenque with its waterfalls and rainforest easily lures the visitor to explore its trails and discover its mysteries. Unfortunately, tourism has, in turn, lured robbers and rapists to this site. It is not advisable to walk alone in the forests around Palenque, especially if you are a woman. This warning extends to the areas around the waterfalls of Aguas Azul and Mishol-Ha.

Getting Around. The **train station** is a couple of kilometers north of town. Taxis run between the station and Palenque. The **1st class bus station** is on 5 de Mayo about four blocks west of the plaza.

Sights. Of course, the thing to see is the archeological zone of **Palenque.** Located six km west of the town, Palenque is a favorite of ruins buffs. While it lacks the minimalist grandeur of Teotihuacán or the massively powerful architecture of Chichén Itzá, Palenque counters with a delicate artistry of stucco and stone and captures an architectural lightness best embodied in the roof combs which top the pyramids.

Palenque was first settled by the Maya around 300 A.D. but its glorious golden age lasted a bare 200 years, from 600 to 800 A.D.

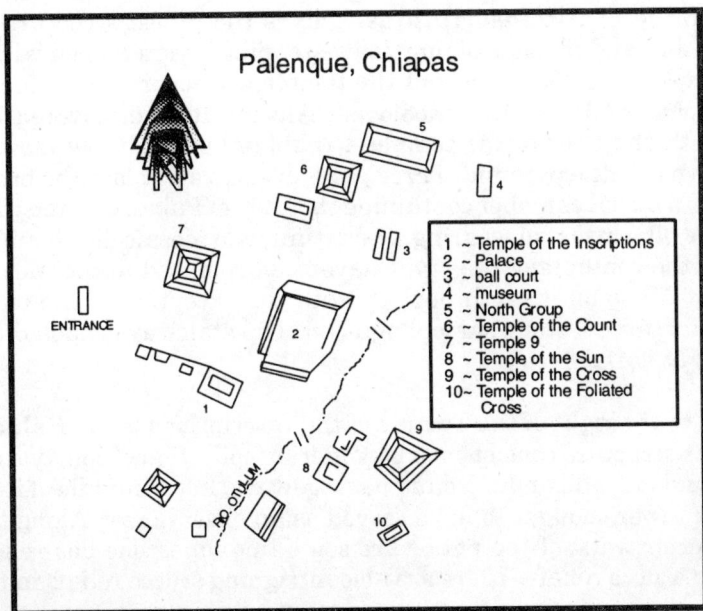

Palenque, Chiapas

1 ~ Temple of the Inscriptions
2 ~ Palace
3 ~ ball court
4 ~ museum
5 ~ North Group
6 ~ Temple of the Count
7 ~ Temple 9
8 ~ Temple of the Sun
9 ~ Temple of the Cross
10~ Temple of the Foliated Cross

ENTRANCE

Pakal's death in 683 A.D. he was succeeded by, first, his eldest son, Chan Bahlum, who died in 702 A.D., and then by his younger son, Kan Xul. During the younger son's reign and for reasons unknown, Palenque entered a period of decline, from which it did not recover. By the 10th Century the city had been abandoned and by the time the Spaniards stepped ashore at Veracruz, Palenque had been swallowed by the rainforest.

The ruins were discovered by the Spanish in the latter 18th Century and became the inspiration for popular fantasies hypothesizing a connection between ancient Egypt and Mexico. The first scientific study of the site was undertaken in 1837 by an American, John Stephens, and an Englishman, Frederick Catherwood.

Today, the site sits nestled at the foot of the Chiapas foothills. The lush rainforest on the hills threatens to take back the structures it had claimed for hundreds of years. Even today, many buildings still belong to the forest, as only a small fraction of Palenque's 500 buildings on 39 acres have been cleared and excavated.

As you enter the site the large pyramid on the right is the **Temple of the Inscriptions**. This is the tallest structure on the site and consists of nine stair-stepping layers topped with a temple. The wall panels of the temple are covered with hieroglyphs. In 1949 an archeologist, Alberto Ruz, discovered beneath the floor of the temple a rubble-filled stairway leading down into the pyramid. Three years of excavation later he broke into a burial chamber containing the body of Pakal, covered with jade offerings and wearing a beautiful jade mosaic death mask. All the contents of the crypt have been removed to the Mexico City Museum of Anthropology with the exception of the enormous carved, stone sarcophagus lid. The stairway is open daily but at variable times.

Off to the right of the Temple of the Inscriptions is the **Palace**. This structure consists of a bewildering collection of courtyards, chambers, and underground passageways. In the middle of it all is a tower thought to have served as an observatory. Along the interior walls of the patios are some fine limestone bas-reliefs and stucco reliefs. There are also intriguing stucco reliefs in the tower. To facilitate examining the underground hallways, bring a flashlight.

Just northeast of the Palace are the ruins of a **ball court** and east of that is the site's small and rather poor **Museum**. It is open daily, 10 a.m. to 1 p.m. and 3 p.m. to 5 p.m.

From between the Palace and the Temple of the Inscriptions a path leads across a small stream and to a complex of buildings. It is thought that the three most impressive of these structures, the **Temple of the Sun**, the **Temple of the Cross**, and the **Temple of the Foliated Cross**, were built by and dedicated to Chan Bahlum. The Temple of the Sun is nearest the stream and is crowned by the best preserved roof comb in the entire zone. Only traces of the original painted stucco covering remain on the structure. Just east of this temple is the large Temple of the Cross which contains some fine historical bas-reliefs and stucco reliefs with the figure of Chan Bahlum. Off the southeast corner of the Temple of the Cross is the Temple of the Foliated Cross. Although the exterior of this temple has decayed considerably, its interior contains an exquisite stone tablet.

The archeological zone is open daily, 8 a.m. to 5 p.m. Vans travel between the town and the ruins and leave from the intersection of Calle Hidalgo and Allende every 15 minutes.

Climate. Palenque is oppressively hot and humid in the summer—also the rainiest time of year. Winters are drier and warm.

Excursions. Las Cascadas Agua Azul consist of a series of waterfalls and swimming holes along a wonderful stream of clear, blue water (except during the rainy season when the waters become furious and brown). Agua Azul is 62 km (37 mi) south of Palenque in the Sierra del Norte de Chiapas. With rapids and placid pools, water-carved rock and lush rainforest, Agua Azul is a delightful place to relax. A campground and restaurant in the area leave much to be desired, however. Vans (*colectivos*) leave for Agua Azul at 10 a.m. from the corner of Hidalgo and Allende in Palenque and return at 3 p.m.

Nearer to town and also a fine swimming hole (though not as spectacular as Agua Azul) is **Cascada Mishol-Ha**, 22 km (13 mi) south of Palenque. Surrounded by tropical forest, the plunge pool of this 35-m waterfall is a fine place to swim and cool off. Mishol-Ha does get crowded on weekends. The same van that goes to Agua Azul stops here on the way. Also, any second class bus traveling from Palenque to Ocosingo or San Cristóbal de las Casas will drop you at the turn off to Mishol-Ha. From there it is a two-km walk to the falls.

Campeche

The town of Campeche was established in 1540 by the Spanish conqueror of the Yucatán, Francisco de Montejo. It was founded on top of an older Mayan settlement called Ah Kin Pech. During the colonial period, the port of Campeche prospered from the export of dyewoods and hardwoods to Spain. However, this prosperity caused the city to suffer often and grievously from pirate attacks. Eventually, and not soon enough for the people of Campeche, the Spanish crown ordered the construction of a defensive wall with regularly placed forts around the port. This wall was completed in the late 17th Century and, in conjunction with aggressive naval actions against the pirates, brought peace to the settlement.

Mexican Independence hit the city hard by freeing slaves previously used on Yucatecan plantations and drastically reducing trade between Mexico and Spain. Campeche's economic slump continued through the 19th Century and into the 20th. There were no land connections between the Yucatán Peninsula and the rest of Mexico so Campeche remained a backwater.

The completion of a highway to the port in the 1950s, the resurgence of the fishing industry, and the discovery of oil offshore all contributed to the economic revitalization of the city. Today Campeche is a city of 150,000 people and, despite its relative prosperity, has managed to retain a tropical but colonial charm. The narrow cobbled streets are lined with 16th, 17th, and 18th Century buildings. Cotton-white clouds dot the forever-blue sky over the green waters of the Gulf of Mexico.

Getting Around. The **train station** is out on the east side of town. Take a taxi or catch a *colectivo* marked "Centro." The **bus**

Campeche, Campeche

Gulf of Mexico

1 ~ bus station
2 ~ Plaza Principal
3 ~ Museo de las Estelas Mayas
       Baluarte de la Soledad
4 ~ tourist office
5 ~ Baluarte de San Carlos
6 ~ Museo Regional de Campeche
7 ~ Baluarte de San Francisco
8 ~ Alameda
9 ~ Baluarte de San Pedro
       Artesanías del Estado
10~ Baluarte de Santiago
       Jardín Botánico Xmuch-Haltún
11~ Cathedral
12~ train station
A ~ Hotel Colonial
B ~ Hotel López
C ~ Hotel América

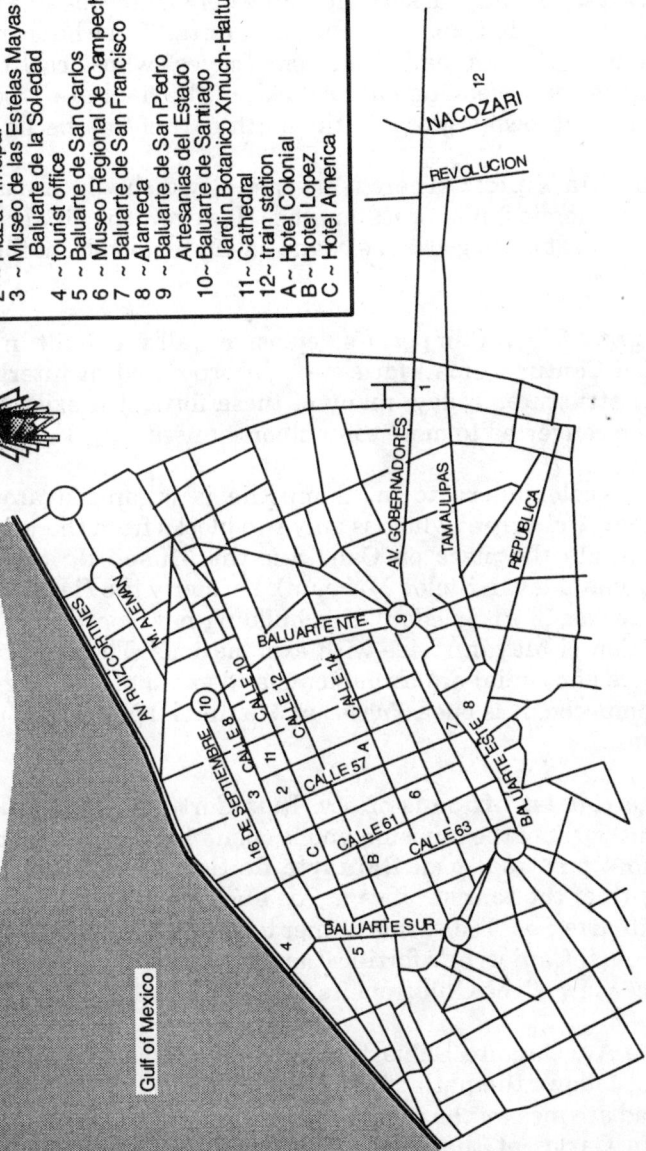

NACOZARI
REVOLUCION
AV. GOBERNADORES
TAMAULIPAS
REPUBLICA
M. ALEMAN
AV. RUIZ CORTINES
BALUARTE NTE.
BALUARTE ESTE
BALUARTE SUR
16 DE SEPTIEMBRE
CALLE 8
CALLE 10
CALLE 12
CALLE 14
CALLE 57
CALLE 57 A
CALLE 61
CALLE 63

station is about 15 blocks east of the plaza. You can walk to the plaza, take a taxi, or catch a bus marked "Centro."

Crafts. In the markets and stores of Campeche one can find excellent and inexpensive **Panama hats**. These hats are manufactured in man-made limestone "caves" whose cool humidity makes their weaving easier. Most of the hats are produced in the small town of Becal in the north part of Campeche state.

Comida Tipica. There is no specialty dish which has earned gastronomic fame for Campeche. However, the city can justifiably boast of its good, basic, and cheap seafood from the Gulf of Mexico.

Sights. When Campeche's defensive wall was built in the late 17th Century, small forts were incorporated at intervals into the structure. Today, many of these forts still exist but have been converted to more contemporary uses.

As a colonial-era town, Campeche is organized around the **Plaza Principal** which is only two blocks from the waterfront. Opposite the plaza on Calle 8 is the **Museo de las Estelas Mayas** (Mayan Stelae Museum). Formerly the **Baluarte de la Soledad** (Fort Soledad), this building now contains a nice collection of Mayan stelae with explanations. There are also displays of colonial-era armaments and exhibits covering colonial Campeche. It is open Tues-Sun, 9 a.m. to 2 p.m. and 3 p.m. to 8 p.m.

The **tourist office** is on Av. Ruíz Cortínez about four blocks southwest of the museum and is open Mon-Sat, 9 a.m. to 2 p.m. and 4 p.m. to 8 p.m. **Baluarte de San Carlos** is two blocks south of the tourist office at Av. Justo Sierra and Av. Circuito Baluarte Sur. Today this former fort contains a model replica of colonial Campeche's fortifications, an authentic dungeon, and a nice view of the Gulf from its roof.

The Av. Circuito Baluarte circles the old center of Campeche and follows the path of the original defensive wall. Along this road are most of the remaining *baluartes* of Campeche. South of San Carlos at the intersection with Calle 14 is Baluarte de Santa Rosa. A few blocks further on is Baluarte de San Juan.

Two blocks north of Av. Circuito Baluarte Este on Calle 59 is the **Museo Regional de Campeche**. This museum contains well organized exhibits covering the pre-Hispanic, colonial, and independence period histories of the state and city. It is open Tues-Sat, 9 a.m. to 8 p.m., and Sun, 9 a.m. to 1 p.m.

Northeast of Baluarte de San Juan along Av. Circuito is **Baluarte de San Francisco**. Beside the fort is **Alameda Park**, a nice place to picnic if you happened to bring a lunch with you.

Baluarte de San Pedro is at the intersection of Av. Circuito with Av. Gobernadores. This former fort now contains the **Artesanías del Estado**, a permanent exhibit of regional crafts. San Pedro is in front of the city's main market, **Mercado Pedro Sáinz de Baranda**.

Baluarte de Santiago is located at the intersection of Av. Circuito and Av. 16 de Septiembre and contains a lovely and soothing garden, the **Jardín Botánico Xmuch-Haltún**. On Calle 55 opposite the plaza is the **Cathedral**. Begun in 1540, the cathedral is noteworthy for being the oldest church in the Yucatán.

Out from the center of town is the **Baluarte de San Miguel**. Surrounded by a moat, this fort is the most distinctive and charming (in a Middle Ages sort of way) of all the remaining fortresses in Campeche. Inside it contains an archeological museum which is open Tues-Sun, 9 a.m. to 1 p.m. and 2 p.m. to 5 p.m. To get there take the "Lerma" bus from the market and tell the driver that you want to get off at the fort ("*Baja en el Baluarte de San Miguel*"). It is about three km from the plaza.

Climate. Warm winters and hot, wet summers characterize Campeche's climate.

Excursions. The archeological zone **Edzná** is 61 km (37 mi) from Campeche. This Mayan site was settled permanently about 200 A.D. and reached the apogee of its power around 450 A.D. With an estimated population of 70,000 people, it was a true city and not just a ceremonial center. For unknown reasons the city had begun a political and economic decline by 650 A.D.

and around 800 A.D. it was invaded by the Maya of Río Bec and Chenes. Much of the city's original architecture was destroyed and reworked by the invaders so the ruins today show a distinct mixture of styles.

The portion of Edzná which has been excavated is dominated by the **Pyramid of the Five Niches**. Located on the eastern margin of the site, this structure is 30 meters high with a base measuring 61 by 59 meters. A central stairway provides access to a temple on the top of the pyramid.

To get there, catch a second class bus in Campeche. The down side is that this bus leaves Campeche at 8 a.m. and returns at 11:30 a.m., which doesn't leave the visitor much time at the site. The only alternatives are to rent a car, join a tour group, or hitchhike. Take your own food and water as there is none at Edzná.

Mérida

The capital of Yucatán state and the most important cultural and economic center on the entire peninsula, Mérida is a wonderful anomaly among Mexico's cities. It is a big city with a gentle spirit. It is also a lovely city, with an architecture boasting Spanish and French influences and an economy not dependent on polluting industries.

Machismo, that irritating and sometimes dangerous component of Mexican culture, is largely absent in Mérida in particular and the Yucatán in general. Without a doubt, this is because of the strength and continuity of Mayan culture. Another key factor in the evolution of Yucatecan culture has been the historical isolation of this region from the political and cultural heartland of the country. Until a road was completed in the 1950s linking Mexico City with the Yucatán Peninsula, it was easier to go from Mérida to Cuba, the United States, or even Europe than to get to Mexico City. For this reason, the city has always looked abroad for economic ties, for the education of its wealthy class, and for ideas in art, science, politics, and architecture. Since the Revolution, Mérida has also looked inward, rediscovering and

Mérida, Yucatan

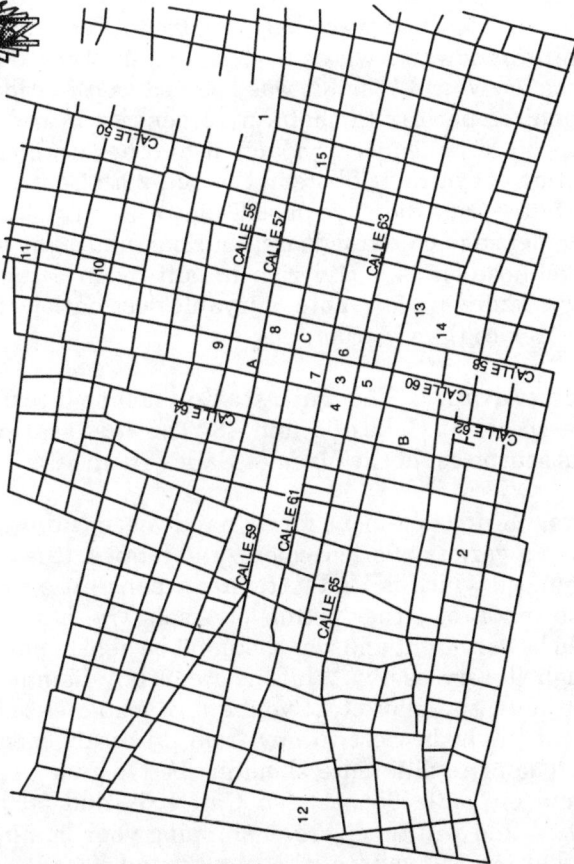

1 ~ train station
2 ~ bus station
3 ~ Plaza de Armas
4 ~ Palacio Municipal
5 ~ Casa de Montejo
6 ~ Cathedral
7 ~ Palacio de Gobierno
8 ~ Teatro Peon Contreras
    tourist office
9 ~ Parque Santa Lucia
10~ Paseo Montejo
11~ Museo de Antropologia
12~ Parque El Centenario
13~ post office
14~ market
15~ Museo de Arte Popular
A ~ Hotel Trinidad
B ~ Hotel Maria Teresa
C ~ Hotel Caribe

institutionalizing its Mayan roots.

Founded in 1542 on top of a long abandoned Mayan center, the town became the commercial center of the agricultural region surrounding it. Unfortunately for the Maya, that agricultural system was based on de facto enslavement of the Indians. Life in the town for the Maya wasn't much better as here they were forced to build the churches, public buildings, and dwellings that, ironically, today make Mérida such a lovely colonial city. European diseases and overwork decimated the indigene population.

Starting in the 19th Century, Mérida began to prosper greatly from the henequen (also called sisal) trade. Fortunes were made by white landowners whose haciendas were worked by dirt poor Indians. By World War I it was boasted that Mérida had more millionaires per capita than any other city in the world. The expansion of henequen production to other countries and the invention of synthetic fibers in the mid-20th Century killed the boom but Mérida didn't go bust. Today, this city of half a million people depends on agriculture, tourism, and light industry for its livelihood. It is a city rich in culture in a region rich in history. There are few more enjoyable destinations for the visitor to Mexico than Mérida.

Getting Around. The **train station** is nine blocks northwest of the zócalo at Calles 55 and 48. The **bus station** is seven blocks southwest of the plaza at Calles 70 and 69.

Crafts. Mérida is famous for its handwoven **hammocks**. They come in a variety of sizes, colors, and fabrics. It is better to get a hammock which is big (extra size means little extra weight) and is made of either cotton or sisal. The hammock weave should be very tight and you shouldn't be able to put your finger through it very easily. While you can buy hammocks on the street or in the market, if you're an inexperienced hammock buyer it might be best to buy from an established hammock shop. The price difference shouldn't be too great. The store La Poblana on Calle 65 between Calles 58 and 60 has a good selection and will take care of shipping your hammock. There are other shops if you want to look around.

Mérida is also the place to buy men's *guayabera* shirts with the classic button-down pockets and *huipiles*, the traditional embroidered blouse worn by Mayan women.

A word of warning: The artisans of Mérida make a number of beautiful objects from coral and tortoise shell. The purchase of such products abets the destruction of coral reefs and the extinction of endangered species.

Comida Tipica. The cuisine of the Yucatán is the richest and most distinctive in Mexico. Its variety is a result of several fortunate conditions: the relative isolation of the Yucatán from the rest of Mexico, the Maya, and the existence of several seasonings grown almost solely on the peninsula. Some of these seasonings are *anchiote*, a sharp-flavored seed from the annatto tree, the bitter Seville orange, a sour lime grown, as far as I know, only in the Yucatán, and the fiery *chile habanero*, the most *picante chile* grown in Mexico.

Specific dishes include *Sopa de Lima* (a chicken soup with lime juice), *Queso Relleno* (stuffed cheese), *Pollo Píbil* (spiced and marinaded chicken baked in banana leaves), *Huevos Motuleños* (fried tortillas covered with beans, eggs, and salsa), *Poc-Chuc* (marinaded and grilled pork), *Relleno Negro* (chicken or turkey with a spicy pork stuffing), *Papadzules* (crumbled hard-boiled egg wrapped in a tortilla and covered with a pumpkin-seed sauce), and *Muk-Bil Pollo* (chicken and pork tamal pie).

Sights. In the center of Mérida is the **Plaza de Armas** or zócalo. This well-shaded plaza is usually full of street vendors and pedestrians and is surrounded by the oldest buildings in Mérida. Just west of the zócalo is the 16th Century **Palacio Municipal** which contains a **tourist information** booth. On the south side is the **Casa de Montejo**. Completed in 1549, this building was the residence of the conqueror of the Yucatán, Francisco de Montejo. The extraordinary plateresque facade was carved by Mayan craftspersons and unashamedly portrays race relations in colonial Mérida: on both sides of the door Spanish conquistadores stand on the heads of vanquished Maya. Today the building is a bank.

On the east side of the Plaza de Armas is the **Cathedral**, an austere and forbidding building with an interior as heavy and plain as the exterior. Finished in 1598, the church was built on the foundation of a Mayan temple and stones from that temple were used in its construction. It was a common practice of the Spanish to build "sacred" structures on top of "profane." A chapel within the cathedral contains a carved wooden image of Christ known as the *"Cristo de las Ampollas"* (Christ of the Blisters). The story goes that some Maya saw a tree which burned intermittantly but was not consumed. So they carved the Christ image from this miraculous tree and placed the image in their small parish church. The church then mysteriously burned to the ground but the image survived. That's right, another miracle. So the Indians brought the carving to the cathedral in 1645 where it is still.

Just north of the plaza is the **Palacio de Gobierno**. This 19th Century building is notable for its powerful and graphic murals by local artist Fernando Castro Pacheco portraying the history of the Yucatán as being based on the brutal exploitation of the Mayas by the Spanish.

On Calle 60 two blocks north of the plaza is the **Teatro Peón Contreras**. Completed in 1900, this theater has a white marble stairway and is the site every Tuesday evening for performances by the university's Ballet Folklorico. Next to the theater is the very helpful **tourist office**. Ask here about upcoming cultural events in town. **Parque Santa Lucía** is one block north of the theater on Calle 60 and is a popular site for cultural events. On Thursday evenings there is the *Serenata Yucateca*, a blend of regional folk music, ballads, and love songs. On Sunday the park becomes an open-air arts and crafts market from 10 a.m. to 2 p.m. Again, there is usually music.

Seven blocks north of the zócalo and between Calles 56 and 58 is the **Paseo Montejo**. The European influence is apparent along this street which the henequen millionaires envisioned as a sort of diminutive Champs Élysées. Their mansions, with Moorish, French, and Mediterranean flourishes, parade along the Paseo accompanied by flower-filled gardens and courtyards. At the north end of Paseo Montejo is the **Monumento a la Patria** (Monument to the Nation), a massive bas-relief sculpture by Rómulo Rosso representing the history of Mexico. In this same area on Av. Colón is the **Parque Las Américas**. This tree-filled and lovely park contains a botanical garden, an open air theater, a salon with changing art exhibits, and a fountain dedicated to Kukulcan, the feathered serpent god.

Toward the south end of the Paseo Montejo at its intersection with Calle 43 is the **Museo de Antropología**. Housed in the beautiful, turn of the century **Palacio Cantón**, this museum contains a fine collection of Mayan artifacts ranging from sculpture to household articles. There is also a gift shop with crafts and some English language archeological guide books for sale. The museum is open Tues-Sat, 8 a.m. to 8 p.m., and Sun, 8 a.m. to 2 p.m.

If you're into zoos, Mérida has one: 11 blocks west of the plaza at Av. de los Itzaes and Calle 59 is the **Parque El Centenario** which contains over 1,000 different animals, specializing in regional and tropical fauna.

The **post office** is southwest of the plaza at Calles 65 and 56. Pretty much surrounding the post office and covering several city blocks is the **mercado**. Filled with Mayan men, women, and children selling everything from crafts to food, clothing to things that defy description. It is one of the finest and most captivating markets in Mexico. Before you buy any *artesanía* in the market, you might want to check out the **Museo de Arte Popular** five blocks east of the plaza on Calle 59 between Calles 48 and 50. This unmarked, hidden, and largely ignored gem contains several scattered rooms full of regional crafts, displays, and crafts-making tools. The *artesanía* is for sale at very reasonable prices. The museum is open Tues-Sat, 8 a.m. to 8 p.m., and Sun, 9 a.m. to 1 p.m.

Fiestas. The most festive celebration in Mérida is that of **Carnival** which takes place the week before Lent. There are parades, regional dances and music, and crafts bazaars. The **Fiesta del Cristo de las Ampollas** celebrates the miraculous properties of the wooden Christ image with processions, masses, and religious drama. It takes place the first two weeks in October.

Classes. The Centro de Idiomas del Sureste offers intensive Spanish classes at all levels. Contact:

> Chloe C. Pacheco
> Ctr. de Idiomas del Sureste
> Calle 14 #106x25, Col. México
> Mérida, Yuc. 97128 México

Climate. Summers are hot and very humid in Mérida. It frequently gets up to 37°C (100°F) with 70 percent or higher humidity. If that doesn't sound pleasant, try visiting the city November through May when the heat is moderated by occa- sional, cool northers. Most of the rainfall comes in May through September.

Excursions. Progresso was Mérida's port town during the henequen boom and is 33 km (20 mi) north of the capital on the Gulf of Mexico. The beaches here are clean, smooth, and pleas- ant but the waters are an opaque green, not the clear turquoise of the Caribbean.

If you feel the need of a close, cooling dip then do as the Meridanos do: go to the quiet beach town of Progresso. To get there, catch one of numerous daily buses which leave from the bus station on Calle 62 at Calle 65 in Mérida. The trip takes about an hour.

For birdwatchers the lagoons and estuaries of the northern Yucatán coast are paradise. The town of **Celestún** is 92 km (57 mi) west of Mérida and is located in a large bird sanctuary. The lagoons and estuaries which surround the town are home to dozens of species of water birds, especially the flamingo, an- hinga, and egret. You can hire a launch at the docks.

A more spectacular sight is the huge flamengo colony at **Río Lagartos**, 250 km (150 mi) east of Mérida on the coast. But flamingoes are not the only birds that call the shallow, marshy estuaries around Río Lagartos home. You can also spot numer- ous varieties of herons, ibis, pelicans, cormorants, plovers, egrets, and other species. Launches to the feeding areas can be hired at the Hotel Nefertiti.

Several buses a day leave Mérida for Celestún from the Autotransportes del Sur station at the intersection of Calles 50 and 67. To get to Río Lagartos, you must first catch a bus to Tizimín from Mérida's main bus terminal. Regular buses run between Tizimín and Río Lagartos.

The state of Yucatán contains numerous Mayan archeological sites. One of the finest is **Uxmal**, 80 km (50 mi) south of the capital. This incredible site contains some of the finest and most detailed Mayan facades on the peninsula. Uxmal was established around 600 A.D. and seems to have been the most important center in the region for about 300 years. The center's distinctive architecture is known as the Puuc style, a name derived from the low relief Puuc Hills of the region. This style is characterized by mosaic-like, fine cut-stone geometric patterns organized in horizontal panels on building facades. Uxmal ultimately succumbed to Chichén Itzá in a series of wars and was abandoned around 850 A.D.

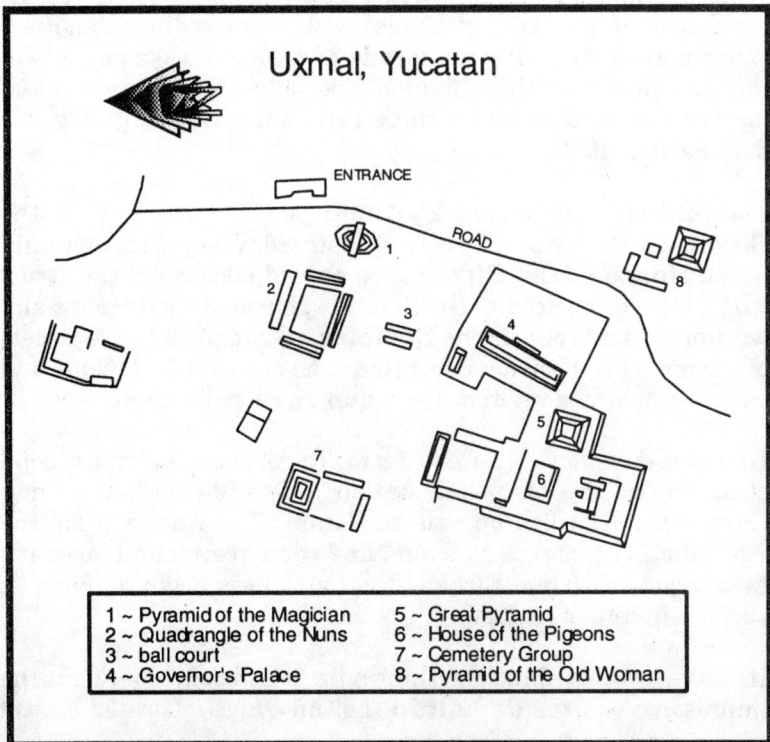

Uxmal, Yucatan

1 ~ Pyramid of the Magician
2 ~ Quadrangle of the Nuns
3 ~ ball court
4 ~ Governor's Palace
5 ~ Great Pyramid
6 ~ House of the Pigeons
7 ~ Cemetery Group
8 ~ Pyramid of the Old Woman

Today the excavated portion of the site covers about 1.5 square kilometers. On the northeast corner of the site, near the parking lot and the tourist center, is the **Pyramid of the Magician**, whose name derives from a Mayan legend that a magical dwarf built this structure overnight. This elliptical pyramid is 39 meters high and crowned by an elegant temple. The doorway of this temple represents the mouth of Chac, the Mayan rain god.

Immediately west of the pyramid is the **Quadrangle of the Nuns**. The building was named by the religion-preoccupied Spanish and its historical function remains unknown. The buildings which make up the four sides of the quadrangle are thought to have been built at different times with the structure on the north side being the oldest. There are hundreds of stone and stucco reliefs decorating the rooms of the quadrangle and many of these reliefs are of Chac.

South of the quadrangle are the remains of a **ball court** and south past these is the **Governor's Palace**. This is perhaps the most elegant structure at Uxmal with its incredible stone mosaic panels dominating the facade and Chac masks embellishing the corners of the building. The palace is more than 100 meters long and sits atop three artificial terraces, giving it a dominating effect.

The 32-meter-tall **Great Pyramid** is just southwest of the Governor's Palace and largely unrestored. West of the pyramid is the **House of the Pigeons**, so named because of the structure's latticed roofcomb. North of the House of the Pigeons and west of the ball court is the **Cemetery Group**. Here the panels of a temple platform are decorated with bas-reliefs of skulls and bones, probably a reference to a human sacrifice ceremony.

Uxmal is open daily 8 a.m. to 5 p.m. To get there, catch a second class bus at the main bus station in Mérida for Kabah and Campeche. It will drop you at Uxmal. The first bus for the 90-minute trip leaves at 7 a.m. and then every two hours. It's best to get to Uxmal early as the tour buses begin arriving at the site in late morning.

If you're interested in something a little different, check out the impressive **Grutas de Loltún** (Loltún Caves). Located east of

Uxmal nestled among other Mayan sites in the Puuc Hills, this cave constitutes an archeological as much as a geological site. Evidence of human presence at Loltún goes back to 500 B.C. and evidence of the Mayas' ceremonial use of the cave abounds. There are also natural secondary rock formations such as stalactites and stalagmites throughout the cave. Tours of the 1.5-km-long Grutas de Loltún begin at 9 a.m. and leave approximately every two hours after that. Wear comfortable shoes and take a flashlight if you have one as the cave's lighting system leaves something to be desired. There is an admission fee and a tip for your tour guide is more than courtesy as they receive no other income.

Getting to Loltún requires some maneuvering. Catch a bus for the town of Oxkutzcab at the Autotransportes del Sur station at Calles 50 and 67. From Oxkutzcab take a taxi the seven km to the cave. There are organized tours from Mérida which also take in various archeological sites.

Another Mayan archeological zone, and the most popular in the Yucatán, is **Chichén Itzá**, 119 km (74 mi) east of Mérida. This is also the best restored Mayan site in the Yucatán. Chichén flourished as a Mayan center from 820 A.D. to 1200 A.D. Evidence of the Puuc architectural style can be seen on many of its older buildings. Other architectural and stylistic elements of the site show an unmistakable resemblance to the Toltec culture at Tula. The reason for this resemblance is a matter of controversy. The original explanation was that a Toltec military force, possibly the exiled party led by Topiltzin-Quetzalcóatl, simply conquered Chichén and the surrounding area. Another theory is that the Itzá, who originated in the region that is now Tabasco, had trading networks extending into central Mexico and through these networks they assimilated elements of Toltec culture and passed these elements on to Chichén.

A final theory is that many of the cultural elements considered to be Toltec in origin were actually developed by the Putún or Itzá. These elements were then translated to the Toltec area through late Classic Maya cities in central Mexico, among them Cacaxtla in the state of Tlaxcala and Xochicalco in Morelos.

The archeological zone is divided into a north group and a south group by the highway. This is convenient because the southern group consists of the older, pure Maya structures at the site while the northern consists of newer, Toltec-Maya additions. The Toltec-Maya group is dominated by the imposing **El Castillo**, also called the **Pyramid of Kukulcan**. Sitting in the middle of a large plaza, this 25-meter-tall structure has a stairway to the top on each of its four sides. Each stairway has 91 steps and the platform at the top yields a total of 365 steps, a reflection of the Mayas' preoccupation with time.

This pyramid is actually built over a smaller pyramid which can be entered only at certain times during the day. Check with the tourist center as to what these hours are. Within this smaller

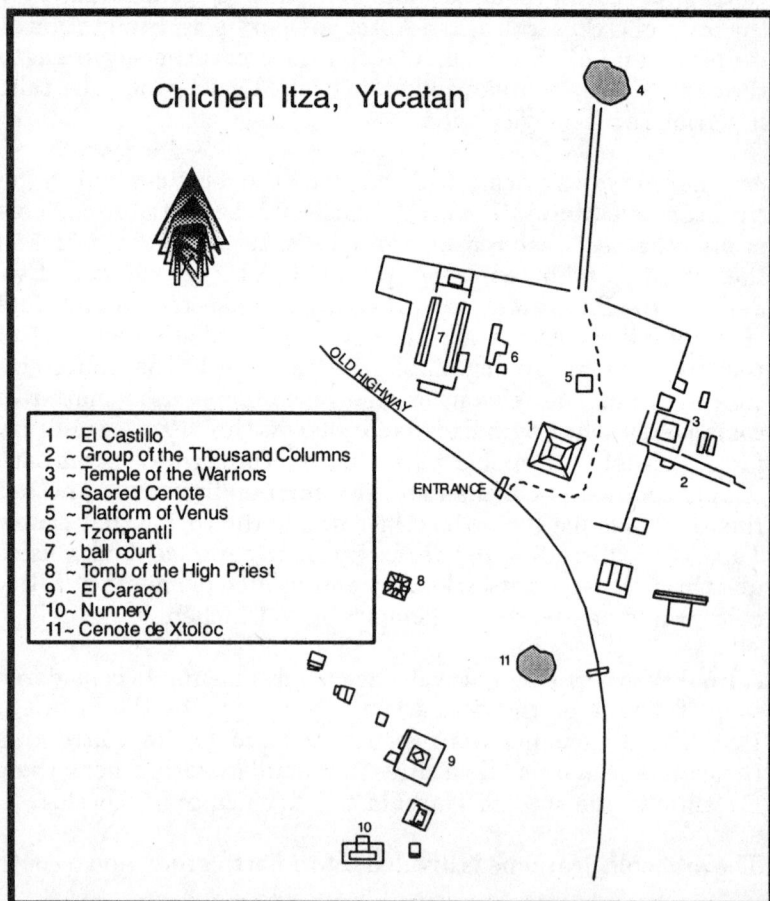

Chichen Itza, Yucatan

OLD HIGHWAY

ENTRANCE

1 ~ El Castillo
2 ~ Group of the Thousand Columns
3 ~ Temple of the Warriors
4 ~ Sacred Cenote
5 ~ Platform of Venus
6 ~ Tzompantli
7 ~ ball court
8 ~ Tomb of the High Priest
9 ~ El Caracol
10~ Nunnery
11~ Cenote de Xtoloc

pyramid is a red stone jaguar throne with jade eyes. There is also a *chac-mool*–a reclining stone figure on which were placed the hearts of sacrificed humans.

Just east of El Castillo is a complex of structures known as the **Group of the Thousand Columns**. This complex includes several ball courts, a steam bath, the **Temple of the Thousand Columns** and the **Temple of the Warriors**. The columns in these latter two temples at one time supported a roof of wood and thatch.

Two hundred meters north of El Castillo is a path that leads to the **Sacred Cenote**. The scummy, green waters of this limestone pit once received bound, human sacrificial victims. Inanimate offerings to the gods such as statuary and jewelry were also tossed into the 35-meter-deep natural well. Several projects have conducted excavations in the cenote and have removed thousands of artifacts and human remains.

Northwest of El Castillo is the **Tzompantli**. This T-shaped platform is decorated with hundreds of bas-relief skulls and was used to hold the heads of sacrificial victims. Just west of the Tzompantli is the largest **ball court** in Mexico, 146 meters long and 36 wide. The **Temple of the Bearded Man** is at the north end of the ball court and the **Temple of the Jaguars** is off its southeast corner.

The most northerly structure in the south group is the **Tomb of the High Priest**. Several richly adorned tombs were found in this dilapidated 10-meter pyramid. About 150 meters south of the pyramid is **El Caracol**, also called the **Observatory**. This structure consists of a cylindrical observatory tower set on a rectangular base. An interior spiral stairway leads to an upper chamber where the narrow windows are aligned with astronomical bodies important to the Mayas' religious and agricultural practices.

South of the Observatory is the **Nunnery** with its beautifully carved facade. This structure measures about 35 meters wide by 65 meters long and, with its many rooms, is thought to have been a residence for royalty. Its architecture is pure Puuc style. There is more to the site but much of the rest is covered by the

Yucatán's ubiquitous scrub jungle. Chichén Itzá is open daily 8 a.m. to 5 p.m. The best time to visit is either early in the morning or late afternoon as during the middle of the day tour buses disgorge swarms of tourists from Mérida and Cancún. First and second class buses make the two-hour trip to Chichén Itzá from the main bus station in Mérida. Sometimes the buses stop at the town of Pisté, which is two km from Chichén, rather than at the ruins.

If you're heading to Cancún from Mérida a nice intermediate place to break up the journey is **Valladolid**. There is little to do but relax in this quiet, colonial town. For most of its history Valladolid was a tiny island of Spaniards in a sea of angry Maya and periodically it was overrun by rebellious Mayan armies. Today, that enmity is gone but the Maya are still everywhere. Lodging is cheap and the food is great. The fort-like **Iglesia de San Bernardino de Siena** was built in 1552. There are also a couple of cenote swimming holes. **Cenote Zaci** with its scummy green water is three blocks from the zócalo on Calle 36. A better choice, though harder to get to, is **Cenote Dzitnup** which boasts cool, transparent waters. To get there, go three km west of town on the Chichén Itzá highway. A sign, saying "Dzitnup," marks the left turn off to the cenote which is two km south of the highway. You can rent bicycles in town.

Both first and second class buses travel between the main bus station in Mérida and Valladolid. The trip takes three hours.

Well, you've come all the way to the Yucatán so you might as well go on to the Caribbean. **Cancún** is only five hours from Mérida by first class bus and once in Cancún other options are available.

This resort city sits on the east coast of the Yucatán Peninsula and up against the transparent turquoise water of the Caribbean. Cancún is a resort, *totalmente*, created largely for foreign tourists. It is comfortable here with amenity-laden hotels, white sand beaches, perfect water, and a lot of pale-faced tourists. But you don't have to be rich to stay here.

A little north and east of Cancún is **Isla Mujeres**. This place is also a resort but its clientele is generally younger and more

Chichen Itza, Yucatan

OLD HIGHWAY

ENTRANCE

1 ~ El Castillo
2 ~ Group of the Thousand Columns
3 ~ Temple of the Warriors
4 ~ Sacred Cenote
5 ~ Platform of Venus
6 ~ Tzompantli
7 ~ ball court
8 ~ Tomb of the High Priest
9 ~ El Caracol
10~ Nunnery
11~ Cenote de Xtoloc

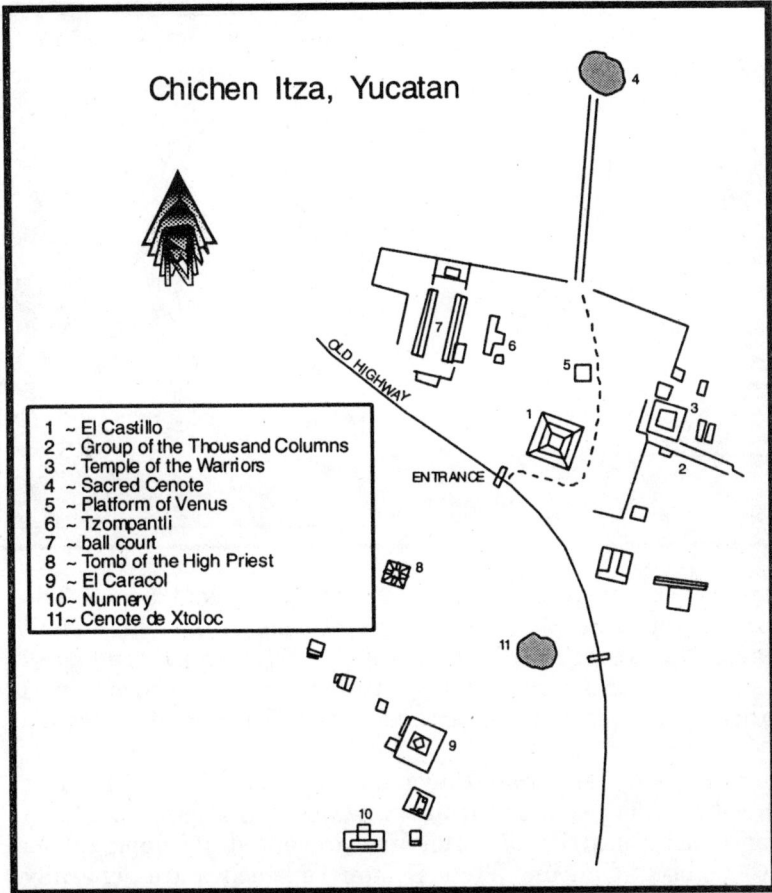

laid-back than the tourists in Cancún. Before the construction boom started on the island, Isla was a kind of counterculture paradise with hippies and fellow travelers camping on its beaches. Those days are gone though some of the relaxed atmosphere remains. There are a number of new hotels, though space is at a premium during the busy winter holiday season. A ferry runs from Puerto Juárez on the mainland to Isla Mujeres, leaving every hour beginning at 8:30 a.m. From Cancún you can take a taxi the three km to Puerto Juárez or the "Ruta 8" bus.

South of Cancún are my favorite beach haunts. **Playa del Carmen** is 66 km (40 mi) south of Cancún and is a quiet,

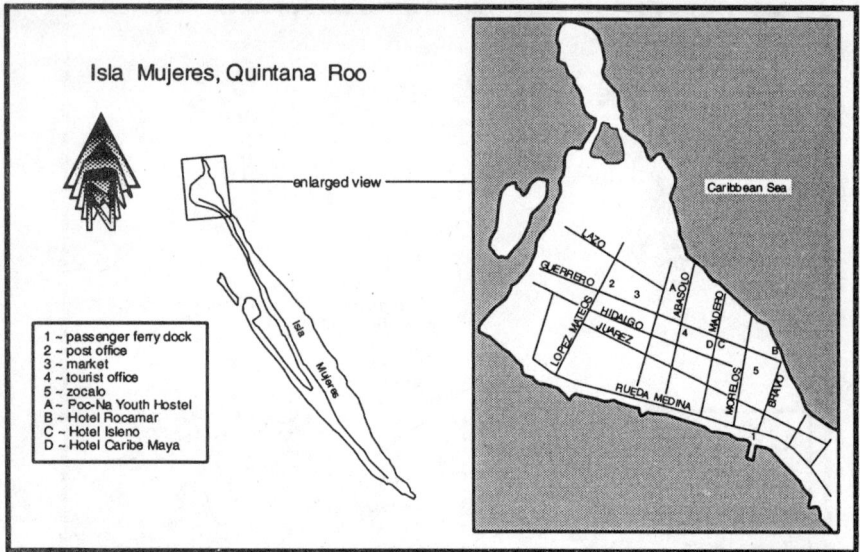

Isla Mujeres, Quintana Roo

enlarged view

Caribbean Sea

1 ~ passenger ferry dock
2 ~ post office
3 ~ market
4 ~ tourist office
5 ~ zocalo
A ~ Poc-Na Youth Hostel
B ~ Hotel Rocamar
C ~ Hotel Isleno
D ~ Hotel Caribe Maya

paradisiacal beach resort well suited to the budget traveler. The same crystalline Caribbean laps at the same white sand beaches but there's no Hilton in sight. First and second class buses run several times a day between Playa del Carmen and Cancún. There is also bus service between Mérida and Playa.

Just off the coast from Playa del Carmen is the island of **Cozumel**. This island, with its town of San Miguel, is also a resort but a scarcity of water has prevented development as intense as at Cancún. While Cozumel's beaches are generally inferior to those on the mainland, the big draw here is spectacular diving and snorkeling opportunities. There are countless dive shops and tour operators. You can also get diving instruction and certification here. Several ferries daily ply the waters between Cozumel and Playa del Carmen.

It is also possible to take **Spanish classes** in Cozumel. Experiencia Centro de Intercambio y Cultura offers classes in languages, both Spanish and Mayan, crafts, culture, and fine arts. Contact: Joan Serino, Mgr., Experiencia, PO Box 6, Cozumel, Quintana Roo, Mexico

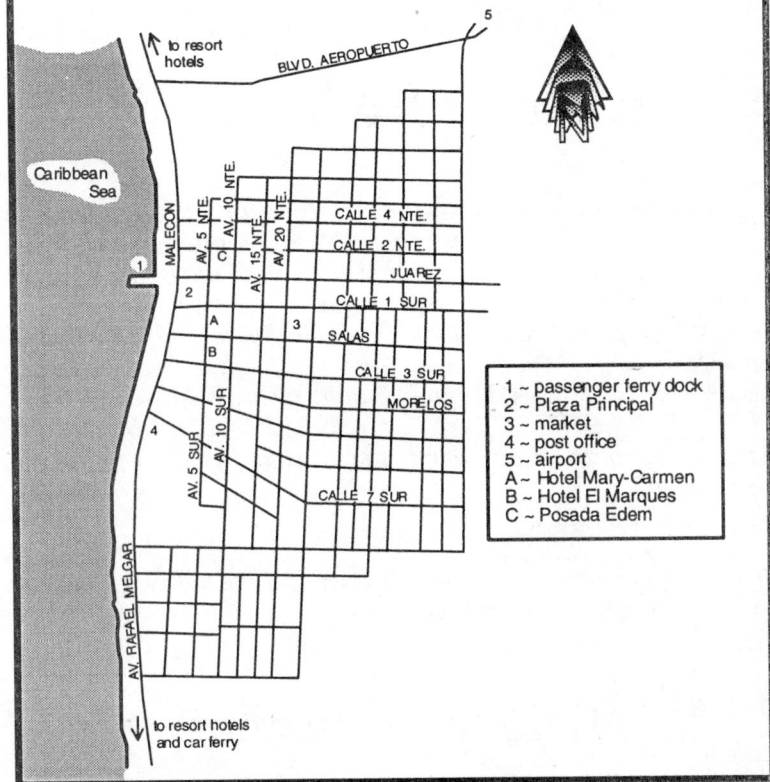

Cozumel, Quintana Roo

to resort
hotels

BLVD. AEROPUERTO

5

Caribbean
Sea

MALECON

AV. 5 NTE.

AV. 10 NTE.

AV. 15 NTE.

AV. 20 NTE.

CALLE 4 NTE.

CALLE 2 NTE.

JUAREZ

CALLE 1 SUR

SALAS

CALLE 3 SUR

MORELOS

CALLE 7 SUR

AV. 5 SUR

AV. 10 SUR

AV. RAFAEL MELGAR

C

A

B

1

2

3

4

to resort hotels
and car ferry

1 ~ passenger ferry dock
2 ~ Plaza Principal
3 ~ market
4 ~ post office
5 ~ airport
A ~ Hotel Mary-Carmen
B ~ Hotel El Marques
C ~ Posada Edem

Chapter 5

Routes North &
Northeast of Mexico City

"My children, a new dispensation comes to us this day. Are you ready to receive it? Will you be free? Will you make the effort to recover from the hated Spaniards the lands stolen from your forefathers three hundred years ago?...Long live our Lady of Guadalupe! Mexicans! Long live Mexico! Death to the Spaniards!"
—the Grito de Dolores, Miguel Hidalgo y Costilla

"Men of the south, it is better to die on your feet than to live on your knees!"
—Emiliano Zapata

"If I must be killed tomorrow, Let them kill me today."
—from "Valentina," a traditional song

Train to Chihuahua

After leaving Mexico City this route angles north-northwestward going through the states of Querétaro, Aguascalientes, Zacatecas, Coahuila, and Chihuahua. The pre-Hispanic history of this region is largely unknown, as the Indians here were nomadic or semi-nomadic people who left few records. On the other hand, the area has a rich history dating from the colonial and independence periods, encompassing many of the events which shaped modern Mexico.

The train climbs out of the Valley of Mexico and leaves the central volcanic belt of Mexico behind. It descends slightly, entering the rolling high plains of first the state of Mexico and then the southern part of Querétaro. This latter state is bordered on the west by Guanajuato, on the north by San Luis

Potosí, on the east by Hidalgo, and on the south by Mexico and Michoacán. The northeastern half of the state extends into the mountains of the Sierra Madre Oriental, while the southwestern half consists of rolling flatlands interrupted by occasional low hills. This southwestern half contains most of the state's population and its capital city, also named Querétaro.

At the time of the conquest Querétaro was occupied primarily by Otomí and Chichimec Indians. In 1529 the Spaniard Hernán Pérez Bocanegra y Córdoba converted the Otomí chief Conín to Catholicism. Conín changed his name to Fernando de Tapia, became a loyal ally of the Spanish crown, and helped establish the town of Querétaro in 1531. The colonial economy of the area depended on mining and agriculture, especially tobacco. It was in Querétaro in 1810 that the Mexican War of Independence began. Later, the infamous Treaty of Guadalupe Hidalgo was signed here on February 2, 1848. This agreement ended the United States-Mexico War and ceded half of Mexico's territory to the U.S. This state was also the site of the execution of the Emperor Maximilian in 1867 and the drafting of Mexico's current constitution in 1917.

At the city of Querétaro the route turns westward through the fertile plains of Guanajuato and then northward again, cutting through eastern Jalisco and passing into the state of Aguascalientes. Originally the home of nomadic Chichimec Indian tribes such as the Guachichiles, Guamares, and Zacatecos, the area was sparsely settled by the Spanish in the middle 1500s. The settlement, which eventually became the city of Aguascalientes, was a defensive maneuver in an effort to protect the trade routes between the silver mines at Zacatecas and the cities of Mexico City and Guadalajara from Indian attacks. Aguascalientes was originally part of Zacatecas. It became one of Mexico's tiniest states in 1823 when the then President of Mexico, Antonio López de Santa Anna, offered to grant the city of Aguascalientes and the surrounding region its statehood in exchange for a kiss from the mayor's wife.

The phrase *aguas calientes* means "hot waters" and refers to the numerous hot springs in the area. Today, this productive agricultural region is well known for grapes and prize winning bulls.

Rail Routes North and Northeast
of Mexico City

---------- ~ train routes

Continuing north from the city of Aguascalientes this route soon crosses into the state of Zacatecas and soon after enters the capital of the same name. This large, irregular state is bordered by Durango on the west, Coahuila on the north, San Luis Potosí on the east, and Guanajuato, Aguascalientes, and Jalisco on the south. Almost all of the state is higher than 2,000 meters above sea level and is roughly bisected by the Tropic of Cancer. The northern half is generally flat and arid, with several small ranges of mountains in the northeast corner. The southern part of the state receives more rainfall and consists of hilly brush-covered land incised by arroyos and river canyons.

Zacatecas was originally home to the Zacateco, Caxcane, and Guachichil Indians. In 1546 silver was discovered at what is today the city of Zacatecas and by 1560 mines had opened up in many other parts of the state. The growing Spanish population of the region and their need for supplies of food and labor transformed the initially friendly relationship between the Europeans and the Indians into one of exploitation and enmity.

In 1550 the Chichimec War began when a band of Zacatecos attacked and massacred a group of Tarascan Indians taking supplies to the miners at Zacatecas. This war lasted 40 years and raged across the mining country of central Mexico, from Jalisco in the west to San Luis Potosí in the east. It involved several Chichimec tribes: the Guamares, Zacatecos, Guachichiles, and Pames.

Even before peace came to the area, the silver barons had established ranches and farms in Zacatecas to provide supplies for their mining operations isolated on this northern frontier of the young colony. By the early 17th Century peace allowed both mining and agriculture to boom. Today the state still depends on these two activities for its economic well-being. However, the rich silver veins that built intricate baroque churches and allowed Spanish royalty to engage in European wars are now a thing of the past. Unless, of course, there are new treasure troves hidden in the dusty hills of Zacatecas waiting to be discovered.

Leaving the city of Zacatecas, the route continues through the flat, northern desert of the state, passes briefly through an eastern arm of the state of Durango, and enters southern Coahuila. This huge, arid state consists of flat-floored valleys and basins separated by numerous discrete mountain ranges. Coahuila is bordered on the north by the United States, on the east by Nuevo León, on the south by Zacatecas, and on the west by Durango and Chihuahua. This harsh land only allowed the barest hand to mouth existence for the indigenous people who called it home. The first Spanish settlement here was at Saltillo, founded in 1577. This town became the administrative center for both Coahuila and the vast territory of Texas to the north.

Coahuila is the birthplace of the revolutionary hero Francisco Madero who in 1908 challenged the dictatorship of Porfirio Díaz and in 1910 declared himself a candidate for the presidency. Arrested and exiled, Madero eventually won the presidency, only to be assassinated a few months into his term.

Today, despite its aridity, Coahuila is a fairly wealthy state, thanks to irrigated agriculture, expanding industry in Torreón and Saltillo, and some mining. There is also a growing *maquiladora* industrial sector along the Mexico-U.S. border.

From Torreón on the western border of Coahuila the train enters eastern Durango and then southern Chihuahua. Chihuahua is the largest state in Mexico with 12.5 percent of the total land area in the country. The eastern half of the state consists of arid flatlands and basins interrupted by occasional hills and short ranges of mountains. The western half grades into the virtually impenetrable, rugged ranges of the Sierra Madre Occidental. With more abundant rainfall, these ranges and the highland valleys between them are covered with forests, grasslands, and, in some places, orchards. The state is bordered on the north by the United States, on the east by Coahuila, on the south by Durango, and on the west by Sinaloa and Sonora.

Chihuahua was originally inhabited by the Tarahumara, Concho, Tepehuan, and Pima Indians. The first Spaniards to enter the area were Nuñez Cabeza de Vaca, Dorantes, Esteban, and Castillo. These were the only survivors of a Spanish expedition which was driven ashore by storms on the Gulf Coast of the southeastern United States in 1528. Cabeza de Vaca and his companions had wandered around the American southwest for seven years before finally making their way through Chihuahua and to the Spanish settlement of Culiacán. These explorers brought back second-hand tales of wealthy Indian civilizations in the north. In the late 1530s and early 1540s expeditions passed northward through Chihuahua in search of these cities of gold, the Seven Cities of Cibola. The cities of gold turned out to be Indian villages of adobe. Finding no treasure, the Spanish turned away from Chihuahua and did not return for over a hundred years.

In the late 17th Century prospectors met some success in the sierras of Chihuahua. Colonists returned to the area, some to mine, others to ranch. The town of Chihuahua was established in 1709 primarily to provide some defense against Apache raids. During the Mexican Revolution most of the Chihuahua country-side was controlled by the revolutionary general Pancho Villa and it was here in the town of Hidalgo del Parral that Villa was finally assassinated in 1923. Today, Chihuahua is one of the wealthiest states in Mexico, with an economy built on mining, timber, and ranching. After leaving Chihuahua City, the route heads north through the Chihuahuan desert and ends at the border town of Juárez.

DIVISIÓN DEL NORTE TRAIN

				1st cl. Reserved	2nd cl. Coach
Train 7		Train 8			
Lv. 8:00 PM	Mexico	9:30 AM	Ar.		
11:30 PM	Querétaro	5:40 AM		$ 7.42	2.06
2:00 AM(+1)	Irapuato	3:10 AM		10.61	2.94
3:35 AM	León	2:02 AM		13.00	3.48
4:35 AM	Lagos de Moreno	1:02 AM(+1)		14.87	3.97
6:50 AM	Aguascalientes	10:30 PM		18.29	4.90
9:30 AM	Zacatecas	8:05 PM		21.90	5.87
11:35 AM	Felipe Pescador	5:45 PM			6.77
12:48 PM	La Colorada	5:09 PM			7.13
5:10 PM	Torreón	12:00 PM			9.48
9:20 PM	Jimenez	7:40 AM			11.48
11:43 PM	Las Delicias	5:29 AM			12.68
1:20 AM(+1)	Chihuahua	3:15 AM(+1)			13.52
Ar. 6:45 AM	Ciudad Juárez	10:00 PM	Lv.		16.52

Train Services. Trains 7 and 8 ("División del Norte") provide special first class reserved and second class coach service between Mexico City and Querétaro, Irapuato, León, Lagos de Moreno, Aguascalientes, and Zacatecas. The route continues on past Zacatecas but only with second class coach service to the following towns: Felipe Pescador, La Colorada, Torreón, Jimenez, Las Delicias, Chihuahua, and Ciudad Juárez.

Querétaro & Irapuato

These towns are discussed in the "Train Through the Bajio" section.

León & Lagos de Moreno

There is little reason to stop in either of these towns.

Aguascalientes

Aguascalientes was founded in 1575 as a defensive measure to protect transportation to and from the Zacatecas silver mines from Indian attacks. However, these same Chichimec raids prevented the new town from growing and it was not until the early 17th Century that the end of the Chichimec War and the expansion of ranching in the area provided the stability necessary for growth. The city was named for the numerous hot springs found in the area.

In 1914 Aguascalientes was the site of a meeting between representatives of the revolutionary leaders Pancho Villa, Emiliano Zapata, and Venustiano Carranza. This meeting, called the Sovereign Revolutionary Convention of 1914, was an unsuccessful attempt to resolve differences among the major revolutionary factions.

Today, with about 400,000 people, the city of Aguascalientes contains about half the state's entire population. The city's prosperity is based on agriculture (grapes, cattle, and orchards) and on a growing industrial and manufacturing sector. While this economic growth has brought prosperity, it has also diminished somewhat the formerly relaxed atmosphere of the city. Pollution and traffic congestion are increasing problems. Despite this, Aguascalientes remains a friendly and largely untouristed town with a number of interesting sights.

Getting Around. The **train station** is 1.5 km east of the plaza and can be reached by taking the "Madero" bus or a cab. I recommend a cab. The **bus station** is one km south of the center, just west of the intersection of Av. de la Convención de 1914 and Chávez. Again, take a cab.

Sights. The zócalo actually consists of two adjacent plazas, the **Plaza Principal** and the **Plaza de la República**. On the south side of the plaza are the 17th Century **Palacio de Gobierno** and the 19th Century **Palacio Municipal**. The Palacio de Gobierno was originally the home of the Marques de Guadalupe. Today this red and pink stone building is strikingly beautiful and becomes even more so when you walk inside, where a spacious and airy courtyard awaits, ornamented with columns, stairways, arches, and murals. The murals occupy the far wall on both the first and second floors. They were painted by the Chilean artist Oswaldo Barra Cunningham, who was a pupil of Diego Rivera. The first floor mural offers a representation of the region's history and contemporary lifestyle, while that on the second floor stylizes the local but famous San Marcos Festival with all its gaiety, exuberance, and "sin."

There is a very friendly **tourist office** on the ground floor of the Palacio de Gobierno.

On the west end of the plaza is the **Cathedral**. This 18th Century structure has an unimpressive exterior but contains a fine collection of religious art including several oils by the Zapotec artist, Miguel Cabrera. Beside the Cathedral is the **Teatro Morelos**. Built in 1885, this was the site of the Sovereign Revolutionary Convention of 1914. Just west of the theater is the **Casa de la Cultura**. Here classes and workshops are offered in dance, music, theater, and painting. The National Plastic Arts Competition is held here every year during the San Marcos Fair. The building also hosts temporary art exhibits and boasts a beautiful stained glass window by Saturnino Herran.

Four blocks south of the plaza at the intersection of Pimental and Chávez is the **Museo José Guadalupe Posada**. A native of Aguascalientes, Guadalupe Posada produced lithographic

Aguascalientes, Aguascalientes

to the bus station

1 ~ train station
2 ~ Plaza Principal
3 ~ Plaza de la Republica
4 ~ Palacio de Gobierno
    Palacio Municipal
    tourist office
5 ~ Cathedral
    Teatro Morelos

6 ~ Casa de la Cultura
7 ~ Museo de Aguascalientes
A ~ Hotel Maser
B ~ Hotel San Jose
C ~ Hotel Rosales
D ~ Hotel Senorial
E ~ Hotel Rio Grande

political cartoons which satirized Mexican society and politics of
the late 19th Century. Two of his frequent targets were the
dictator, Porfirio Díaz, and the Mexican ruling class. The propa-
ganda produced by this artist was instrumental in popularizing
criticism of the Porfiriato. The museum contains a large collection of Guadalupe Posada's work. It is open Tues-Sun, 10 a.m.
to 2 p.m. and 4:30 p.m. to 8 p.m.

Approximately 10 blocks west of the Posada Museum on Av.
Adolfo López is the **Centro de Diseño y Artesanal** (Design
and Crafts Center). Here local crafts are exhibited and sold and
you can actually watch potters and weavers at work. The center
is open Tues-Sat, 10 a.m. to 8 p.m., and Sun, 10 a.m. to 2 p.m.
Four blocks east of the plaza on Madero and then four blocks
north on Zaragoza is the **Museo de Aguascalientes**. Built in
the early 20th Century, this lovely neoclassical building houses
a nice collection of contemporary, mostly Mexican, art. The
foremost personality represented is native son, Saturnino Herran. It is open Tues-Sun, 10 a.m. to 1 p.m. and 5 p.m. to 9 p.m.

Fiestas. The **Fair of San Marcos** is famous throughout Mexico. It begins on April 25, the feast day of Saint Mark, and
continues into May. Entertainment is quite varied during the
festival and consists of such activities and events as: cock fights
in the city's modern arena; gambling in the Casino de la Feria;
bullfights; agriculture and industry exhibitions; and cultural

programs ranging from plays and musical performances to costume displays.

Climate. In general the climate is semi-arid and most of the area's precipitation results from violent summer thunderstorms. Winters are dry and temperate with night time frosts common.

Excursions. The towns of **Jesús María** and **Valladolid**, 14 km and 21 km north of Aguascalientes respectively, have nice spas with hot spring-fed pools, dressing rooms, and picnic areas. Second class buses go there from the Aguascalientes bus station.

The small town of **Pabellon de Hidalgo** is 36 km north of Aguascalientes just west off Hwy 45. Here is the **Museo de la Insurgencia** on the grounds of the former hacienda of San Blas. It was here in 1811 that troops under Miguel Hidalgo and Ignacio Allende camped as they fled from the royalist forces. Today the hacienda is a museum containing documents and artifacts from the War for Independence. Also in Pabellon is the **Instituto Aguascalentense de Bellas Artes** which contains locally produced yarns and weavings on display and for sale.

Pabellon de Hidalgo can be reached by second class bus from Aguascalientes.

Zacatecas

Like few other cities, Zacatecas embodies the spirit of colonial Mexico in its history, architecture, and atmosphere. There are no level streets, as the city is built on the slopes and in the ravines of the Cerro de la Bufa, a rocky igneous hill that towers 200 meters over Zacatecas. Narrow streets struggle through a jumble of colorful houses, baroque churches, and colonial mansions. At 2,474 meters this is the second highest capital city in Mexico.

On September 8, 1546, Spanish troops under the command of Captain Juan de Tolosa camped at Cerro de la Bufa. Engaged in exploration, these Spaniards were on the unknown and uncivilized northern frontier of New Spain, many kilometers from the nearest Spanish settlement. To get off on the right foot with the Zacateco Indians which inhabited the area, Tolosa gave the indigenes some trinkets. Probably knowing of the Spaniards' preoccupation with precious metals, the Zacatecos gave the Europeans several pieces of silver ore. That was a mistake. Immediately Zacatecas was established and mines were sunk in the area. Other prospectors soon found other ore bodies in the hills of the surrounding region. Zacatecas grew quickly. The silver, gold, zinc, and lead removed from the earth made some Spaniards very wealthy and built magnificent churches and colonial houses.

The discovery of silver also changed the lives of the Indians, but for the worse. The Europeans needed laborers to work in the mines, to provide food, and to do all the mundane and back-breaking tasks required in a growing city. And the way the Spaniards saw it, the Indian tribes were the perfect laborers. The Native Americans didn't see it that way and sent such a message, when in 1550 a band of Zacatecos massacred a trading party on the road to Zacatecas. This was the beginning of the 40 year Chichimec War. This war slowed the rate of growth of the town, but with the resolution of the conflict in the early 17th Century, Zacatecas grew quickly. For a time in the 1600s, the town was the third largest in all of New Spain. However, the War of Independence and the tumultuous events of the 19th Century crippled the mining industry in the area. During the Porfiriato stability and new investment sparked a revival of the industry, but mining again regressed during the decade of revolution in the early 20th Century.

Today, most of the mines have long since played out. The economy of the city is now based on irrigated farming and ranching. While the day of the silver barons is past, the legacy of their wealth lives on in the architecture and atmosphere of Zacatecas.

Getting Around. The **train station** is at the southern tip of Av. González Ortega about 20 blocks or more from the plaza. Taxis are cheap and buses marked "Hidalgo" or "Centro" are even cheaper. The city's new bus station is miles from the center of town, well beyond walking distance. Buses and taxis travel

Zacatecas, Zacatecas

CERRO LA BUFA

1 ~ train station
2 ~ Plaza de Armas
    Palacio de Gobierno
3 ~ Museo Rafael Coronel
4 ~ Cathedral
5 ~ tourist office
6 ~ Teatro Calderon
7 ~ Mercado Gonzalez Ortega
8 ~ Templo de San Agustin
9 ~ post office
10~ Iglesia de Santo Domingo

11~ Museo Pedro Coronel
12~ Teleferico Estacion
13~ Capilla de la Virgen
14~ Museo de la Toma de Zacatecas
15~ Mina del Eden
16~ Parque Enrique Estrada
17~ aqueduct
18~ Museo Francisco Goitia
A ~ Hotel Rio Grande
B ~ Hotel Colon
C ~ Hotel Condesa

Cathedral facade, Zacatecas

between the station and the central area.

Crafts. Looking to buy a saddle to carry on the train? You'll be able to find a good one, and a variety of other **leather goods**, in Zacatecas. The city is also well known for its colorful **wool sarapes** and **turquoise jewelry**.

Sights. Built on hills and in ravines, Zacatecas is a bit confusing. Streets don't follow a nice grid pattern, they follow the path of least resistance. Despite this, you can still walk to most locations of interest in the city. As usual, the best place to start is the main plaza, here called the **Plaza de Armas**. On the east side of this largely treeless square is the **Palacio de Gobierno**. Originally the home of the Count of Santiago de la Laguna, this 18th Century building now houses government offices and contains a mural representing the history of Zacatecas by local artist Antonio Pintor Rodríguez.

About eight blocks north of the plaza on Calle Abasolo is the **Museo Rafael Coronel**. This fantastic new museum is in the 16th Century **Ex-Templo de San Francisco** and contains perhaps the finest collection of masks in the country. There are thousands of them in countless styles and from every historical period and geographical region of Mexico. There are also displays of pre-Hispanic pottery and terracotta colonial figurines. The exhibits are superbly designed and very modern. When inside it's hard to believe that the outside of the building is a crumbling structure 400 years old. The museum is open daily, except Wed, 10 a.m. to 2 p.m. and 4 p.m. to 7 p.m. The "Ruta 8" bus goes past the museum.

Immediately south of the plaza is the **Cathedral**. This 18th Century church is one of the finest examples of Mexican baroque

Zacatecas Cathedral

and in its form embodies the symbolism of the Holy Trinity: three facades and in the interior three naves. The facades, especially that which opens onto Av. Hidalgo, are intricately carved from pink stone and are especially beautiful in the rich light of late afternoon. The interior of the church was originally ostentatiously furnished by the silver wealth of Zacatecas but revolutions and anticlerical movements have left only a shadow of that former wealth.

Across the street from the Cathedral on Hidalgo is the **tourist office**. Two blocks south of the plaza and facing each other across Av. Hidalgo are the **Teatro Calderón** and the **Mercado González Ortega**. The theater was built during the Porfiriato in 1891 and shows that era's preference for French neoclassical architecture. The market was built in the same period and is today more a shopping mall than a traditional Mexican market.

The **Templo de San Agustín** is one block west and south of the Teatro Calderón on Calle Miguel Auza. This former church, dedicated to Saint Augustine, was built in the 17th Century, served for a time as a casino, and today is used for exhibits and conferences. The **post office** is two blocks south of the Mercado

Bell tower, Santo Domingo
Church

González Ortega on Allende between Hidalgo and Tacuba. Just east of it on Tacuba is the **Palacio Municipal**.

Returning to the Plaza de Armas area, the **Iglesia de Santo Domingo** is a block west of the plaza on Calle Codina. This 18th Century church has an unimpressive exterior but a nice interior. Next door is the **Museo Pedro Coronel**. This fine museum contains the personal art collection which the Zacatecan painter and sculptor, Pedro Coronel, bequeathed to the city. There is a wonderful group of ceremonial masks and pieces by such artists as Picasso, Dali, Miro, and Chagall. There is also art from Africa, Asia, and the Middle East. Open Fri-Wed, 10-2 and 4-7.

Four blocks west of the museum on Calle Ramos is the **Teleférico Estación** (Cable Car Station). The station is normally open Tues-Sun, 12 p.m. to 7 p.m. but may be closed when weather conditions warrant. The "Ruta 7" bus goes to the station. The cable car runs from this station to the one on top of Cerro de la Bufa and offers a spectacular perspective on the city and surrounding countryside. On top of La Bufa is the **Capilla de la Virgen del Patrocinio**, a small chapel with a miraculous portrait of the Virgin, and the **Museo de la Toma de Zacatecas** (Museum of the Capture of Zacatecas). This museum, with documents, newspapers, and artifacts, commemorates the 1914 battle in which Pancho Villa defeated Mexican federal troops and captured the city. It is open Tues-Sun, 10 a.m. to 5 p.m. There are also several crafts shops on top of La Bufa.

Near the Teleférico Estación is the **Mina del Eden**. From the plaza, go south on Hidalgo and turn right (west) on Juárez. Take another right at the Seguro Social Hospital (I.M.S.S.), a left on

Calle de la Loma and you're at the mine entrance and ticket office. The "Ruta 7" bus will take you as far as the hospital. Access to the mine proper is via a mining train which rattles through a 520-meter man-made tunnel and deposits visitors at the beginning of the pedestrian section of the tour. Here there is a small shop selling jewelry and mineral specimens from the mine.

As you walk through the mine the tour guide recounts, in Spanish, the history of the operation and details the grim working conditions faced by the miners, mostly Indians and African slaves. As they worked to produce silver, gold, zinc, and lead for the clerical and secular aristocracies of Spain and New Spain, these miners, some only children, faced the prospect of short and/or crippled lives from accidents, tuberculosis, and silicosis. Over the 300-year history of the mine, an estimated half-million miners, mostly Indians, died here. Such was the economic foundation of colonial Mexico.

The mine cuts diagonally through the rock, a three- to four-meter-wide crevice. There are seven levels, with the tour following a specially constructed pathway built into the sloping wall on the fourth level. Looking down, one can see the flooded lower levels, eerily filled with transparent green water. At the end of the tour, you have the option of returning to the entrance or taking an elevator from the back of the mine to the surface. This elevator exits at the Teleférico Estación. La Mina del Eden is open daily, 12 p.m. to 7:30 p.m.

Ten blocks south of the plaza on Av. González Ortega (which is what Av. Hidalgo turns into) is **Parque Enrique Estrada**. This hilly, forested park is a nice place to sit and relax after your long walk south from the Plaza de Armas. On the east side of the park is a portion of Zacatecas' 18th Century **aqueduct**.

On the northwest corner of the park is the **Museo Francisco Goitia**. This attractive pink neoclassic structure was built in 1948 and originally served as the governor's mansion. In 1978 it became a museum dedicated to the work of Zacatecan artists: Julio Ruelas, Pedro and Rafael Coronel, Manuel Felguerez, José Kuri Breña, and, naturally, Francisco Goitia. The ground floor contains the paintings of Ruelas, Felguerez, and Pedro Coronel, while the second floor exhibits the paintings of Goitia and Rafael Coronel and sculpture by Breña. The museum is open Tues-Sun, 10 a.m. to 2 p.m. and 5 p.m. to 8 p.m.

Fiestas. The **Festival of La Morisma** takes place August 27-29 and consists of a three-day mock battle between Christian Spaniards and Moors. The **National Fair** takes place September 1-16. During this period various events are held throughout the city including fine arts presentations, bullfights, and handicrafts and agriculture exhibits.

Climate. Zacatecas can be windy, dusty, and hot in the summer. Occasional violent thunderstorms turn the streets into rivers and the heat into a memory. Winters are mild and nights can be cold and frosty. If you have just arrived in Zacatecas (elev. 2,474 m or 8,100 ft) from a much lower altitude, remember to take it easy until you acclimate to this elevation.

Excursions. The town of **Guadalupe** is now more like a neighborhood, having been "captured" and enveloped by Zacatecas. It is six km to the east on Hwy 45. The **Museo de Arte Virreinal** (Museum of Viceregal Art) is on the town plaza, the **Jardín Juárez.** The museum contains a fine collection of religious paintings and other art by some of the finest Mexican artists of the colonial period, among them Miguel Cabrera, Juan Correa, Cristóbal de Villalpando, and José de Ibarra. The building itself is a former Franciscan convent founded in 1707. It is open Tues-Sun, 10 a.m. to 5 p.m.

Next to the Viceregal Museum is the **Museo Regional** with its transportation exhibits and artifacts. There is also a small collection of Huichol art. It is open Tues-Sun, 10 a.m. to 5 p.m. To get to Guadalupe catch the "Guadalupe" bus on Blvd. Adolfo López Mateos.

The **Chicomostoc** ruins, also known as **La Quemada**, are 56 km south of Zacatecas on Hwy 54. Though difficult to get to, poorly restored, and expensive, these ruins are interesting for what they represent. The site consists of a walled, fortified outpost positioned on top of a strategic hill. Chicomostoc dates to about 1000 A.D. and, although there are some ceremonial structures, it is thought to have been primarily a defensive outpost established by the Toltecs to protect the trade routes to the turquoise deposits of what is now the southwestern United States. Chichimec Indian tribes would have made unprotected travel through this desolate region extremely dangerous.

The ruins are unrestored and you will probably have the site all to yourself. On the summit of the hill within the wall are the remains of several platforms and building complexes. Outside the wall and at the bottom of the hill is a small pyramid.

Expensive tours to Chicomostoc can be arranged. The other option is to take a second class bus to the village of La Quemada and walk the three km to the ruins. Give yourself plenty of time to explore the ruins, then get back to La Quemada to catch a Zacatecas-bound bus later in the day.

Felipe Pescador and La Colorada

These are tiny towns in the Zacatecan wasteland. If the train didn't stop you would never notice them.

Torreón

Torreón is a modern city of half a million people and with an economy based on irrigated agriculture, food processing, and minerals. The city is on the Coahuila-Durango state border and is of little interest to the traveler unless one wants to catch a bus to Saltillo, three hours east of here.

Jimenez and Las Delicias

Just keep going.

Chihuahua

Chihuahua was founded in 1709 by prospectors and missionaries. It quickly became the major settlement in the northern portion of the colony and was the administrative center for the region known as Nueva Vizcaya. As mining and ranching grew, Chihuahua followed the pattern established 150 years earlier at Zacatecas: exploitation and brutalization of the local indigenous people led to long-running and violent Indian wars.

Despite this turmoil, Chihuahua grew right along with the output of its mines and cattle ranches. In 1811, the revolutionary priest, Miguel Hidalgo, was tried, executed, and beheaded here, his head being taken to Guanajuato for display. During the period of the French Intervention (1862 to 1867) Benito Juárez made the city headquarters of his government. During part of the Mexican Revolution, Chihuahua served as the headquarters of Pancho Villa's army, the División del Norte.

Today Chihuahua is a city of 700,000, the commercial center of northwestern Mexico. Timber, mines, and agriculture have combined to make it prosperous. While it lacks the colonial intensity of Oaxaca or Zacatecas, it does have its share of period architecture and is inhabited by the open, friendly people of Mexico's frontier. You won't be disappointed by a couple of days spent in this pleasant city.

Getting Around. There are two train stations in Chihuahua. The **División del Norte station**, which is on the line connecting the border with Mexico City, is two km north of the plaza just off the intersection of Av. Colón and Av. División del Norte. From downtown take the bus marked "Colón."

The **Chihuahua-Pacífico station**, otherwise known as the Copper Canyon train station, is two km south of the plaza near the intersection of Calle 22 and Av. Carlos Fuero and behind a castle-like prison. To get there, catch the bus "Colonia Rosario" on Av. Ocampo and, after it turns on 20 de Noviembre, get off on Calle 30. The station is two blocks to the southeast. The **bus station** is nine blocks northwest of the plaza and two blocks south of Av. Ocampo. It's within walking distance.

Crafts. Chihuahua is known for its fine **wool ponchos** and **sweaters** and for **silver jewelry**. It is also a good place to buy crafts produced by the Tarahumara Indians such as **woven straw baskets** and carved **wooden objects**.

Comida Tipica. Chihuahua is beef country and it is said that the meat here has a distinctive flavor because the animals graze on wild oregano. Chihuahua is also known for its cheeses and

Chihuahua, Chihuahua

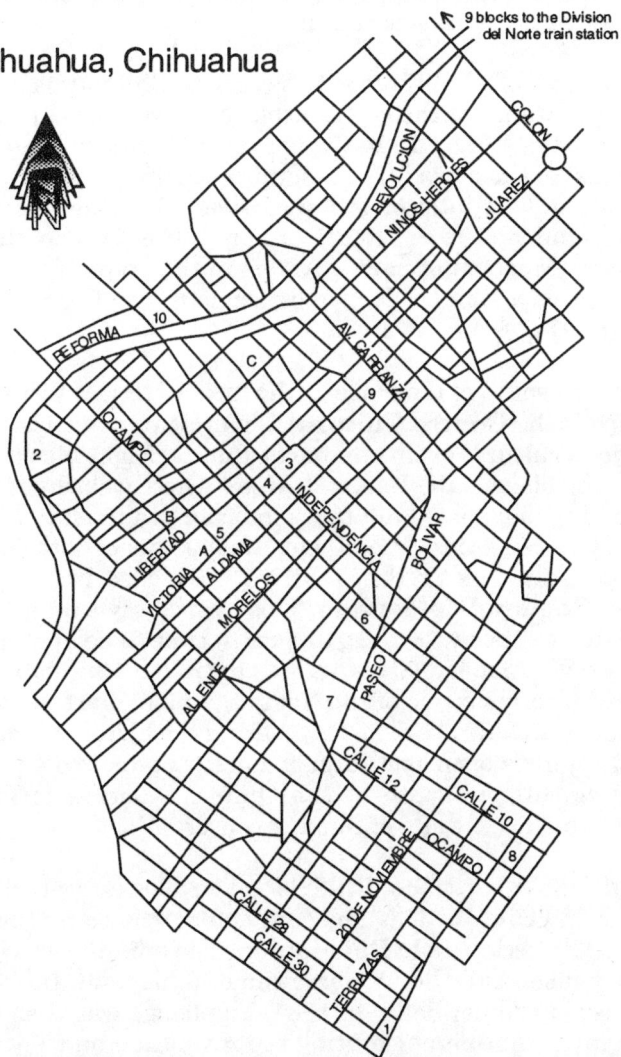

9 blocks to the Division
del Norte train station

REVOLUCION
NIÑOS HEROES
COLON
JUAREZ
REFORMA
10
AV. CARRANZA
C
9
OCAMPO
2
3
4
INDEPENDENCIA
8
5
LIBERTAD
ALDAMA
BOLIVAR
VICTORIA
MORELOS
6
PASEO
ALLENDE
7
CALLE 12
CALLE 10
20 DE NOVIEMBRE
OCAMPO
8
CALLE 28
CALLE 30
TERRAZAS
1

1 ~ train station--Chihuahua-Pacifico	8 ~ Museo Francisco Villa
2 ~ bus station	9 ~ post office
3 ~ Plaza de la Constitucion	Palacio de Gobierno
4 ~ Cathedral	10~ Museo de Arte Popular
5 ~ Centro Cultural Chihuahua	A ~ Hotel San Juan
6 ~ Museo Regional del Estado	B ~ Nuevo Hotel Turista
7 ~ Parque Lerdo	C ~ Hotel Balflo

dairy products, a continuing legacy of the productive Mennonite communities just outside the city.

Sights. Most of what there is to be seen in Chihuahua is within walking distance of the city's rather average zócalo, otherwise known as the **Plaza de la Constitución.** Immediately to the southwest of the plaza is the magnificent 18th Century baroque **Cathedral.** The interior is impressively festooned with gold, marble, and an organ from Germany. The **Museo de Arte Sagrado** (Museum of Sacred Art) is in the crypt of the church and contains a small collection of religious art. The museum is open Mon-Fri, 9 a.m. to 3 p.m.

Two blocks south of the plaza at the intersection of Victoria and Ocampo is the **Centro Cultural Chihuahua** which is the site of various cultural events and art exhibits. Eight blocks southeast of the plaza is the **Paseo Bolívar** where wealthy ranching and mining magnates built fancy mansions in the late 19th and early 20th centuries. Prominent among these is the **Museo Quinta Gameros** at Paseo Bolívar 401, also known as the **Museo Regional del Estado.** This French-style mansion was completed by its owner in 1910, just in time to be appropriated by the revolutionary forces which controlled Chihuahua. The restored interior is one of the finest example of art nouveau in the country. There are exhibits covering the history of the state. The museum is open Tues-Sun, 9 a.m. to 2 p.m. and 4 p.m. to 7 p.m. Immediately south of the Quinta Gameros is **Parque Lerdo** which is the site of Sunday concerts.

The **Museo Francisco Villa** is seven blocks east of Paseo Bolívar on Calle 10. This museum is also known by the name **Museo Histórico de la Revolución.** The building was Pancho Villa's house. After he was assassinated his wife, Luz Corral, lived here until her death in 1981. The house was then turned into a museum commemorating the revolution and Villa's role in it. Here is the bullet-ridden car that Villa was driving when he was killed. There are also weapons, photos, documents, and other artifacts from that bloody period of Mexico's history. The museum is open Tues-Sun, 9 a.m. to 2 p.m. and 4 p.m. to 7 p.m.

The **post office** is four blocks northeast of the plaza at Av. Juárez and Av. Carranza. Next to it is the **Palacio de Go-**

bierno. The most interesting things about this 19th Century building are the ground floor murals by Aarón Piña Mora representing the history of the state.

The **Museo de Arte Popular** is at the intersection of Reforma and Independencia, six blocks northwest of the plaza. Here there are permanent exhibits of Tarahumara costumes, crafts, and folklore. Some crafts are for sale.

Climate. Summers in Chihuahua are hot, with temperatures often exceeding 40°C (105°F). Two-thirds of the city's annual rainfall, which only averages 39 cm (16 in) per year, comes in the form of thunderstorms in July, August, and September. Since Chihuahua is at 1,430 m (4,690 ft) above sea level and is in northern Mexico, winters here can be quite cold, with temperatures often below freezing.

Ciudad Juárez

Juárez is the border town opposite El Paso, Texas. Actually, it's a big city and, with a population of around one million people, it is twice as large as El Paso. Although more Mexican than most border towns, Juárez still satisfies the adage that the only good border town is one that's receding behind you.

Copper Canyon Train

The Chihuahua-Pacífico railway, also known as the Copper Canyon train, is the most spectacular trip in Mexico and one of the most scenic in the world. It is also a wonder of engineering, its construction requiring 90 years to cross the most rugged chain of mountains in Mexico. Even today in this region there are no roads connecting the interior of Mexico with the coast, only a lonely ribbon of steel twisting through the crumpled landscape of the Sierra Madre Occidental.

The train connects Chihuahua in the east with the port of Topolobampo in the west and was originally the idea of an

American, Albert Owen, in 1872. He wanted to build a line connecting the midwestern grain belt of the United States with the Mexican port and envisioned a utopian socialist community at Topolobampo. Owen actually succeeded in founding a community but, over a period of 20 years, the settlement fell apart.

After Owen, other entrepreneurs and companies completed pieces of the route through the mountains but were unable fully to overcome the difficulties of the terrain. Finally, in the 1950s, the Mexican government took over. Anxious to succeed where the gringo entrepreneurs had failed, the Mexicans treated the project as a matter of national pride and eventually did succeed in blasting, tunneling, and building a way through that unforgiving landscape. In 1961 the finished railway opened. It meanders for 650 kilometers west and southwest of Chihuahua, clinging to the sides of volcanic cliffs, plunging through the darkness of man-made tunnels, and hurtling across steel bridges, which look flimsy against the massive majesty of the mountains. The fact that there are 86 tunnels and 59 bridges on this route gives some insight into the difficulty of the project.

This route heads west from Chihuahua city, leaving the dry, rolling plains of the state behind and entering the foothills of the Sierra Madre Occidental. Oak trees crowd the hilltops while ranches and small farms fill the valleys. The train passes through the town of Cuauhtémoc, famous for the prosperous Mennonite communities in this area. Apple orchards, an uncommon sight in Mexico, stretch out alongside the tracks as do fertile fields full of tall, green grass and fat horses. Hawks define lazy patterns in the cloudless blue sky. At La Junta the railway turns south and follows the Papagochic River valley upstream as it climbs into the sierras. On the hilltops the hardwoods have given way to pines and junipers and in the valleys log houses sit beside scattered, plowed fields.

At Creel the paved road ends and ahead of you lies the heart of the canyonlands. Although the region is called Copper Canyon, or Barranca del Cobre, in reality it is comprised of a network of canyons, chief among them Copper, Urique, and Batopilas canyons. The canyon is four times larger than the Grand Canyon and, at its deepest point, is about 100 meters deeper. Creel also marks the beginning of Tarahumara Indian country.

The train continues southwest from Creel and stops for 20 minutes at Divisadero, allowing passengers barely enough time for photo opportunities at the incredible overlook of Urique Canyon. Between Divisadero and Temoris lies the most spectacular section of the route. The vegetation also changes, going from pine and oak to spiny brush and cacti. Several hours out of Temoris the track exits from the sierras and enters the wide, flat valley of the Río Fuerte. Warmed by the proximity of the west coast and well-watered by the streams emerging from the highlands to the east, the valley is distinctly sub-tropical and is covered by irrigated croplands. The train stops briefly at El Fuerte, the last pleasant town on the route, and then continues on to Sufragio, the intersection of this route with that of the Pacific coast. The terminus of the passenger route is in the unappealing city of Los Mochis, while the freight train continues another 25 km to the port of Topolobampo.

Train Services. Trains 73 and 74 ("Chihuahua-Pacífico") provide special first class service between Chihuahua and Creel, Divisadero, Posada Barrancas, Bahuichivo, Sufragio, and Los Mochis. Second class coach service along this same route is provided by trains 75 and 76.

CHIHUAHUA-PACÍFICO TRAIN

	Train 74		Train 73		1st cl. Reserved
Lv.	7:00 AM	Chihuahua	8:50 PM	Ar.	
	12:26 PM	Creel	3:14 PM		$ 11.81
	1:45 PM	Divisadero	1:35 PM		14.19
	2:10 PM	Posada B.	1:30 PM		14.39
	3:32 PM	Bahuichivo	12:12 PM		16.00
	7:59 PM	Sufragio	7:43 AM		24.61
Ar.	8:50 PM	Los Mochis	7:00 AM	Lv.	26.19

	Train 76		Train 75		2nd cls. Coach
Lv.	8:00 AM	Chihuahua	11:25 PM	Ar.	
	2:00 PM	Creel	5:05 PM		$ 2.48
	3:30 PM	Divisadero	3:25 PM		2.97
	3:58 PM	Posada B.	3:10 PM		3.03
	5:25 PM	Bahuichivo	1:45 PM		3.35
	10:25 PM	Sufragio	8:45 AM		5.16
Ar.	11:25 PM	Los Mochis	8:00 AM	Lv.	5.48

Creel

For those who wish to spend some time exploring the Copper Canyon area, Creel is an excellent base of operations. Although the town is not located immediately on any of the canyons, it does offer lodging, supplies, and transportation into the surrounding area. Creel was at one time the terminus of the railroad and based its economy on logging. Nowadays, Creel is no longer the end of the line and depends more on tourist revenues and less on logging income.

Getting Around. With only 16,000 people Creel is an eminently walkable town.

Crafts. At the **Tarahumara Mission Store** on the plaza one can find Tarahumara crafts such as **carved wooden objects**, **jewelry**, and wonderful **woven baskets** with double walls and bottoms. The store is run by Catholic missionaries and all profits are invested in education and health programs for the Indians. The store also sells maps of the Copper Canyon area.

Sights. There are few points of interest within Creel itself. The **post office** is on the plaza. A Jesuit Tarahumara **mission** is also located on the plaza.

Climate. Summers can be quite hot. Frequent thunderstorms also make travelling into the backcountry problematic as trails and dirt roads are often washed out or, at the very least, made more treacherous. On the other hand, winters in Creel (at 2,200 m elev.) can be windy and cold, with occasional snow. The best time to visit Creel is September to November or February to May though snow may fall any time between November and March.

Excursions. A number of intriguing excursions are possible from Creel. Unfortunately, public transportation is minimal. It consists of a bus which travels between Creel and the town of Batopilas, 118 km to the south. The bus leaves Creel at 7 a.m. on Tuesday, Thursday, and Saturday and then leaves Batopilas for the return at 4 a.m on Monday, Wednesday, and Friday. The trip takes seven hours under good conditions and gives the visitor a wonderful overview of the countryside. Alternatives to this marginal public transport are hiking and private tours. These tours are organized by several hotels in Creel, chief among them the Hotel Parador, Hotel Nuevo, and the Casa de Margarita on the plaza. It is wise to shop around.

The village of **San Ignacio** is only five km south of Creel along Av. Mateos, an easy hike. The little settlement contains a 400-year-old Jesuit mission. The walk to the town goes through beautiful countryside and passes several Tarahumara caves. A couple of kilometers past the village is **Lago de Arareco** (Arareco Lake). In the midst of an oak and pine forest, this lovely lake contains cold, blue water.

The village of **Cusarare** is 13 km south of San Ignacio and just east of the main road. Here is another 17th Century Jesuit mission and across the street from the church is a small Tarahumara museum containing household utensils and other ethnographic exhibits on this indigenous culture. There is also a waterfall near the town, the **Cascada Cusarare**. Just before you get to the town, a small sign saying "cascada" signals a trail to the right. Follow this trail for three km to the falls.

While the bus to Batopilas will drop you at the turnoff to Cusarare, getting back to Creel can be a problem. The occasional logging truck may give you a lift back. There is one fairly expensive hotel in Cusarare.

Batopilas is 118 km south of Creel and is, as has already been mentioned, at the end of a rugged, seven-hour bus ride. The small town is actually at the bottom of Batopilas Canyon, right on the shore of the river. Subtropical vegetation, including avocados, guayabas, and mangoes, grows along the narrow riverbank. There are a couple of basic hotels. For travellers prepared to do some heavy duty backpacking or hiking, Batopilas can be an ideal headquarters, situated as it is in the heart of the canyonlands. The bus ride to the town, especially the descent to the river bottom, is an eye-opening, and sometimes white-knuckled, experience.

The **Cascada Basaseachic** (Basaseachic Falls) is 140 km northwest of Creel. At 310 meters, this waterfall is not only the highest in Mexico but is also the second highest in the world.

The river shoots out over the cliff from a deep groove worn into the volcanic bedrock and falls in an uninterrupted cascade to the jumble of rock and logs below. A trail from the top of the falls, where the camping and parking areas are located, leads to a vantage point near the bottom. There is no public transportation to this fantastic display. There are, however, hotel tours, most of which take about four hours each way.

Divisadero

Divisadero is perched right on the edge of **Urique Canyon** and at 2,460 m is the highest stop on the route. The train stops here for 20 minutes allowing passengers just enough time to become frustrated by the task of adequately photographing the spectacular canyon at their feet. There is also a mini-market run by Tarahumara women along the tracks and walkways of the town, selling food and crafts and hoping to capture a few tourist pesos through the only employment available to them.

Getting Around. This village is so small you can almost see it all by stretching.

Crafts. Same Tarahumara crafts as in Creel.

Sights. The only "sight" in town is the magnificent overlook of Urique Canyon.

Climate. Pretty much the same climate as Creel with the exception that winters at Divisadero tend to be colder.

Excursions. A half-hour walk from town is the **Mesa de Divisadero** (2,370 m elev.) which offers a magnificent view of the Tararecua, Urique, and Cobre canyons.

In Divisadero it is also possible to hire guides, horses, or jeeps for the trip to the bottom of the Urique Canyon.

Posada Barrancas

Just down the track from Divisadero, Posada Barrancas sits literally on the edge of the vast canyon system. There are two good, though fairly expensive, hotels here and it is easy to rent burros or guides for expeditions into the canyons.

Bahuichivo

Bahuichivo is little more than a station for the village of **Cerocahui**, 12 km south. In Cerocahui excursions to Urique Canyon, waterfalls, and abandoned mines can be booked through the Mission Hotel. If the hotel knows you're coming, they will send a car to pick you up. Otherwise, it's a pleasant, if longish, walk.

Sufragio

This station marks the intersection of the Chihuahua-Pacífico and the Pacífico railways. To make a connection from one to the other is the only reason I can conceive of to stop in this place.

Los Mochis

There are no two ways about it: Los Mochis sucks. It's a big, modern, dirty, confusing city with no charm. It's also a place where you pay through the nose for a hotel room w/out a bath. Avoid if possible.

Train to Monterrey

After passing through several states of central Mexico, this route enters the state of San Luis Potosí, the gateway to northern Mexico. Conversely, if you're coming from the north, San Luis Potosí is the gateway to colonial Mexico. I prefer to think of it as the latter. This state encompasses a variety of terrains. The western portion is a flat brush land covered by Joshua trees, mesquite, ocotillo and other plants you wouldn't stuff a mattress with. The central corridor is slightly more hilly, with occasional short ridges of hills and low mountains breaking up the monotonous landscape.

Both the western and central sections are part of Mexico's central plateau. As you move eastward you enter the margin of the plateau, defined by canyons and the mountains of the Sierra Madre Oriental. Thanks to moist winds coming off the Gulf of Mexico, there are lush forests, springs, and waterfalls. Crystalline rivers beneath green canopies race to the Gulf of Mexico.

Before the Spanish arrived the dry, highland part of San Luis Potosí was inhabited by a Chichimec tribe called the Guachichil. Totonac Indians lived in the forested eastern margins of the state. The Spaniards first appeared in 1522 when Cortés led an expedition to conquer the Huasteca, an area along the Gulf Coast which includes part of San Luis Potosí. An Augustinian convent was built in 1557 at what is now Xilitla in the eastern mountains and a Franciscan mission was founded at Santa María de las Charcas in 1574.

But it was not until silver was discovered in the Cerro de San Pedro in the late 16th Century that Spanish colonization of the area began in earnest. The town of San Luis Potosí was founded in 1592 near the mining area. During the colonial period important mines operated at Charcas, Real de Catorce, Cerro de San Pedro, and Guadalcazar. Only Zacatecas and Guanajuato produced more silver. Although mining has declined in economic importance in recent years, livestock raising on the plateau and agriculture in the southern and eastern parts of the state have grown. Industry, especially in the city of San Luis Potosí, has also expanded over the last couple of decades.

The train route continues northward through the Valle del Salado and passes just west of the Sierra de Catorce. The railway enters the southern part of the state of Coahuila and finds a landscape similar to that in San Luis Potosí: semi-arid, brushy flatland. Soon, however, the character of the terrain changes as mountain ranges formed of severely tilted limestone strata appear. The track goes through a narrow pass in one of these ranges, the Sierra la Concordia, and soon after arrives at the capital of Coahuila, Saltillo.

From Saltillo, the railway angles eastward, entering the state of Nuevo León and that state's capital, Monterrey. Nuevo León is only slightly less arid than Coahuila and is covered for the most part by low forests of mesquite and huisache. On the higher mountains juniper and pine predominate. Portions of the sierras west and south of Monterrey have been designated as a national park, **Cumbres de Monterrey** (Heights of Monterrey). Also, along the eastern face of the Sierra Madre Oriental numerous springs and rivers create lush valleys full of cypress, oak, and willow trees.

Nuevo León is roughly linear, trending north-south with a small knob of territory jutting east from the state's midsection. The northern section of the state consists of small ranges of short mountains alternating with valleys and basins. The eastern midsection of the state is part of the flat, Gulf coast plain. Entering the state from the west and then running south along the state's southeastern margin is the Sierra Madre Oriental with its picturesquely tilted beds of limestones and shales. This rugged country was originally inhabited by tribes of the Chichimec group. In 1577, the first Spanish settlements were founded in the area, Villa de Santiago de Saltillo and Santa Lucía. Nineteen years later Diego de Montemayor established the town of Monterrey.

The colonial era economy was based almost entirely on cattle, goats and wheat. Today, the agriculture sector has diversified into citrus, apples, peaches, nuts, plums, apricots, sorghum and avocadoes. As a complement to this agricultural growth, the city of Monterrey has developed into Mexico's second most important industrial center with the production of beer, steel, and glass products.

After leaving Monterrey the railway heads north toward the United States border. About 30 kilometers before reaching the border the train enters the state of Tamaulipas and soon after arrives in the border town and terminus of this route, Nuevo Laredo.

It is important to note that there are two other routes to the Texas border which branch off this main route. One railway covers the distance between Saltillo and the border town of Piedras Negras. The other route links Monterrey with Reynosa and Matamoros which are both entry points into Mexico.

Train Services. Trains 71 and 72 ("Regiomontano") provide special first class service between Mexico City and San Luis

Potosí, Saltillo, and Monterrey. The train includes both a dining car and a sleeping car. Trains 181 and 182 ("Coahuilense") provide the same services between Saltillo and the border town of Piedras Negras.

REGIOMONTANO TRAIN

Train 71		Train 72	
Lv. 6:00 PM	Mexico City	10:00 AM	Ar.
0:01 AM(+1)	San Luis Potosí	3:45 AM(+1)	
5:44 AM	Saltillo	10:00 PM	
Ar. 8:10 AM	Monterrey	7:50 PM	Lv.

COAHUILENSE TRAIN

Train 181		Train 182	
Lv. 8:15 AM	Saltillo	6:55 PM	Ar.
Ar. 5:35 PM	Piedras Negras	9:15 AM	Lv.

RATES FROM MEXICO CITY TO:	1st cl. Reserved	Rmtte (1)	Rmtte (2)	Bedrm (3)	Bedrm (4)
Piedras Negras	$38.52	78.65	129.77	157.32	275.29
Monterrey	27.90	57.90	95.55	115.84	202.71
Saltillo	24.65	51.13	84.39	102.29	179.00
S.Luis Potosí	13.06	27.10	44.74	54.23	94.87

Train 1		Train 2		1st cl. Reserved	2nd cl. Coach
Lv. 9:00 AM	Mexico City	7:00 PM	Ar.		
12:56 PM	Querétaro	2:42 PM		$ 7.42	$ 2.06
2:35 PM	S.M. Allende	1:09 PM		9.84	2.71
5:10 PM	S.L. Potosí	10:05 AM		13.06	4.23
11:55 PM	Saltillo	2:35 AM(+1)			7.45
2:22 AM(+1)	Monterrey	11:30 PM			8.39
Ar. 7:20 AM	N. Laredo	6:55 PM	Lv.		10.65

TAMAULIPECO TRAIN

Train 141		Train 142		1st.cl. Reserved
Lv. 10:30 AM	Monterrey	4:00 PM	Ar.	
2:45 PM	Reynosa	11:25 AM		$ 7.74
Ar. 5:10 PM	Matamoros	9:20 AM	Lv.	10.58

Trains 1 and 2 offer special first class reserved and second class coach service between Mexico City and Querétaro, San Miguel de Allende, and San Luis Potosí. These trains continue with only second class service to Saltillo, Monterrey, and Nuevo Laredo. Trains 141 and 142 ("Tamaulipeco") provide special first class service between Monterrey, Reynosa, and Matamoros.

Querétaro

This town is discussed in the "Train Through the Bajio" section.

San Miguel de Allende

San Miguel de Allende is a pretty colonial town which for 50 years has enjoyed a reputation as an art colony. The place just seems conducive to a variety of art forms. At 1,870 m elevation the town enjoys a climate which is almost always spring-like. Overhead a deep violet-blue sky contrasts with cottony clouds. Baroque facades crowd narrow, winding streets and huge carved wooden doors hundreds of years old open reluctantly to reveal hidden courtyards erupting with flowery color. With only 30,000 people, there are few of the modern diversions to which we have grown addicted. Perhaps all this allows artists the creative space and inspiration to create the works they do. And it also allows those who think they are artists the creative space to imagine that they are.

A Franciscan priest, Juan de San Miguel, established a settlement here in 1542. It was a settlement of Native Americans, chiefly Guamares, Otomíes, and Tarascans. After the discovery of silver at Zacatecas in 1546, San Miguel began to grow as a result of commerce between the mines and Mexico City. But a raid by Guamar-Chichimeca Indians in 1551 forced the abandonment of the site. San Miguel was reestablished in 1555 and this time a military garrison was included. Because of its pleasant climate, San Miguel became home to many wealthy mine and ranch owners. Their refurbished mansions are still there.

San Miguel was the first town captured by Hidalgo's independence forces in 1810. It was also the hometown of Hidalgo's co-commander, Ignacio Allende, who loaned his surname to the modern incarnation of the town. The War of Independence severely disrupted the patterns of wealth accumulation in the mining areas. The condition of the wealthy class further deteriorated during the Mexican Revolution. The result was that by the 1920s most of San Miguel's colonial mansions, churches, and even public buildings were in a state of serious decay.

In 1926 the Mexican government declared the city a national monument and that declaration might have been San Miguel's epitaph but for the action of two artists. In 1938 Stirling Dickinson of the United States and Cossio de Pomar of Peru founded a school of fine arts known as the Instituto Allende. From that point on it seems San Miguel de Allende's future was assured. Slowly at first, but then in droves, artists of all types began spending time there. Many North American and European artists settled there as did their groupies and imitators. The locals benefited from the construction and commerce generated by the wealthier emigres.

Today San Miguel is an amalgam of nationalities with Mexican clearly predominating. It is a friendly, comfortable mix of working class people, students, artists, and shop owners. Perhaps as much as one-tenth of the population consists of foreigners. The town also has one of the highest art gallery to population ratios in the world.

Getting Around. The **train station** is two km west of the plaza out Canal street. There is no local bus service so you can walk or take a taxi. The new **bus station** is also west of town along that same road but only about a kilometer from the center.

Crafts. Aside from formal art, San Miguel is known for its colorful **tinwork** fashioned into, among other things, Christmas ornaments, masks, and dioramas.

Sights. There is nothing extraordinary or fascinating in San Miguel, except the town itself. It is primarily a place to walk and sit and observe. It is a place which seems to inspire reflection and thought. It is, also, an easy place to get around.

At the center of town is the **Jardín Principal**, a small but lively plaza graced with cast-iron street lamps, conveniently

San Miguel de Allende, Guanajuato

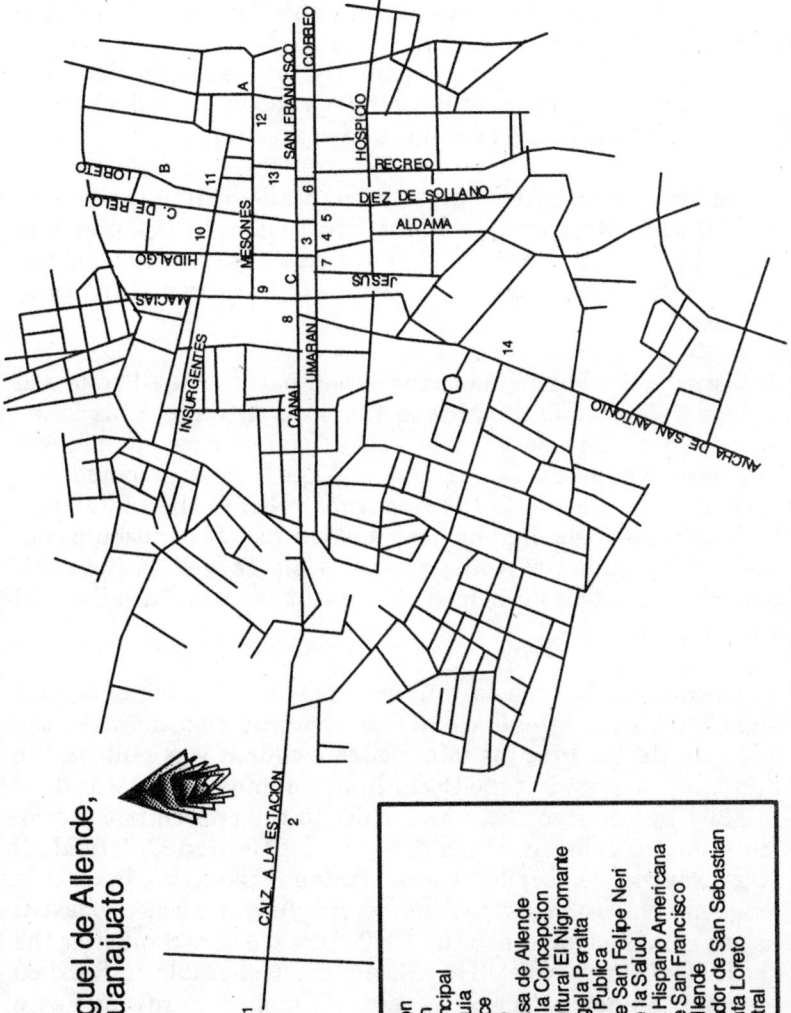

1 ~ train station
2 ~ bus station
3 ~ Jardin Principal
4 ~ La Parroquia
5 ~ tourist office
6 ~ post office
7 ~ Museo Casa de Allende
8 ~ Iglesia de la Concepcion
       Centro Cultural El Nigromante
9 ~ Teatro Angela Peralta
10~ Biblioteca Publica
11~ Oratorio de San Felipe Neri
       Templo de la Salud
12~ Academia Hispano Americana
13~ Templo de San Francisco
14~ Instituto Allende
A ~ Hotel Parador de San Sebastian
B ~ Hotel Quinta Loreto
C ~ Hotel Central

placed park benches, and a cluster of well manicured trees. Easily dominating the small plaza is **La Parroquia**, the parish church. This unique structure was originally built in the 17th Century as a plain Franciscan church. However, in 1880, a self-taught Indian architect, Zeferino Gutiérrez, added the facade and towers. Gutiérrez apparently got his inspiration from postcards of European gothic churches though it looks like La Parroquia is a mixture of gothic and spaceship.

Immediately east of La Parroquia on Calle Correo is the very helpful **tourist office**, open Mon-Fri, 10 a.m. to 2:30 p.m. and 5 p.m. to 7 p.m. and Sat, 10 a.m. to 1 p.m. One block east of the tourist office and on the opposite side of the street is the **post office**.

Just west of La Parroquia at the corner of Cuna de Allende and Calle de Umaran is the **Museo Casa de Allende**. This is the house where Ignacio Allende, one of the leaders of the 1810 rebellion, was born. Like Hidalgo, Allende was executed and beheaded for his efforts to bring some relief to the Indian and *mestizo* masses slaving for King and church. The museum contains memorabilia covering Allende's life as well as the independence struggle he helped initiate. It is open Tues-Sun, 10 a.m. to 4 p.m.

Two blocks west of the Jardín Principal at the corner of Macias and Canal is the **Iglesia de la Concepción**, also known as the **Templo de las Monjas**. Most of this church was built in the mid-18th Century but the Corinthian-columned dome was done in 1891 by Zeferino Gutiérrez. Next to the church is the two-story former convent which today is the **Centro Cultural El Nigromante**, also called **Bellas Artes** (Fine Arts). Second in longevity only to Instituto Allende, this fine arts school boasted as one of its instructors in the 1940s David Alfaro Siqueiros, the great Mexican muralist. There is an undecipherable, unfinished mural by Siqueiros as well as several finished murals by Pedro Martínez.

Just around the corner from Bellas Artes on Calle de Mesones is the 19th Century **Teatro Angela Peralta**. There are frequent concerts in this neoclassical theater. Two blocks northeast of the theater is the **Biblioteca Pública** (Public Library) at Insurgentes 25 with over 30,000 volumes in English. This is a lending library so if you're going to be in town for a while check it out.

Also on Insurgentes and two blocks east of the library is the **Oratorio de San Felipe Neri**. Originally the church of San Miguel's poor mulattos, in the early 18th Century this structure was extensively remodeled, given a new baroque facade, and taken over by the town's aristocracy. The interior's crowning glory is the chapel of **Santa Casa de Loreto**. Financed by the elite of San Miguel's elite, Don Manuel Tomás de la Canal, the chapel is a replica of the Holy House in Loreto, Italy, which is supposed to be the original house of the Virgin Mary. The chapel is full of gilt, velvet, ornate columns, reliefs, and oil paintings depicting the life of Mary. Beneath the chamber are the tombs of its benefactors, Don Manuel de la Canal and his wife Dona María de Hervas de Flores.

Beside the Oratorio is the more subdued **Templo de la Salud**. This 18th Century church is interesting for its Churrigueresque facade crowned with a large, stylized shell. The shell motif was fairly common in San Miguel's architecture but was rarely employed elsewhere in New Spain. One block south and east of the Templo de la Salud on Mesones is the **Academia Hispano Americana**, a school offering primarily language and Latin American culture classes.

One block east of the Jardín Principal is the **Templo de San Francisco**. Its energetic Churrigueresque facade contrasts sharply with its neoclassical tower. The interior follows the neoclassical pattern of the tower. The **Instituto Allende** is 6 blocks south of the plaza at Calle Ancha de San Antonio 4. This is the oldest fine arts school in San Miguel and occupies an 18th Century former mansion of the wealthy Canal family. This building is a work of art itself with its bougainvillea-filled and arcaded courtyard as well as its outstanding views of the town. Within its stone walls the institute contains classrooms, galleries, an art library, and studios. The galleries exhibit the work of students and other local artists.

Fiestas. No Mexican town has more festivals per capita than San Miguel. Chief among its celebrations is that of the town's namesake and patron saint, **Saint Michael the Archangel**. The festivities, taking place around the saint's feast day, September 29, include fireworks, concerts, and mariachis. The highlight of the festival is a series of dances performed by Indian dance troupes from Guanajuato and other Mexican states. These dancers gather at the *Cruz del Cuarto* on the road to the train station and, amidst the burning of copal incense and before a Christian cross, the dancers promise to forget old grievances. Then the ritual dances start. The dance groups are composed of men, women, and children but all have taken a religious vow to make this pilgrimage and learn the dances. No amateurs are permitted to disturb the dignity and solemnity of the ceremony. Each group carries an offering constructed of flowers, a *xuchil*, and when the first ritual dance is completed these *xuchiles* are deposited in the atrium of La Parroquia. After the offerings are made, the dancing continues for the rest of the day in front of the parish church. One of the dances is the **Danza Guerrera** which represents the war between the Chichimecs and the Spanish.

Las Yuntas is celebrated on May 3, the Day of the Holy Cross. The name derives from the yokes decorated with flowers and fruit which are placed on oxen at this time. The oxen are also decked out with lime necklaces and an ornament made of painted tortillas. You'll have to trust me on this.

The heart of the celebration is a mock battle between Indians and Federales, both groups being inspired to fight by pulque liquor and the sounds of an animated musical march called "El Culebras," the Snake Man. After the mock battle is over and the dead and dying are scattered about, the "wizard" appears. He heals the dead and injured whereupon both "armies" celebrate their victory.

Classes. Centro Cultural El Nigromante, or Bellas Artes, offers classes in plastic arts, music, and crafts. Classes are taught in Spanish. Contact:

> Centro Cultural El Nigromante
> Hernández Macias 75
> San Miguel de Allende
> Guanajuato, 37700 Mexico

The Instituto Allende offers Spanish, fine art, and various craft classes. Most of the instruction is in English. Contact:

> Sr. Rudy Fernández
> Instituto Allende
> San Miguel de Allende
> Guanajuato, 37700 Mexico

The Academia Hispano Americana has Spanish language classes at all levels as well as classes on various aspects of Mexican culture. Language classes are conducted in the flower-filled courtyard of a beautifully renovated colonial mansion. Contact:

> Academia Hispano Americana
> Mesones 4
> San Miguel de Allende
> Guanajuato, 37700 Mexico

Climate. San Miguel generally manages to avoid the extremes of temperature. Summer days are warm and the nights are cool. Most afternoons a thunderstorm will pass across town, dropping temperatures and settling the dust. Winters are dry with cool days and chilly nights. However, temperatures very rarely drop below freezing.

Excursions. There are a couple of hot spring spas only a few minutes outside of San Miguel. The closest is at **Taboada**, eight km north of the town on the road to Dolores Hidalgo. Here there are large, spring-fed pools and changing rooms. Entry is cheap and there is a restaurant and hotel (expensive) in town.

About five km further north along the same road is **La Gruta**. Here there are three small hot-spring-fed pools. Although smaller than the spa at Taboada, La Gruta is more interesting in one respect: you can actually go into a cave and sit in the water of the hottest spring. One kilometer from La Gruta is the town of **Atotonilco**, famous for its village church. The building is not spectacular. It was built in 1740 as a retreat and it was here in 1802 that Ignacio Allende was married. On his way from Dolores to capture San Miguel and thus to launch the War for Independence, Miguel Hidalgo first stopped here, at Atotonilco.

He went into the church and removed the Virgin of Guadalupe banner from above the altar, converting it from a religious to a powerful political icon. The church has six chapels and the walls and floors of virtually all available space have been covered with various forms of folk art.

To get to Taboada, La Gruta, or Atotonilco, either negotiate with a taxi driver or try to catch what is often an irregularly running bus. The bus is supposed to leave every couple of hours from in front of the Oratorio de San Felipe Neri.

San Luis Potosí

The first settlement on this spot was founded in 1583 when Father Diego de la Magdalena settled a group of Guachichil Indians here and called the town San Luis. Then, in 1592, after silver was discovered at nearby Cerro de San Pedro, the calm of the religious community was shattered by an overwhelming influx of miners and others drawn by the promise of silver wealth. The term "Potosí" was added to the town's name in the hope that the Mexican Potosí would produce as much wealth as the legendary Bolivian mining town of the same name.

The town grew quickly, fueled by silver, other metals, and cattle. San Luis Potosí also became a jumping off point for Spanish expeditions to the northern frontier of the colony. It was in San Luis in 1854 that González Bocanegra composed the Mexican National Anthem and during the French Intervention (1861-1867) Benito Juárez twice located his government here.

In the early 20th Century San Luis became a hotbed of liberalism and opposition to the dictator Porfirio Díaz. Francisco Madero, the chief liberal opponent of Díaz, formulated his Plan de San Luis here in 1910 while in jail. After his release, Madero went to San Antonio, Texas, from the safety of which he proclaimed himself provisional president and called on the Mexican people to rise in revolt. Eventually, some did.

Although for most of the colonial and independence periods San Luis Potosí was the preeminent urban center in northern Mexico, by the early 20th Century the city's growth had been outpaced by that of Monterrey. Today, San Luis is a city of about 600,000 people and has a diversified economy based on commerce, residual mining, and a fast-growing industrial sector including textiles, beer, and food and mineral processing.

Getting Around. The **train station** is six blocks east of the main plaza on the north side of the Alameda. The **bus station** is three km east of the center just south of the Glorieta Juárez traffic circle on Hwy 57. Buses from the plaza to the bus station are marked "Central" and run on Iturbide.

Crafts. San Luis is famous for its fine silk **rebozos**, or shawls. These are actually made in the nearby town of Santa María del Río and are so delicate that they can be pulled through a wedding ring. While some are still made from imported silk, many are now made from cotton and rayon. Inlaid wood objects, jewelry, and leather crafts are also regional products.

Comida Tipica. A distinctive candy produced here is *queso de tuna* which is made from the fruit of the prickly pear cactus. The fruit, or tuna, is mashed into a paste, cooked with raw sugar, and then dried in the sun. Two other local specialties are *fiambre potosino*, a dish of cold meats marinaded in a vinaigrette sauce, and *enchiladas potosinas*, rolled and fried tortillas stuffed with cheese.

Sights. As you pass through the outskirts of San Luis Potosí on the train you have to think you've made a mistake in deciding to disembark here. Slowly moving past your window are overcrowded neighborhoods, ugly warehouses, and busily polluting factories. Piles of cars and trucks, halted by the train's slow passage, seem to glower at you through the dust. But the compact center of this busy city is a different world, a world of balconied mansions overlooking colonial streets, of pedestrian malls, of baroque churches carved from pink stone and wearing tiled domes. There is a surprising and relative calm in the center though it is by no means quiet.

The focus of the city is the **Plaza de Armas**, also called the **Jardín Hidalgo**. With benches for relaxation and trees for protection from the strong sun of the plateau, the plaza is a favorite of Potosinos. There are also cafes and restaurants

San Luis Potosi, San Luis Potosi

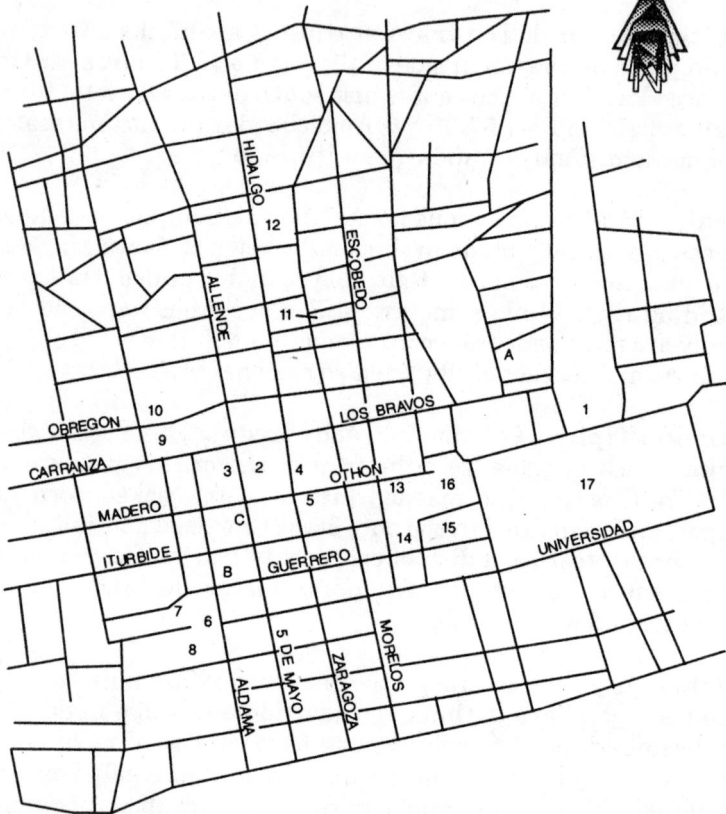

1 ~ train station
2 ~ Plaza de Armas
3 ~ Palacio de Gobierno
4 ~ Cathedral
  Palacio Municipal
5 ~ tourist office
6 ~ Plaza San Francisco
7 ~ Museo de Artesanias
8 ~ Iglesia de San Francisco
  Museo Regional Potosino
9 ~ Plaza de los Fundadores

10 ~ Capilla de Loreto
  Iglesia de la Compania
11 ~ post office
12 ~ Mercado Hidalgo
13 ~ Plaza del Carmen
14 ~ Museo Nacional de la Mascara
15 ~ Teatro de la Paz
16 ~ Iglesia del Carmen
17 ~ Alameda
A ~ Hotel Anahuac
B ~ Hotel Progresso
C ~ Hotel de Gante

located around the square for those leisurely, people-watching meals and refreshments.

Immediately west of the plaza is the **Palacio de Gobierno**. This 18th Century, neoclassical building was occupied by Benito Juárez twice when his government was located in San Luis Potosí. In the Juárez Room there is a life size diorama depicting Juárez making his decision on the execution of Maximilian. Just east of the Jardín Hidalgo is the **Cathedral**. Completed in 1710, this baroque church boasts four marble statues of the apostles on its facade and a beautiful carved wooden choir in its interior. Next to the Cathedral is the **Palacio Municipal**. Also, the very helpful **tourist office** is on the south side of the church at Othon 130. It is open Mon-Fri, 9 a.m. to 8 p.m. and Sat, 9 a.m. to 2 p.m. Ask here about cultural events in the city.

The **Plaza San Francisco** is four blocks south of the Jardín Hidalgo. On the western side of this pleasant park are three buildings of interest: the **Museo de Artesanías** (also called **Casa de las Artesanías**), the **Iglesia de San Francisco**, and the **Museo Regional Potosino**. The Museo de Artesanías exhibits and sells crafts from around the state, including the much-prized silk rebozos from Santa María del Río. Though more expensive than those sold in the market, these crafts are of higher quality on average. The museum is open Tues-Sat, 10 a.m. to 2 p.m. and 4 p.m. to 6 p.m. and Sun, 10 a.m. to 2:30 p.m.

Next to the museum is the 18th Century Iglesia de San Francisco, a rather low-key, baroque church built of pink stone. Just south of the church is the Museo Regional Potosino which is housed in the former monastery of the San Francisco church. Most of the exhibits consist of artifacts from the pre-Hispanic Huastec culture of eastern San Luis Potosí. Other exhibits cover the colonial and independence history of the state and the ethnography of its indigenous peoples.

One block northwest of the **Jardín Hidalgo** is the **Plaza de los Fundadores** which was the center of the original town. On the north side of the plaza are a couple of 17th Century Jesuit churches, the **Capilla de Loreto** and the **Iglesia de la Compañía**.

The **post office** is three blocks north of the Jardín Hidalgo on Morelos. Another two blocks north of the post office is the **Mercado Hidalgo**.

The **Plaza del Carmen** is two blocks southeast of the Jardín Hidalgo. At the southern end of this plaza is the **Museo Nacional de la Máscara** (National Mask Museum). This museum houses an outstanding collection of ceremonial masks from all over Mexico. It is one of the two finest collections of its type in the country and is open Tues-Sun, 10 a.m. to 2 p.m. and 4 p.m. to 6 p.m. Just east of the museum is the 19th Century **Teatro de la Paz** (Peace Theater). Almost every evening there is something going on in this neoclassical theater.

The **Iglesia del Carmen** is immediately east of the plaza of the same name. This very ornate 18th Century baroque church has domes covered with yellow, green, blue, and white tiles, as well as an intricately carved and decorated facade. The riot of decoration continues on the inside. Two gold-covered retablos flank the neoclassical altar designed by Eduardo Tresguerras. The highlight of the interior is the megabaroque Chapel of the Virgin.

Behind the Teatro de la Paz is the large park known as the **Alameda**. This area used to be orchards and gardens for the Carmelite monastery but now it's a pleasant urban park with trees, benches, paths, and a small pond.

A little less than one kilometer east from the Jardín Hidalgo on Universidad at Triana is the **Museo Taurino** (Bullfighting Museum). This museum has an interesting collection of posters, equipment, and photographs relative to bullfighting and to famous matadors. There are occasional bullfights at the nearby **Plaza de Toros** on Universidad.

The **Casa de la Cultura** is two km west of the center on Av. Carranza (No. 1815) and contains an assortment of exhibits including crafts, contemporary art, and archeological artifacts. Some exhibits are permanent while others are temporary.

Fiestas. There is no shortage of festivals in San Luis Potosí. During the **Semana Santa** (Holy Week) prior to Easter, there are concerts, festivities, and dances all over town. Then, on Good Friday, there is the **Procession of Silence** where costumed figures representing different neighborhoods march silently through the streets. On August 25 is the celebration of the **Patron Saint of the City** with parades and music. This is also the time of the **National Fair** which consists primarily of agricultural, industrial, and handicrafts exhibits, various cultural events, bullfights, and rodeos (charreadas).

Climate. The city has hot summers with thunderstorms and temperate, dry winters. Winter nights can get cold and frost is not uncommon.

Excursions. The spa at **Gogorrón**, otherwise known as the **Centro Vacacional Gogorrón**, is about 59 km south of San Luis Potosí and a couple of kilometers north of the town of Villa de Reyes. The spa is fueled by a set of hot springs whose temperatures reach 41°C. There are swimming pools for adults and children, Roman baths (which are hotter than the pools), a restaurant, gardens, and cabins. For overnight visits you can make reservations through the tourist office in San Luis.

Buses bound for San Felipe, Guanajuato, will stop at Gogorrón. Flecha Amarilla runs buses every half hour from the bus station in San Luis.

The picturesque village of **Santa María del Río** is 50 km south of San Luis on Hwy 57. This town's chief claim to fame is as the source of the high quality silk rebozos known throughout Mexico. The **Escuela del Rebozo** (Rebozo School) is located on the town's zócalo and here the visitor can view and purchase rebozos. Prices are considerably lower than in San Luis Potosí.

There are other things to do and see in Santa María besides the rebozos. There is a colonial stone aqueduct, **El Arquillo**, which crosses the river. On the other side of the river is a wonderful picnic spot, covered with grass and shaded by a grove of ancient walnut trees. If you follow the river past El Arquillo you will come to a 15-m waterfall with a very inviting plunge pool. There are a couple of hotels in town, all basic. Several bus lines connect San Luis Potosí with Santa María.

On the western margin of the Huasteca region and 135 km east of San Luis on Hwy 70 is **Río Verde**. This is an unexceptional town located in the midst of numerous orange groves. However, this is a nice area if you want to do some backpacking. There are several caves, waterfalls, and springs within 20 km of the town.

The **Laguna de la Media Luna** is near the village of San Diego 16 km from Río Verde. The lake is fed by three springs and contains smooth, transparent water. Its maximum depth is 36 meters and it is full of fish and ancient red cedar tree trunks. Archeological remains have been found in the lake. There are undeveloped camping sites around the lake. The springs of **Los Anteojitos** are four km south of Río Verde over an unpaved road. This swimming hole consists of two spring-fed pools, each about 15 m across. Several bus lines connect San Luis Potosí with Río Verde.

Saltillo

Saltillo is set in a wide valley surrounded by mountains and is on the northeastern margin of Mexico's central plateau. The highway to Monterrey in the east drops 1,000 meters in 80 km. Saltillo was founded in 1578 during the Chichimec War as a defensive outpost against the Guachichiles. At the time it was also hoped that grain production from the area could supply the needs of the mining towns. Isolated on the frontier and beset by the Indians, Saltillo grew hardly at all.

That changed in 1591 when a group of 932 Tlaxcalan Indian settlers arrived. The Spanish government had made them a number of attractive promises if they would agree to the long migration from their homeland in south central Mexico. The hard working Indians stabilized the community and set an example for the Chichimec still raiding the nearby countryside. Soon, many of the Chichimecs were asking if the Spanish would give them land and teach them how to farm.

By the early 19th Century Saltillo was the capital of the province of Coahuila and after Mexican independence its domain included Texas as well. Mexico's later wars with Texas and with the United States cost Saltillo over half its administrative territory. In 1847 the city was occupied by United States troops after they decisively defeated the Mexican army under General Santa Anna. This bloody battle took place at Buenavista, 10 km south of Saltillo.

It was in Saltillo in 1908 that Francisco Madero published the document that would spark the Mexican Revolution, *The Presidential Succession of 1910*. (It doesn't sound very revolutionary, does it?) It was also here a year later that Madero announced himself a candidate running against Díaz in the 1910 presidential election. Today, Saltillo has a population of about 300,000 and is the capital of Coahuila. It is a commercial and communications center for an agricultural region that produces wool, cotton, wheat, and alfalfa. The city also has a dynamic industrial sector manufacturing pharmaceuticals, textiles, engines, and chemicals. Despite this industrial growth, Saltillo has managed to retain a low-key, laid-back atmosphere.

Getting Around. The **train station** is southwest of the center just off Emilio Carranza. It's a 15-minute walk or an even shorter taxi ride between downtown and the station. The **bus station** is way out on the southwestern outskirts of town. To get from the station to downtown, take a *colectivo* marked "Centro" or the No. 9 bus. To know when you've reached the center of town, look for the large cathedral. To go from the center to the bus station, catch the No. 9 bus at the corner of Aldama and Hidalgo.

Crafts. The Tlaxcalan Indian colonists that moved to Saltillo in the late 16th Century developed a distinctive style of weaving. Today, that style is embodied in the **Saltillo wool sarape** which is famous throughout Mexico. Saltillo is also known for its blankets and silver work.

Sights. The **Plaza de Armas** is austere as zócalos go in Mexico. Just east of it is the 18th Century **Cathedral**. With its ornately, even exuberantly, carved facade, this church is a fine example of Churrigueresque architecture. In its interior the altar and pulpit are covered with gold leaf. If you ask, you will probably receive permission to climb the Cathedral's main tower for a nice view of the city.

On the other side of the plaza from the Cathedral is the **Palacio de Gobierno**. This pink stone, three-story structure was originally built in 1808 and then reconstructed in 1928. Inside the Palacio are murals depicting the history of the state by Salvador Tarazona. The interior courtyard also contains a fountain. Behind the Palacio de Gobierno on Calle Victoria are the **Taller de Plateria** (Silver Workshop) and the **Taller de Sarapes**. The **post office** is also located here.

The **Alameda Zaragoza** is six blocks west of the plaza on Victoria. This large public park is full of paths, shade trees, and benches. There is a monument honoring Ignacio Zaragoza, the Mexican hero of the Battle of Puebla. Two blocks northwest of the Plaza de Armas is the **Plaza Acuña** which is the center of a bustling, commercial neighborhood.

The **Universidad Autonoma de Coahuila** (Autonomous University of Coahuila) is one km north of the main plaza along Allende (which changes to Av. Carranza). On campus is the **Ateneo Fuente y Pinacoteca** (Athenaeum Fountain and Art Museum) with a collection of art works by both Mexican and European painters.

On the south side of the plaza is the **Centro de Artes Visuales** (Visual Art Center). The center houses temporary art exhibits, shows films, and has its own permanent art collection. Three blocks northeast of the plaza on Av. Bravo is the **Museo de Arte Rubén Herrera** (Ruben Herrera Art Museum). Located in the former home of Rubén Herrera (1888-1933), this museum contains several hundred of his paintings.

Fiestas. **La Feria del Estado** (State Fair) takes place from July 23 to August 6 and includes rodeos, cock fights, and exhibits of agricultural and industrial products.

Climate. Saltillo is hot and dry in the summer and cold and dry in the winter. Snow, while uncommon, is not unknown.

Saltillo, Coahuila

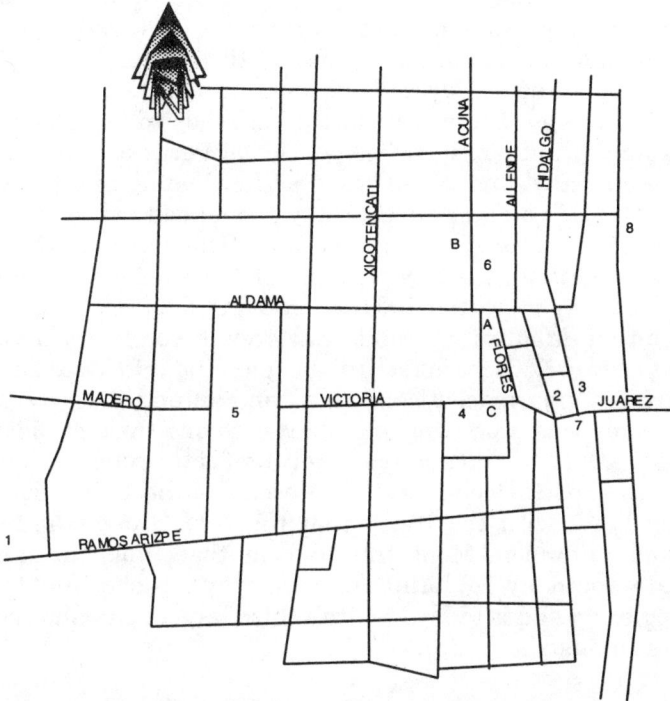

1 ~ train station	5 ~ Alameda Zaragoza
2 ~ Plaza de Armas	6 ~ Plaza Acuna
Palacio de Gobierno	7 ~ Centro de Artes Visuales
3 ~ Cathedral	8 ~ Museo de Arte Ruben Herrera
4 ~ post office	A ~ Hotel Saade
Taller de Plateria	B ~ Hotel de Avila
Taller de Sarapes	C ~ Plaza Urdinola

Piedras Negras

Spend as little time here as possible. The **train station** is 1.5 km (one mi) south of the plaza at the end of Calle Zaragoza.

Monterrey

Diego de Montemayor founded the town of Nuestra Señora de Monterrey in 1596. The town grew very slowly for 250 years with an economy based on sheep ranching and trade with the settlements in Tamaulipas to the northeast. In the mid-19th Century Monterrey began to develop its textile and iron and steel industries. The arrival of the railroads in the 1880s and the stability and pro-business policies of Porfirio Díaz accelerated Monterrey's industrial growth. The Cuauhtémoc Brewery, today Mexico's oldest and largest, was founded in the 1890s by the Mexican of German ancestry, José Schneider. By the time of the revolution, the city was one of Mexico's largest with a population approaching 100,000. Pausing during the Mexican Revolution, Monterrey's industrial growth continued into the 20th Century with manufacturing expanding into areas such as electronics, pharmaceuticals, glass, and automobiles. By 1980, Monterrey was producing one-quarter to one-third of Mexico's industrial output and approximately half of the country's manufactured exports. However, the recession of the 1980s hit Monterrey hard, with the result that the Alfa Group, the major economic group in Monterrey and, at that time, the largest private company in Latin America, went broke. Monterrey struggles on and is today Mexico's third largest city and second largest industrial center.

Since at least the beginning of this century there has existed a great rivalry between Monterrey and Mexico City. Having been left to its own devices on the frontier for hundreds of years, Monterrey developed an independence of spirit that has carried over to modern times. This spirit conflicts strongly with the over-bureaucratized, all-powerful Mexican central government. It also conflicts with the domination of politics through fraud and cooptation by the PRI. As a result, many in Monterrey regard Mexico City as a parasite on the national economy. These people are often also supporters of the PAN, the right-wing, pro-business opposition party to the PRI. Regardless of their political affiliations, most Monterreños are friendly, modern, and open to English-speaking travelers.

Getting Around. The **train station** is about three km northwest of the Macro Plaza on Av. Nieto, three blocks north of Calle

Colón. Take a taxi. The bus routes are contorted and confusing. The **bus station** is only about 2.5 km northwest of the city's center at Colón and Amado Nervo. Again, a taxi is a good choice but bus No. 17 is also fairly direct. Going from downtown to the station you can catch the bus heading north on Cuauhtémoc.

Crafts. There are many things to buy in Monterrey but few of them are locally produced crafts. One exception is **lead crystal** produced at Cristaleria Kristalux, although this product is produced by wage-laborers rather than independent artisans.

Comida Tipica. Monterrey is the goat meat *(cabrito)* capital of Mexico. The cabrito is prepared in a variety of ways, but most often barbecued. Another meat used in Monterrey cuisine is dried beef, *carne seca*. This is used in *machaca de Monterrey*, where the beef is fried with eggs, tomatoes, onions, and peppers.

Sights. Monterrey is a difficult city for the traveler afoot. Historically, most of the city's energy has gone into industry and growth with little left over for art, museums, or recreation. In recent years that focus has altered somewhat but the size of the city has meant that when new museums or the like are built, they are established away from the city's center.

What is of interest in downtown Monterrey is found around the city's huge zócalo, called the **Gran Plaza** or **Macro Plaza**. This modern construction is 11 blocks long and fronted by several government buildings, palaces, and shops. Bands play in the plaza on Thursday and Sunday. On the east side of the plaza near Ocampo is the 17th Century baroque **Cathedral**. Opposite it on the other side of the plaza is the **Palacio Municipal Viejo** (Old City Hall). Halfway up the plaza on the east side near Matamoros is the **Teatro de la Ciudad** (City Theater). The **tourist office** is on the other side of the plaza at Matamoros and Zaragoza. At the north end of Macro Plaza is the **Palacio de Gobierno**, built in 1908 of pink stone from San Luis Potosí. Behind the Palacio de Gobierno is the **post office**.

Like Mexico City, Monterrey has its own **Zona Rosa**, an exclusive area of expensive shops, restaurants, and hotels. In Monterrey it is just west of Macro Plaza between Calle Padre Mier on the north and Ocampo on the south.

Monterrey, Nuevo Leon

1 ~ train station
2 ~ bus station
3 ~ Gran Plaza
4 ~ Cathedral
5 ~ Palacio Municipal Viejo
6 ~ Teatro de la Ciudad
7 ~ tourist office
8 ~ Palacio de Gobierno
9 ~ post office
10~ Mercado Colon
11~ Mercado Juarez
A ~ Hotel Los Reyes
B ~ Hotel Colonial
C ~ Hotel Nuevo Leon
D ~ Hotel Patricia
E ~ Hotel Yamallel
F ~ Hotel Posada

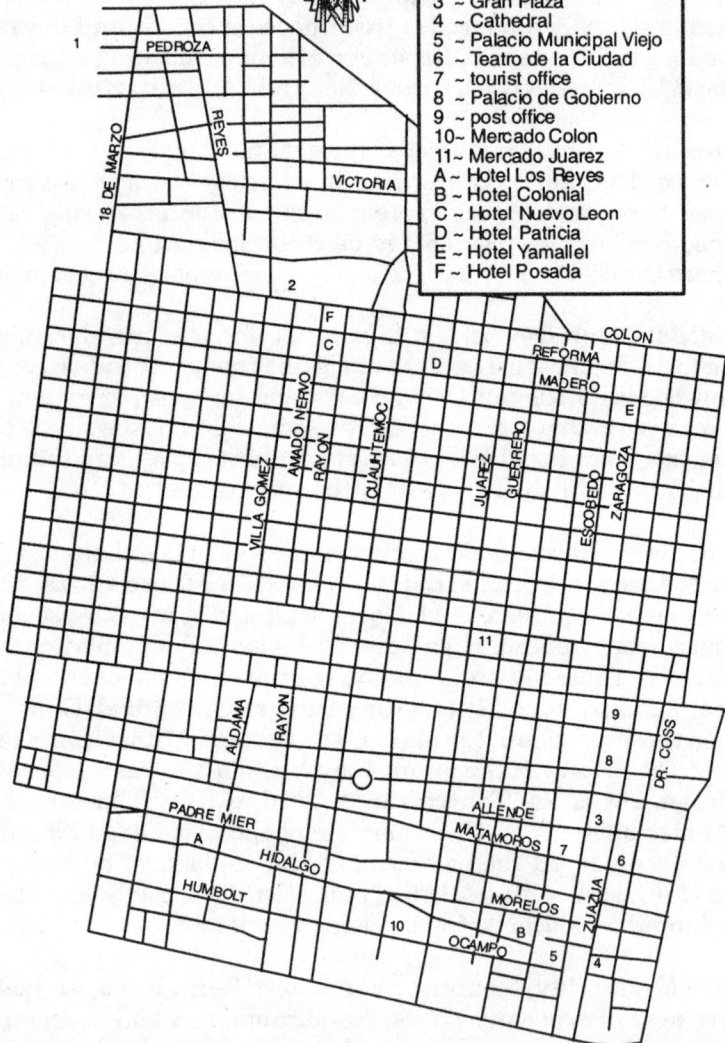

Monterrey also has several traditional Mexican markets. One is the **Mercado Colón** four blocks west of the Macro Plaza near Ocampo and Juárez. The **Mercado Juárez** is 12 blocks north of the Colón market along Av. Juárez.

The **Obispado** (Bishop's Palace) is at the west end of Padre Mier approximately three km from the Gran Plaza. The structure was built in the late 18th Century and served with distinction as a fort in the United States assault on Monterrey during the Mexican-American War and again when Maximilian's French troops attacked Monterrey. Today the building serves as the **Museo Regional de Nuevo León**. Its exhibits chronicle the ethnographical, political, and economical history of the region. The Obispado is open Tues-Sun, 10 a.m. to 6 p.m. To get there, take bus No. 4 on Padre Mier and get off when the bus turns off that road. Then climb the hill.

The **Cerveceria Cuauhtémoc** (Cuauhtémoc Brewery) is on the north side of town along Av. Universidad. Founded in the 1890s, this is Mexico's oldest and largest brewery, the home of Tecate, Bohemia, and Carta Blanca beers. There are tours of the brewing facilities at 11 a.m., noon, and 3 p.m. At the end of the tour there is the obligatory free beer which, of course, one must imbibe in the spirit of international cooperation. But there is much more here than just a brewery. There is the **Museo de Monterrey** with a permanent collection of art by Mexican and Latin American artists and occasional visiting exhibits. There is also a **Baseball Hall of Fame Museum** with exhibits covering the history of Mexican baseball. The complex is open Tues-Sun, 9:30 a.m. to 5:30 p.m. To get there, take bus No. 1 north on Juárez.

Climate. In the summer Monterrey is hot and polluted. Winters are cold and polluted. This semi-arid region receives most of its rain in September and October.

Excursions. Las Grutas de García (García Caves) are about 30 km northwest of Monterrey and about eight km east of the small town of Villa de García. There is actually only one cave and it consists of 16 chambers stretched out over 2.5 km. Tour guides take you along incandescently lit paths and past an assortment of stalagmites, stalactites, and columns. At times it's a bit surreal. If my memory serves me correctly, the tour ends in a large chamber lit by a distant skylight where everyone stands around a Christmas-light-decorated stalagmite as, from somewhere in the darkness, the song "Ave María" plays. Easily one of the highlights of the trip is getting to the cave entrance. From the valley floor a tracked cable car takes the visitor almost straight up 700 meters to the shadowed entrance high on the mountainside. The cave is open Tues-Sun, 9 a.m. to 4:30 p.m. Getting there is difficult. Fairly expensive tours can be arranged in Monterrey. Cheap, quasi-public transportation to the cave is provided by Transportes Monterrey-Saltillo but only on Saturday. Buses leave from the main bus station at 9 a.m., 10 a.m., 11 a.m. and noon.

Nuevo Laredo

Nuevo Laredo is one of the busiest entry points on the Mexican

Nuevo Laredo, Tamaulipas

United States

to Laredo, Texas

RIO BRAVO (RIO GRANDE)

INTERNATIONAL BLVD.

BRAVO   VICTORIA

BELDEN

SUAREZ
MIER
GONZALEZ
CANALES
MINA

L. DE LARA

JUAREZ   MATAMOROS   GUERRERO   OCAMPO   GALEANA

1 ~ train station
2 ~ bus station
3 ~ Mexican Immigration
      tourist office
4 ~ Plaza Principal
5 ~ International Bridge (old)
6 ~ International Bridge (new)
A ~ Hotel Calderon
B ~ Hotel Don Antonio

border. So, like most other border towns, it has developed a distinctive economy based on restaurants, curio shops, hotels, and gambling. It is a dusty ramshackle town and if you are entering here, don't let it scare you. Mexico gets better.

You can walk to the **train station** from the International Bridge. After crossing the bridge and going through immigration, take a right onto International Boulevard. Continue on this street until you reach the train tracks and take a left on Av. César López de Lara. After about .8 km you reach the station.

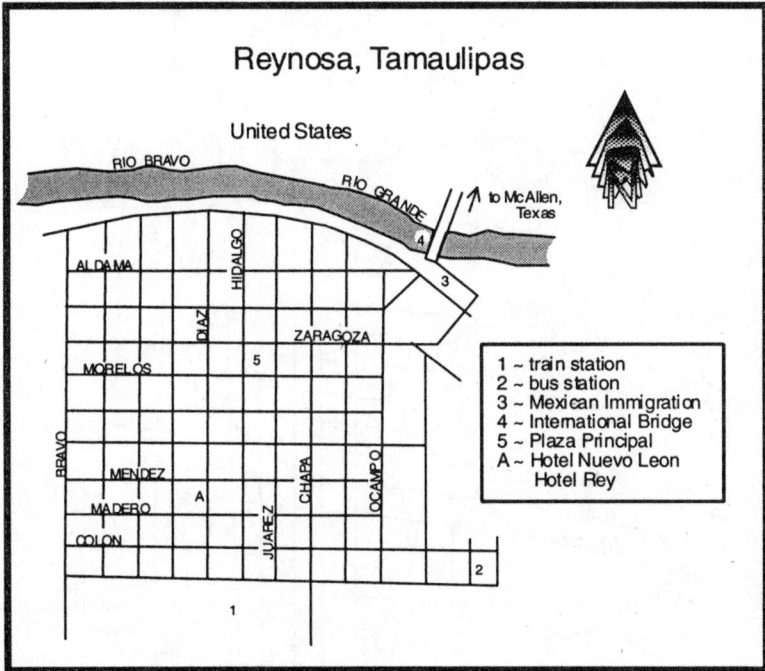

Reynosa, Tamaulipas

United States

RIO BRAVO

RIO GRANDE

to McAllen, Texas

ALDAMA

HIDALGO

DIAZ

ZARAGOZA

MORELOS

5

BRAVO

MENDEZ

CHAPA

OCAMPO

MADERO

A

COLON

JUAREZ

1

2

3

1 ~ train station
2 ~ bus station
3 ~ Mexican Immigration
4 ~ International Bridge
5 ~ Plaza Principal
A ~ Hotel Nuevo Leon
     Hotel Rey

Reynosa

The border town of Reynosa is about 10 km (six mi) from the Texas city of McAllen. With almost half a million people, Reynosa is an important commercial and industrial center in northern Mexico. While it is a pleasant town by border standards, there is little to do here but eat, sleep, and buy liquor.

Matamoros, Tamaulipas

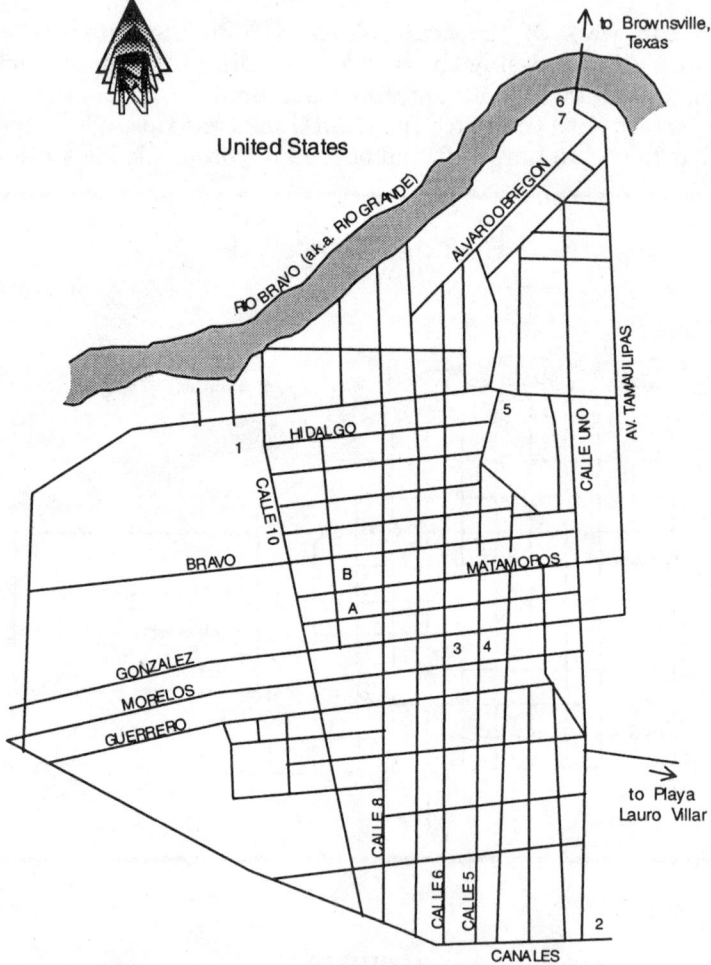

to Brownsville, Texas

United States

RIO BRAVO (a.k.a. RIO GRANDE)

ALVARO OBREGON

AV. TAMAULIPAS

CALLE UNO

HIDALGO

CALLE 10

1

5

BRAVO

B

A

MATAMOROS

3 4

6
7

GONZALEZ

MORELOS

GUERRERO

to Playa
Lauro Villar

CALLE 8

CALLE 6

CALLE 5

2

CANALES

1 ~ train station	6 ~ International Bridge
2 ~ bus station	7 ~ Mexican Immigration
3 ~ Plaza Principal	A ~ Hotel Majestic
4 ~ Cathedral	B ~ Hotel Roma
5 ~ Museo del Maiz	

Getting Around. The **train station** is six blocks south of the main plaza. The **bus station** is a little over a kilometer southeast of the plaza. Take a cab.

Matamoros

Opposite the city of Brownsville, Texas, Matamoros is similar to Reynosa in population and commercial importance but is somewhat less important as a jump-across-the-border destination for tourists. This fact works to the city's advantage, for while Matamoros is still unmistakably a border town it manages to feel more like a Mexican city than a curio bazaar. If you end up staying a night here, you'll find that the hotels are more reasonably priced than in other towns along the border.

Getting Around. The **train station** is on Hidalgo, one km northwest of the plaza. The **bus station** is on Canales, about the same distance southeast of the plaza. Either walk or take a cab.

Sights. There is actually something specific to see here though I wouldn't go very far out of my way to see it. The **Museo del Maíz** (Maize Museum) is about seven blocks north of the main plaza. Domesticated by indigenous people thousands of years ago, maize has always been the lifeblood of Mexican civilizations. This museum's fine displays examine the history of the plant and its role in Mexican religion, culture, and politics. The museum is open Tues-Sun, 9:30 a.m. to 5 p.m.

About 38 km (23 mi) east of Matamoros is **Playa Lauro Villar** (Lauro Villar Beach). This is a rather nice beach for the Gulf Coast and it is never crowded. To get there catch the "Playa" bus on Abasolo, one block north of the plaza.

Train Through The Bajio

The Bajio is often considered the breadbasket of Mexico but in the country's history it is much more. Geographically, the region includes the southern part of the state of Querétaro and most of the state of Guanajuato. It consists of a basin of fertile land caught between the central volcanic cordillera to the south and the Sierra Madre Oriental to the east and north. Before the Spanish came this area was a buffer between the settled, agricultural Indians to the south and the nomadic Chichimecs to the north. The region was inhabited primarily by the semi-settled Otomí Indians and assorted Chichimec tribes. By the late 15th Century both the Aztecs and the Tarascans had extended their influence into the area. The names of both states are derived from Tarascan words. Querétaro means "Place of the Ball Game" and Guanajuato means "Hill of the Frogs."

The town of Querétaro was founded in 1531 by Christianized Otomí and Spaniards. In what is today the state of Guanajuato the first colonial towns were established between 1526 and 1528 by two Otomí and recently baptized allies of the Spaniards, Nicolás de San Luis Montañés and Fernando de Tapia. Acámbaro is one of the towns they founded. In 1548 the first of several silver mines was found in the area and in that year the city of Guanajuato was established. Silver was not the only mineral found here in abundance as iron, zinc, copper, and lead were also taken from the richly mineralized igneous bedrock. But silver was the most lucrative and Guanajuato became Mexico's most prolific producer of the white metal.

During the Chichimec War (1550-1600) the population grew slowly but relentlessly. The conclusion of the conflict resulted in an orgy of growth in the Bajio. Mines, ranches, and farms doubled, then tripled, their production, size, and number. While the *peninsulares* and criollos prospered, the Indians suffered, deprived of their lands, crippled and killed in the mines, overworked on the haciendas. Perhaps it should come as no surprise, then, that Mexico's War of Independence began here.

Mexico's struggle for independence from Spain was not a vector, a force of defined strength and direction. It was a whirlwind, an explosion of divergent motivations, origins, and tactics responding to conditions in both Mexico and Europe. It also presaged the next whirlwind, the Mexican Revolution.

For the most part the leaders of the War for Independence were *criollos*, born in Mexico but with pure Spanish blood. Such privileged whites were also the leaders here but in the Bajio these leaders unleashed the angry passion of the Indian and *mestizo* peasants and almost brought down the colonial government that ruled New Spain. Under the guise of a literary society these middle class revolutionaries met periodically in Querétaro to brainstorm their vision of independence. In late 1810 they were discovered and several arrested. This prompted Miguel Hidalgo y Costilla, a parish priest in the town of Dolores, to accelerate the plan so he immediately declared Mexican independence from his pulpit with the *Grito de Dolores* (Shout from Dolores).

Hidalgo and Ignacio Allende, another *criollo* revolutionary, led an ever-growing army of peasants and Indians and captured town after town in the Bajio. San Miguel fell first and without a struggle as the garrison there joined the rebel force. Then came Celaya and Guanajuato. Though Hidalgo's army was eventually defeated, the struggle continued and the Bajio is revered by many Mexicans as the birthplace of Mexican independence.

Other memories are also associated with this area: in 1848 Mexico was forced to sign the hated Treaty of Guadalupe Hidalgo in Querétaro. This treaty ceded over half of Mexico's territory to the United States. Also, in 1867, the puppet Emperor Maximilian was executed at Cerro de las Companas (Hill of the Bells) just outside Querétaro and it was in that same town in 1917 that the current Mexican Constitution was written.

There is still mining in both the states of Querétaro and Guanajuato but production has declined considerable since the heady days of the 17th Century. Today, agriculture dominates this fertile basin and the region is responsible for a good fraction of Mexico's production of wheat, sorghum, alfalfa, and barley. Dairy, cattle, and swine are also important.

Industry is growing fast on the outskirts of the city of Querétaro–spillover from nearby Mexico City. The state of Guanajuato also has its industrial centers: León with shoes and other leather goods, Irapuato with food processing, and Salamanca with its huge oil refinery.

The Bajio is a wonderful place to visit. It is full of character and history. It is not full of tourists. Many who come to visit return again and again. Others never leave.

Train Services. Trains 9 and 10 ("Constitucionalista") provide special first class service between Mexico City and Tula, Querétaro, Celaya, Salamanca, Irapuato, and Guanajuato. Trains 1 and 2, mentioned in the "Train to Monterrey" section, provide special first class reserved and second class coach service between Mexico City, Querétaro, and San Miguel de Allende.

CONSTITUCIONALISTA TRAIN

Train 9		Train 10		1st cl. Reserved
Lv. 7:00 AM	Mexico City	9:15 PM	Ar.	
8:03 AM	Tula	7:54 PM		$3.03
10:20 AM	Querétaro	5:35 PM		7.42
11:00 AM	Celaya	4:50 PM		8.81
11:44 AM	Salamanca	4:15 PM		10.00
12:05 PM	Irapuato	3:40 PM		10.61
Ar. 1:25 PM	Guanajuato	2:25 PM	Lv.	12.29

Tula

For information on Tula see "Excursions" in the Mexico City section.

Querétaro

Querétaro was founded by Spaniards and Christianized Otomí Indians in 1531. During the colonial period the town served as a defensive and commercial center for the mining areas to the north. It was in Querétaro in 1810 that the first serious independence movement in New Spain was organized. Under the guise of a "literary club" this group would meet to plot the independence of Mexico. The Spanish authorities discovered their intentions and moved to arrest them but before this could be effected, Doña Josefa Ortiz, one of the plotters and the wife of Querétaro's mayor, managed to get word to Miguel Hidalgo y Costilla, another plotter and the parish priest in the small town of Dolores nearby. With nothing to lose and independence to win, Miguel Hidalgo proclaimed the independence of Mexico on September 16, 1810, with the *Grito de Dolores*, organized the astonished Indian peasants of his parish into a rude army, and began Mexico's 12-year anti-colonial struggle.

On February 2, 1848, Mexican President Peña y Peña signed the Treaty of Guadalupe Hidalgo in Querétaro. This infamous agreement ended the U.S.-Mexico War and ceded half of Mexico's territory to the United States. Ironically, a few months after the transfer of sovereignty, gold was discovered in California.

Querétaro also served briefly as the capital of Mexico in 1848 when Mexico City was occupied by U.S. troops. Also, during the War of Reform (1857-1859) Benito Juárez located his government here. In the spring of 1867 the imposed Emperor Maximilian was besieged and then captured at Querétaro by the republican troops of Benito Juárez. The Hapsburg would-be monarch was tried and sentenced to death. Because 50,000 Mexicans died in the struggle to oust the French, Juárez ignored the many pleas of clemency from around the world. Maximilian was executed at Cerro de Companas just outside Querétaro.

In 1917 a convention of revolutionaries drew up Mexico's current constitution in Querétaro and in 1929 an almost equally significant political event occurred here: the Institutional Revolutionary Party (PRI) was formally organized in Querétaro.

Today the city retains a Spanish center well blessed with colonial structures, while on its outskirts new industrial and manufacturing plants sprawl, spillover from nearby Mexico City. If you avoid the suburbs, the old heart of Querétaro makes a pleasant and interesting foray into Mexico's past.

Getting Around. The **train station** is seven blocks north of the Jardín Obregón. The **bus station** is about seven blocks southeast of the Jardín at the intersection of Av. Constituyentes and Pasteur.

Crafts. Querétaro is a good place to find **jewelry** made from locally mined gems, particularly opals, topaz, and amethyst.

Comida Tipica. As Querétaro is in the center of a grape growing region, it's not too unexpected to find that a local food specialty is *pechugas de pollo a la uva*, or chicken breasts covered with a grape sauce.

Sights. It's hard to believe that within the industrial suburbs of Querétaro there could be a pretty and very Spanish colonial town with tree-lined paseos, baroque mansions, and quiet, flower-filled city plazas. Yet that is the case. At the center of it all is the **Plaza Principal**, also called the **Jardín Obregón**. There are band concerts and folk music performances on Thursday and Sunday evenings in the plaza. One block north of the plaza on Angela Peralta is the **Teatro de la República** where in 1917 delegates gathered to write Mexico's constitution.

On the east side of Jardín Obregón is the **Church of San Francisco** with its beautifully tiled domes. Inside the church is a fine collection of religious art from the 17th, 18th, and 19th centuries and beside it is the very helpful **tourist office**. Free tours of the city leave here every day at 10 a.m. The office also has information on cultural events in the city. Also beside the Church of San Francisco and housed in that church's former monastery is the **Museo Regional**. It contains a number of colonial and independence period artifacts and documents. Most of the displays relate to Querétaro's role in the making of Mexican history. The museum is open Tues-Sat, 10 a.m. to 3:30 p.m. and Sun, 10 a.m. to 3:30 p.m.

East of the Museo Regional on Av. 5 de Mayo is the **Plaza de la Independencia**, which sits in the midst of a lovely colonial neighborhood. On the south side of this plaza is the **Casa de Ecala**. This striking baroque mansion has been converted into the **Casa de la Cultura** and now contains exhibits of local crafts. On the north side of the Plaza de la Independencia is the **Casa de la Corregidora**. This 18th Century building was traditionally the home of the mayor and it was here that the mayor's wife and revolutionary, Doña Josefa Ortiz de Domín-guez was held under house arrest. Despite this she managed to get word to Miguel Hidalgo that they had been discovered. Today this building serves as the **Palacio Municipal.**

Five blocks east of the Plaza de la Independencia is the **Templo y Convento de la Cruz** (Church and Convent of the Cross). During the 17th and 18th Centuries this was the most active monastery in Mexico and served as a religious base of operations for the "spiritual conquest" of what is today northern Mexico and western and southwestern United States. Later, the monastery housed Maximilian's troops and served briefly as the "Emperor's" jail. Today, the monastery contains flower-filled courtyards, Maximilian's cell, and assorted colonial-era arti-facts. The monastery also contains part of Querétaro's **aque-duct.** This was built in 1738 to bring water into the town. It is nine km long and consists of 74 arches.

Two blocks west of the Jardín Obregón is the **Church of Santa Clara.** Built in 1633, this church has an effusively carved interior. One block south of the church on Guerrero is the **Palacio Federal,** which also contains the city's main **post office.** This 18th Century building was formerly an Augustinian monastery and, with its carved gargoyles and in-tricately decorated arcades, it is a delightful example of Querétaro baroque. Two blocks west of Santa Clara are the unremarkable **Palacio de Gobierno** and the **Cathedral.**

Three blocks south of the Palacio Federal at Gral. Arteaga and Calle Ezequiel Montes is the **Church of Santa Rosa.** This church was finished in 1752 and is considered by many to be the finest example of colonial baroque in Querétaro. Santa Rosa exhibits a distinct Moorish influence in its tower and arched doorways. Its interior is covered with gilt and marble. The **market** is two blocks east of Santa Rosa Church and contains mostly food.

About 10 blocks west of downtown is the **Cerro de las Com-panas** (Hill of the Bells). It was here in 1867 that Maximilian was executed. Today that historical event is marked by a small chapel and a large statue of Benito Juárez. To get there from the center catch a bus marked "Carillo."

Queretaro, Queretaro

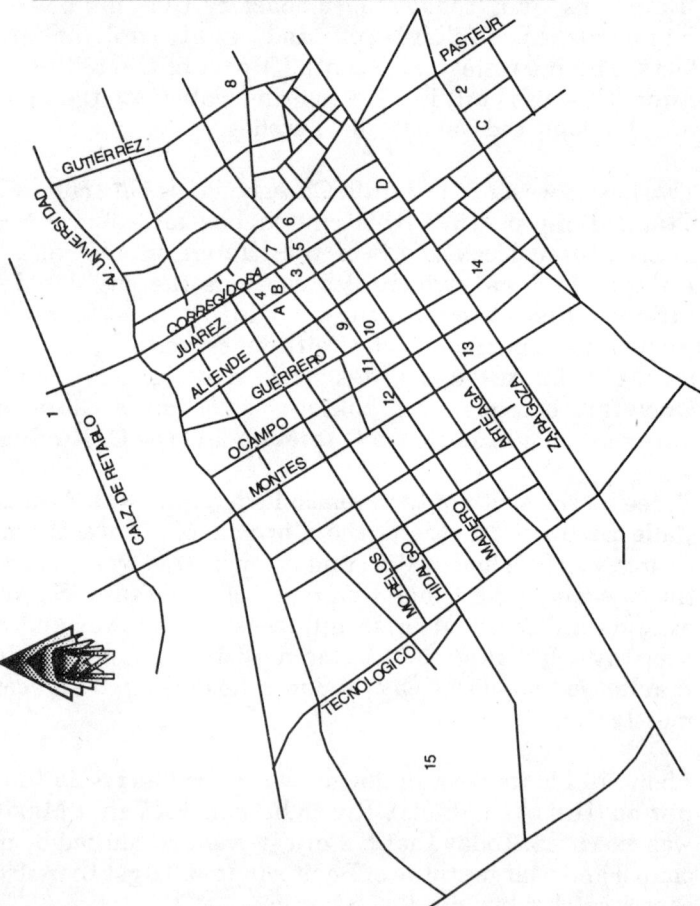

Legend:

1 ~ train station
2 ~ bus station
3 ~ Plaza Principal
4 ~ Teatro de la Republica
5 ~ Church of San Francisco
       Museo Regional
       tourist office
6 ~ Plaza de la Independencia
       Casa de la Cultura
7 ~ Casa de la Corregidora
       Palacio Municipal
8 ~ Templo y Convento de la
       Cruz
9 ~ Church of Santa Clara
10~ post office
11~ Palacio de Gobierno
12~ Cathedral
13~ Church of Santa Rosa
14~ market
15~ Cerro de las Companas
A ~ Hotel Hidalgo
B ~ Hotel Plaza
C ~ Hotel Mirabel
D ~ Hotel Impala

Climate. At 1,853 meters above sea level, Querétaro often experiences frost on winter nights but is hot in the summer. Almost all of the area's rain falls during the summer months.

Celaya

There are no compelling reasons to stop in this pleasant town. Celaya sits in the middle of a very productive agricultural area and its chief industry is food processing. It was here in 1915 that Alvaro Obregón defeated the troops of Pancho Villa and by doing so eliminated Villa as a threat to the Constitutionalist revolutionary faction led by Venustiano Carranza.

Salamanca

Salamanca is also set in a rich agricultural region but, in addition, boasts a huge petroleum refinery. There is even less reason to stop here than in Celaya.

Irapuato

Other than delicious strawberries, there's little to recommend Irapuato to the visitor. Only about four blocks separate the train station from the bus station in town.

Guanajuato

Scattered among the slopes and ravines of the Sierra de Guanajuato like a collection of so many pastel and more violently colored boxes, the town of Guanajuato has witnessed the same boom and bust pattern as Zacatecas. In 1548 a fabulous vein of silver was discovered at La Valenciana so the town was established as near the mine as possible given the terrain. Over two and a half centuries La Valenciana produced an immense quantity of silver. An estimated 20 percent of world production during this period came from La Valenciana. Other mines were dug into the sierras and Guanajuato became one of the wealthi-

Guanajuato

est cities in New Spain. As was the case everywhere, that
wealth was built on the suffering of the mine workers.

So by 1810, when Miguel Hidalgo's peasant army marched on
Guanajuato, the terrible exploitation of the Indians and *mestizo*s had been going on for 250 years, more than enough time to
build a revolutionary level of anger. The Spanish royalists knew
they were in trouble so they took refuge in the seemingly
impenetrable Alhóndiga de Granaditos, a massive granary.
Legend has it that a young miner called El Pipila, on a suicide
mission, managed to burn down the Alhóndiga's huge wooden
doors. Exacting vengeance for hundreds of years of misery, the
peasants slaughtered all the besieged. Later, after Spain had
crushed the first flurry of insurrection and executed the main
rebel leaders, the government hung the heads of these rebels–
Hidalgo, Allende, Aldama, and Jiménez–from the four corners
of the Alhóndiga.

When independence finally came it only amounted to the sub-
stitution of *criollos* for *peninsulares* in positions of power. This
type of independence was fine with the elite of Guanajuato since
they no longer had to send a sizable fraction of their production

to the bloated aristocracy of Spain and they could continue to extract as much labor from their miners as human tissue could bear.

By the late 19th Century, however, the richest veins had been played out and the economic base of Guanajuato weakened. When the Mexican Revolution came along in the early 20th Century and radically altered the power relationship between the working class and the financial elite, mining in Guanajuato seriously declined.

One can only be thankful that Guanajuato didn't experience a Monterrey-like burst of industrialization, a burst which would have replaced intricate baroque facades with warehouse wall panels and filled the violet-blue sky with yellow particulate clouds. Along with towns like Oaxaca, Zacatecas, and San Miguel, Guanajuato is a time capsule of an earlier era. Its twisting, hilly streets and alleyways add a pleasant physical dimensionality to a town that already has a rich historical texture. With treasures lurking around every corner and within every nuance of light and color, Guanajuato is perhaps the best town in all of Mexico to explore afoot.

Getting Around. The **train station** is one km west of the Jardín Unión on the way to the Museo de las Momias and just south of Tepetlapa. Buses labelled "Momias" run past the station. Or you can walk or take a taxi. Guanajuato has a new **bus station** located on the toll road to Silao about 6.5 km (4 mi) from the center of town. Taxi is the best way to get there but local buses marked "Central Camionera" or "Central de Autobuses" will get you there, too.

Crafts. Guanajuato is well known for its **maiolica ceramics** similar to the Talavera tile of Puebla. The traditional design consists of an opaque, white glaze overlain by a second glaze which incorporates blue and green patterns. The town is also famous for the quality and design of its gold and silver jewelry, especially its earrings.

Sights. Guanajuato follows the path of least resistance as it snakes through its valley. There is no semblance of a grid pattern here. There are no straight streets and no central

Guanajuato, Guanajuato

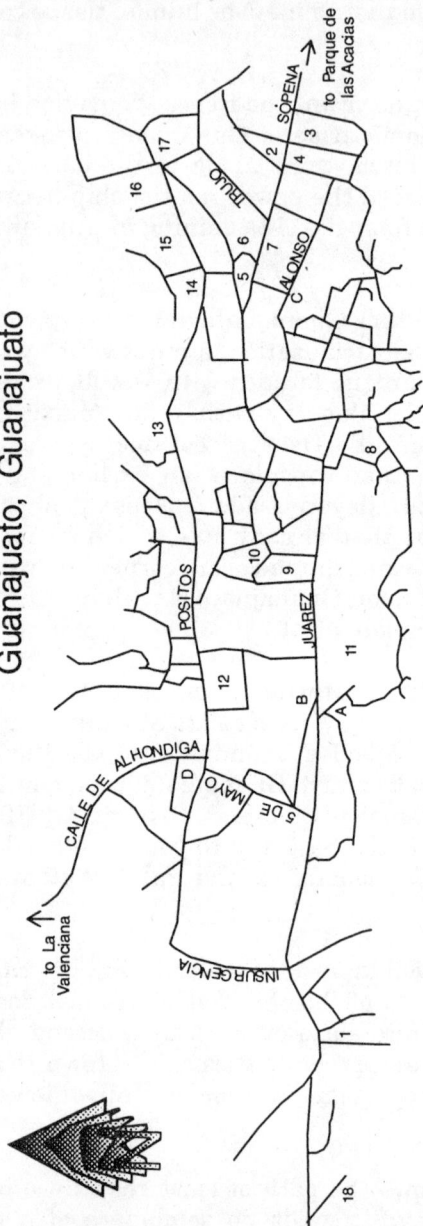

1 ~ train station
2 ~ Jardin Union
3 ~ Teatro Juarez
4 ~ Iglesia de San Diego
5 ~ Plaza de la Paz
6 ~ Basilica de Nuestra Senora de Guanajuato
7 ~ tourist office
8 ~ Callejon del Beso
9 ~ Jardin de la Reforma
10~ Plaza de San Roque
11~ Mercado Hidalgo

12~ Alhondiga
13~ Museo y Casa de Diego Rivera
14~ Museo de Pueblo de Guanajuato
15~ Universidad de Guanajuato
16~ Iglesia de la Compania
17~ post office
18~ Museo de las Momias
A ~ Posada San Francisco
B ~ Hotel Central
C ~ Casa Kloster
D ~ Hotel Alhondiga

zócalo. Instead there is a series of small parks and plazas, most of which are on or are near Guanajuato's main street, Juárez. There is also a system of streets beneath the city but, with the exception of catching certain buses, you need have little to do with them. Despite its convolutions, Guanajuato is an easy city to explore on foot.

A good place to start your exploration is the **Jardín Unión**, a small, pleasant plaza filled with trees and lined with cafes and ice cream shops. Located on the east end of downtown, the Jardín is the heart of Guanajuato and is the scene of band concerts on Tuesday, Thursday, and Sunday evenings.

Baroque facade, Church of San Diego, Guanajuato

Across Juárez from the Jardín is the 19th Century **Teatro Juárez** with its neoclassical exterior and Moorish interior. Built of local green sandstone, the theater hosts most of the performances during the Cervantino Festival. Beside the theater is the **Iglesia de San Diego**. This Franciscan church dates from the 16th Century and is one of the oldest churches in the city. Behind the church on Calle Alonzo is the **Casa de las Artesanías** which displays and sells local crafts such as ceramics, glassware, textiles, and copperware.

One block west of the Jardín along Juárez is the **Plaza de la Paz** with its Monument to Peace. On one side of the plaza is the saffron-hued **Basílica de Nuestra Señora de Guanajuato** (Church of Our Lady of Guanajuato). The church's namesake is inside on a silver pedestal: a jewel-inlaid wooden statue of the Virgin Mary. It was a gift to the town from King Philip II of Spain in 1557 in appreciation for all the wealth that had flowed into royal coffers from Guanajuato's mines. According to legend the statue dates from the 7th Century. The church also contains the mummified body of Saint Faustina.

On both sides of the Plaza de la Paz are beautifully preserved and restored colonial mansions, some of which have been converted into boutiques, shops, and restaurants. The **tourist office** is also located here on Juárez across from the basílica. Av. Juárez continues west for a couple of blocks past the plaza, then curves first left and then right. Just southwest of this last curve is the **Callejón del Beso** (Alley of the Kiss), a narrow pedestrian alleyway where opposite balconies are so close that two people could kiss by simply leaning out a little. There is, naturally, a tragic Romeo and Juliet-type legend concerning this spot. Guanajuato, like Zacatecas, is full of pedestrian *callejones* whose twisting passageways make the city fun to explore. A little farther along Juárez is the **Jardín de la Reforma** and one block northeast (right) of Juárez at this point are the **Plaza de San Roque** and the **Plaza de San Fernando**. The former plaza is the site of occasional plays put on by the university and, during the Cervantes festival, it is the location for dramatic "playlets" called *entremeses* which involve costumed actors and horses.

A long block west of the Jardín de la Reforma on the left side of Juárez is the hanger-like **Mercado Hidalgo**. One block northeast of the market at the corner of Positos and Mendizabal is the **Alhóndiga**. Originally a granary and the site of the 1810 massacre of Spanish and Mexican royalists by Hidalgo's peasant army, the Alhondiga is today a museum. The first floor contains a permanent collection of works by Mexican artists and exhibit space for temporary displays. There is also a mural by Chávez Morado depicting the region's history. Upstairs Guanajuato's history is covered by exhibits of antiques, documents, and photographs. There is also a collection of pre-Hispanic artifacts with emphasis on the local Chupicuaro culture. The museum is open Tues-Sat, 9 a.m. to 2 p.m. and 4 p.m. to 6 p.m.

Five blocks southeast along Positos is the **Museo y Casa de Diego Rivera** at Calle Juan Valle. This was the house of the great Mexican muralist and communist, Diego Rivera (1886-1957). However, he only lived here until he was seven, when his family moved to Mexico City in 1903. The first floor rooms are

filled with period furniture. Upstairs is more interesting, with
a fairly good collection of Rivera's sketches and paintings. The
museum is open Tues-Sat, 10 a.m. to 1 p.m. and 4 p.m. to 6 p.m.
and Sun, 10 a.m. to 2:30 p.m.

Another couple of blocks southeast along Positos near Estudi-
ante is the **Museo de Pueblo de Guanajuato**. This museum
contains a fine collection of both pre-Hispanic and local, contemporary pottery and ceramics. Even better are the murals and
paintings by Chávez Morado and Olga Costa. The museum is
housed in a former church and is open Tues-Sun, 10 a.m. to 2
p.m. and 4 p.m. to 7 p.m. Beside the Museo del Pueblo on Calle
Lascurain de Retana is the **Universidad de Guanajuato**. The
university dates to 1732, when it was founded by the Jesuits,
and has long been one of the premier institutions in Mexico for
fine arts. In 1945 it became a state school and most of the
construction dates from the 1950s. There is also a **Mining
Museum** within the university.

A block east of the university at Positos and Navarro is the
Iglesia de la Compañía. Built in the mid-18th Century by the
Jesuits, the church contains a collection of religious paintings
by Miguel Cabrera. Nearby is the **post office**.

The **Monumento a El Pipila** is southwest of the Jardín Unión
on a cliff overlooking the town. This nine-meter statue commemorates Juan José de los Reyes Martínez, otherwise known
as El Pipila, who sacrificed his life so that Hidalgo's insurrec-
tionary army could take the Alhóndiga. The main point to
coming here, however, is the panoramic view of the city the
monument offers. To get here, take a bus marked "Pipila" from
the Jardín Unión or walk southeast from the Jardín along Calle
Sopena and take a right on Callejón de Calvario. Just keep
climbing up.

On the southeast outskirts of town are a lake, **Presa de la Olla**,
and a park, **Parque de las Acacias**. This is a lovely area in
which to relax, picnic, or rent a rowboat. While weekends are
crowded, weekdays allow you almost unlimited choices in pick-
ing a spot for your picnic. Getting there requires about a 45-min-
ute walk southeast from the Jardín Unión along Juárez, which
turns into Sopena, which turns into Paseo de la Olla. Or you can

catch a bus marked "Presa" or "Olla" on the underground street below Iglesia de San Diego.

One of the most unusual museums in all Mexico is the **Museo de las Momias** (Museum of the Mummies). In the late 19th Century the Guanajuato cemetery, the *Panteón*, began to run out of room, so the authorities began to disinter the corpses of families which could not afford to pay to keep their departed in the ground. To the amazement and horror of some, a peculiar combination of climate and soil composition had mummified the corpses and not allowed them to decay gracefully. Some enterprising, unknown and long dead (mummified?) individual, understanding the Mexicans' fascination with death, decided to display the leathery remains to the public for a fee. Only the most "interesting" corpses were kept. The rest were cremated. At first the bodies were stacked like so much cord wood in a storage warehouse. Today, these grotesque and fascinating reminders of our own mortality have a special exhibit hall beside the *Panteón* and recline within glass cases.

It is a strange experience to file through hallways and into rooms lined with these almost skeletal but identifiably human remains. It is a stranger experience to wait in line at the entrance with the Mexican crowds, with the kids who suck on candy skulls and skeletons, with the parents holding babies and nervous with a circus-like excitement.

The museum is open daily, 9 a.m. to 6 p.m. It is about 1.5 km west of the Jardín Unión and is up a considerable hill. You can walk there by heading west on Juárez and by staying on it after the street changes to Calz. Tepetlapa. Look for signs to the "Panteón" or "Momias." Or you can catch a bus on Juárez marked "Panteón/La Rocha" or "Momias."

The **Mina de la Valenciana** and the nearby **Iglesia la Valenciana** are about 10 km north of the Jardín on the road to Dolores Hidalgo. This silver mine was Mexico's richest and produced until the Mexican Revolution shut it down. It reopened in the 1960s as a cooperative venture and is still in operation. It's about a 10-minute walk from the church.

The 18th Century Church of La Valenciana was built by the

*La Valenciana Church,
intricate retablo*

owner of the mine as a way of giving thanks to God for his unbelievable wealth. He should have thanked his miners, but instead he made them not only build the church but also contribute silver for its construction. The result of their double labor is an impressive structure with an intricate though subdued Churrigueresque facade. The interior cannot be called subdued. It is a carnival of gilded retablos and delicately carved pink stone.

There are several craft stores and vendors in the small plaza in front of the church. There are also nice views of distant Guanajuato from the vantage point of the road beside the church. To get to La Valenciana, catch a bus marked "Valenciana." The bus stop (*parada*) is one-half block north of the Alhóndiga on Calle de la Alhóndiga. There is a sign that says "La Valenciana." The trip takes about 15 minutes.

Fiestas. Without a doubt the **Festival Cervantino de Guanajuato** is the most important festival in the city and is famous throughout the Spanish-speaking world. The festival takes place in early October and is a celebration of the life and work of Cervantes. The festivities include plays, poetry, music, song, dance, parades, and anything else that seems spontaneously appropriate. The action takes place all over the city but the Teatro Juárez and the Plaza San Roque see the bulk of it.

Classes. Instituto Falcón offers Spanish language classes at all levels. Contact:

Instituto Falcón
Callejón de la Mora 158
Guanajuato, Gto. Mexico 36000

Climate. Almost all of Guanajuato's rain falls in June through September, brought by afternoon thunderstorms. Summers are warm but rarely oppressively hot. Winter days are mild and nights can be cold but freezing temperatures are uncommon.

Excursions. The towns of **San Miguel de Allende** and **Dolores Hidalgo** are both within about an hour of Guanajuato by second class bus. If history lights your fire then you should make the easy journey to **Dolores Hidalgo**, 50 km (30 mi) to the east. Here in the small parish church on September 16, 1810, Miguel Hidalgo issued the *Grito de Dolores*. As he addressed his

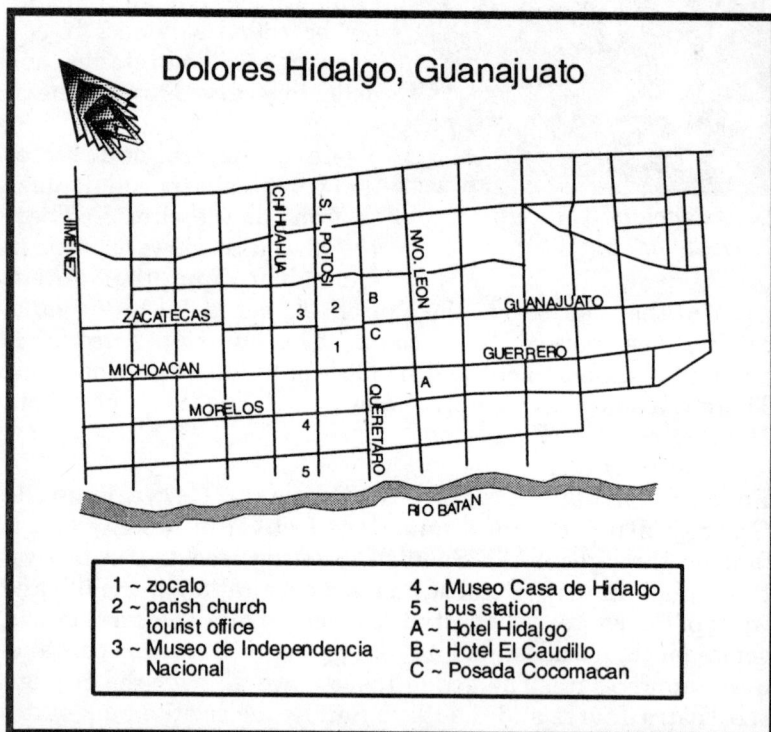

astonished Indian congregation, Hidalgo told them that they had been slaves for 300 years and that the Spanish had deprived them of their lands, history, and culture. It was, Hidalgo said, time for them to rise up against the oppressive government, to destroy it, and take back their lands and heritage. While no one knows the exact words Hidalgo used, this is the gist of it.

Miguel Hidalgo's background and religious education had prepared him for a life among the Catholic church's elite but his intellectual courage and skepticism doomed him. He questioned church dogma such as the authority of the Pope, the virgin birth of Christ, and the Inquisition and he was punished for his doubts by assignment to the Indian parish of Dolores. Hidalgo used his punishment as an opportunity to minister to the economic as well as the spiritual needs of his parishioners. In defiance of Spanish law, he introduced silk production and vineyards to the people of Dolores. He also started a pottery and ceramics industry which remains today the town's chief manufacturing occupation.

Mexico's independence struggle was led by white-skinned *criollos*, many of whom favored independence only because it would allow Mexican-born whites to assume the positions of power and wealth then held by European-born whites. Such "revolutionaries" favored a change of regimes, not policies, and for this reason commanded little respect and inspired little passion among the Indian and Mestizo peasants. Hidalgo, on the other hand, did command and did inspire. He was respected and loved by his parishioners who were willing to go to war under his leadership. Hidalgo's participation in the independence struggle transformed that struggle from discussion groups into armies, transferred it from parlor rooms to battle fields. And all this began at Dolores when Ignacio Allende recruited the iconoclastic priest, Miguel Hidalgo, into the independence fold.

Again, unless you're interested in Mexican history there's not much reason to go to Dolores Hidalgo. The **parish church** from which Hidalgo issued the *Grito* is on the northeast side of the zócalo. Although it has a nice Churrigueresque facade, there is little to suggest the incredible drama that began here almost 200 years ago. The **tourist office** is beside the church facing the plaza.

The **Museo de Independencia Nacional** is one block northwest of the tourist office on Calle Zacatecas. There is a lot of information in this smallish museum covering the origins and history of the independence struggle. It is open Tues-Sat, 9 a.m. to 2 p.m. and 4 p.m. to 7 p.m., Sun, 9 a.m. to 3 p.m.

The **Museo Casa de Hidalgo** is one block southwest of the plaza at the corner of Morelos and Hidalgo. This was, of course, Miguel Hidalgo's residence and contains his personal effects and furniture as well as exhibits about his life and the War for Independence. It is open Tues-Sat, 10 a.m. to 6 p.m., Sun, 10 a.m. to 5 p.m.

Dolores is served by second class buses of the Flecha Amarilla line from both Guanajuato and San Miguel de Allende.

Cerro de Cubilete is a 90-minute second class bus ride from Guanajuato. At the 2,878-meter summit of this mountain there is a large statue of Christ and a spectacular view of the fertile Bajio. Buses run to the overlook from the bus station.

Appendix

Reading List

Michael D. Coe, *Mexico* and *The Maya* (both Thames and Hudson). These are both excellent overviews of the pre-Hispanic cultures of Mexico with the former focusing on the Indian cultures outside the Maya area and the latter dealing with the Maya themselves.

Bernal Díaz del Castillo, *The True History of the Conquest of New Spain* (Penguin). This compelling and detailed book is an eyewitness account of Cortés' conquest of the Aztecs by one of the conquistadors.

Carl Franz, *The People's Guide to Mexico* (John Muir Publications). No reading list would be complete without this, the best travel book I have ever read. *The People's Guide* doesn't tell you where to go but how to go and how to survive.

Eduardo Galeano, *Memory of Fire* (Pantheon). Actually a trilogy, *Memory of Fire* is a brilliant and very readable history of the Americas before, during, and after the Conquest. Not specifically Mexican, it offers important insights into Mexico's origins.

Diana Kennedy, *The Cuisines of Mexico* (Harper & Row). More than a book of recipes, this classic work constitutes a valuable introduction to the culture and content of Mexican food.

Daniel Levy and **Gabriel Szekely**, *Mexico: Paradoxes of Stability and Change* (Westview Press). This readable academic book examines the evolution of Mexico's political, economic, and foreign policy.

Oscar Lewis, *The Children of Sanchez*. This sociological study offers an enlightening view of Mexican society in the mid-20th Century through interviews with an extended working class family.

Lonely Planet, *Mexico: A Travel Survival Guide* (Lonely Planet). This very comprehensive guidebook contains abundant historical and background information as well as a plethora of maps.

Henry Bamford Parkes, *A History of Mexico* (Houghton Mifflin). This very readable and complete history of the region avoids dry, scholarly prose and concentrates on human values, motivations, and personalities.

Octavio Paz, *The Labyrinth of Solitude* (Grove Press). *Labyrinth* is an abstruse but brilliant collection of essays which explores the soul of modern Mexico.

Dick J. Reavis, *Conversations with Moctezuma* (Quill). Reavis, a veteran journalist, illuminates the character of and contradictions within Mexican society through his close, human portrayals of everyday people.

John Reed, *Insurgent Mexico* (Penguin). Reporter Reed accompanied the revolutionary general and occasional bandit Pancho Villa in 1913 and 1914. The result was this book with its fascinating depictions of life with Villa's northern army during the Mexican Revolution.

Alan Riding, *Distant Neighbors* (Vintage). In this very readable book Riding searches for modern Mexico's identity within the panorama of that country's history, politics, psychology, and relationship with the United States.

Chloë Sayer, *Arts and Crafts of Mexico* (Chronicle Books). There is no more comprehensive book in English on this subject. It is full of wonderful color photographs.

Linda Schele and **David Freidel,** *A Forest of Kings* (Quill). Based on interpretation of Maya hieroglyphs, the authors have constructed a detailed history of the Maya kingdoms spanning 1,500 years.

R.J. Secor, *Mexico's Volcanoes: A Climbing Guide* (The Mountaineers). This book contains comprehensive climbing information on seven Mexican volcanoes and includes route details, maps, and a bilingual mountaineering glossary.

John L. Stephens, *Incidents of Travel in Central America, Chiapas, and the Yucatán* (Dover). This North American's explorations in the early 19th Century brought the lands and ruined cities of the Maya to the attention of the world.

Frances Toor, *A Treasury of Mexican Folkways* (Bonanza Books). This classic book from the late 1940s is an encyclopedic compilation of modern Mexican customs, folklore, fiestas, and more.

Jack Weatherford, *Indian Givers* (Fawcett Columbine). This long overdue book chronicles the contributions of Native Americans to modern world civilization.

The best of the Mexican fiction writers which have been translated into English are **Carlos Fuentes** (*The Death of Artemio Cruz* and *Where the Air Is Clear*) and **Juan Rulfo** (*Pedro Paramo* and *The Burning Plain and Other Stories*). As with most national fiction, these works offer important insights into different aspects of Mexican regional culture and life.

Hotels and Accommodations

The accommodations listed here are intended as a starting point for the traveler, not as an exhaustive or comprehensive data base. I would encourage you to explore the hotel options available at your destinations and to select an accommodation that more precisely meets your budget, amenity, and logistical needs.

I have employed the same ranking system used by the Mexican Ministry of Tourism to indicate the cost category of each establishment. Following the name of each hotel is a number in parentheses. The system ranks accommodations from 1 (cheapest) to 5 (most expensive). I have tried to include mostly Category 1 and 2 hotels with a small number of 3s. In some places, such as some of the Copper Canyon Train towns, there are no budget hotels at all, so I have listed Category 4 accommodations.

These numeric rankings are relative and make sense only when establishments within the same town are compared. A Category 2 hotel in Cancún will be more expensive than a similarly ranked hotel in Querétaro because the cost of living is higher in the former.

The price of accommodations in resort areas varies by season. During the tourist season, which corresponds to the North American winter, prices can be anywhere from 30 to 100 percent higher than during the off-season.

Aguascalientes
Hotel Maser (2), Juan de Montoro #303, 5-35-62
H. San José (2), Hidalgo #207, 5-51-30

H. Rosales (1), Victoria #104, 5-21-65
H. Señorial (1), Juan de Montoro and Colón, 5-16-30
H. Río Grande (3), José María Chávez #101, 6-16-66
Alamos
H. Los Portales (3), Juárez #60, 8-02-01
Doliza Motel (2), Madero #72, 8-01-31
Bahuichivo (hotel is in town of Cerocahui, 10 km to the south)
H. Misión (4), for reservations contact: Hotel Santa Anita,
Box 159, Los Mochis, Sin. 81200, tel. 681/2-00-46
Campeche
H. México (1), Calle 10 #329, 6-27-13
H. López (2), Calle 12 #189, 6-33-44
H. América (2), Calle 10 #252, 6-45-88
H. Colonial (2), Calle 14 #122, 6-22-22
Cancún (these are on shore, not on the expensive Isla Cancún)
H. Parador (2), Av. Tulum #26, 4-19-22
Novotel en Cancún (2), Av. Tulum #12, 4-29-99
H. Rivemar (2), Av. Tulum #49, 4-17-08
Celestún
H. San Julio (1), Calle 12 #92, 1-85-89
Chichén Itzá (these are located in the nearby town of Pisté)
Pirámide Inn (3), Pisté, 5
Posada El Paso (1), Pisté, N/A
Posada Novela (1), Pisté, N/A
Chihuahua
H. San Juan (2), Victoria #823, 12-84-91
Nvo. Hotel Turista (1), Juárez #817, 12-08-12
H. Balflo (3), Niños Héroes and Calle 5 #702, 16-03-00
Ciudad Guzmán
Flamingos (2), Federico del Toro #133, 2-01-03
Zapotlán (1), Federico del Toro #65, 2-00-40
Ciudad Juárez
H. Plaza (1), Ugarte #239, 2-68-61
H. Impala (2), Lerdo #670 Norte, 15-04-31
H. Juárez (1), Lerdo #143 Norte, 2-99-85
Colima
H. Ceballos (2), Portal Medellín #12, 2-13-54
H. San Cristóbal (1), Reforma #98, 2-05-15
H. Impala (1), Moctezuma #93 (at Independencia), 2-15-12
Córdoba
H. Virreynal (3), Av. 1 and Calle 5, 2-23-77
H. Iberia (2), Av. 2 #919, 2-13-01

H. Manzur (3), Av. 1 #301, 2-66-00
Cozumel
H. Mary-Carmen (3), 5a Av. Sur #4, 2-05-81
H. El Marqués (3), 5a Av. Sur #8, 2-05-37
Posada Edem (2), Calle 2 Norte #12, 2-11-66
Creel
Casa de Huéspedes Margarita (1), López Mateos #11, 6-00-45
Parador de la Montaña (3), López Mateos #41, 6-00-75
H. Nuevo Barrancas (2), Francisco Villa #121, 6-00-22
Cuernavaca
H. Iberia (2), Rayón #9, 12-60-40
H. Palacio (2), Morrow #204, 12-05-53
H. Colonial (1), Aragon y León #104, 12-00-99
Cusarare
Cabañas Cañon del Cobre (3), N/A, 15-82-14
Divisadero
Cabañas Divisadero-Barrancas (4), reservations: Cabañas, Calle Aldama 407-C, Box 661, Chihuahua, Chih. 31300, tel.14/2-33-62
Dolores Hidalgo
H. Hidalgo (1), Veracruz #5, 2-08-52
H. El Caudillo (1), Querétaro #8, 2-01-98
Posada Cocomacán (2), Plaza Principal #4, 2-00-18
Fortín de las Flores
Posada la Marina (1), Av. 1 and Calle 3, N/A
H. Fortín de las Flores (3), Av. 2 betw. Calles 5 & 7, 3-00-55
Guadalajara
H. Maya (1), López Cotillo #38, 14-54-54
H. Hamilton (2), Madero #381, 40-67-26
H. Las Américas (2), Hidalgo #61, 14-16-04
H. Universo (3), López Cotillo #161, 13-28-15
Gran Hotel Canada (2), R. Michel #218, 19-20-92
Guanajuato
Posada San Francisco (2), Av. Juárez and Calle Gavira, 2-24-67
H. Central (2), Juárez #111, 2-00-80
Casa Kloster (1), Alonso #32, 2-00-88
H. Alhóndiga (1), Insurgencia #49, 2-05-25
Guaymas
H. Impala (3), Calle 21 #40, 2-13-35
H. Rubi (3), Av. Serdán and Calle 29, 2-01-69
Hermosillo
H. Kino (3), Pino Suárez #151, 2-45-99

H. Monte Carlo (2), Av. Juárez and Sonora, 2-08-53
Isla Mujeres
Poc-Na Youth Hostel (1), Calle Matamores, 2-00-90
H. Rocamar (3), Av. Nicolás Bravo and Guerrero, 2-01-01
H. Isleño (1), Calle Madero, 0-08-03
H. Caribe Maya (2), Madero #9, 2-01-90
La Paz
Pensión California (1), Calle Degollado #209, 2-28-96
H. La Perla (3), Alvaro Obregón #570, 2-07-77
H. Purísima (2), 16 de Septiembre #408, 2-34-44
Posada San Miguel (1), Belisario Domínguez #15140, 2-18-02
Lázaro Cárdenas
H. Costa de Marfil (1), Lerdo de Tejada #650, N/A
H. Plaza (3), Av. Morelos and Nicolás Bravo, 2-03-18
Los Mochis
H. Lorena (2), Obregón #786, 2-09-58
H. América (2), Allende #655 Sur, 2-13-55
Manzanillo
H. Colonial (3), Av. México #100, 2-10-80
H. Emperador (1), Davalos #291, 2-23-74
H. Los Flamingos (1), Madero #72, 2-10-37
Matamoros
H. Majestic (1), Abasolo #89, 3-36-80
H. Roma (3), Av. Nueve Bravo and Matamoros, 6-05-37
Mazatlán
H. Siesta (3), Olas Altas #2 Sur, 1-26-40
H. Milan (1), Canizales #10, 1-35-88
H. San Jorge (1), Serdán #2710, 1-36-95
Mérida
H. Trinidad (1), Calle 62 betw. C. 55 & 57, 1-30-29
H. María Teresa (1), Calle 64 #520, 1-10-39
H. Caribe (3), Calle 59 #500, 1-92-32
Mexicali
H. Azteca de Oro (2), Calle de la Industria #600, 57-14-33
H. Fortín de las Flores (1), Cristóbal Colón #612, 52-45-22
H. Las Fuentes (1), López Mateos #1655, 57-15-25
Mexico City
H. Conde (2), Pescaditos #15, 585-23-88
H. La Avenida (1), Lázaro Cárdenas #38, 518-10-07
H. Hidalgo (2), Santa Veracruz #37, 521-87-71
Posada de Don Enrique (2), Dinamarca #42, 566-84-03
H. Carlton (2), Ignacio Mariscal #32, 566-29-11

H. Regente (2), Paris #9, 566-89-33
H. New York (4), Edison #45, 566-97-00
Monterrey
H. Los Reyes (2), Hidalgo #543 Poniente, 43-61-68
H. Colonial (3), Hidalgo #475 Oriente, 43-67-91
H. Nuevo León (2), Amado Nervo #1007 Norte, 74-19-00
H. Patricia (1), Madero #123 Oriente, 75-07-50
H. Yamallel (3), Zaragoza #90 Norte, 75-35-00
H. Posada (3), Amado Nervo #1138 Norte, 72-39-08
Morelia
H. Mintzicuri (2), Vasco de Quiroga #227, 2-06-64
H. Concordia (2), Gómez Farías #328, 2-30-52
Posada Don Vasco (2), Vasco de Quiroga #232, 2-14-84
H. Casino (3), Portal Hidalgo #229, 3-10-03
Navojoa
H. Aduana (1), Av. Allende and Pesqueira, 2-00-69
H. Colonial (3), Pesqueira Sur, 2-19-19
Nogales
H. Granada (3), López Mateos and González, 2-29-11
H. Olivia (3), Obregón #125, 2-22-00
Nuevo Laredo
H. Calderón (1), Juárez #313, 2-00-04
H. Don Antonio (2), González #2435, 2-11-40
Oaxaca
H. Reforma (1), Reforma #102, 6-71-44
Mesón del Rey (2), Trujano #212, 6-00-33
H. Principal (2), 5 de Mayo #208, 6-25-35
H. Colón (1), Colón #120, 6-47-26
Orizaba
H. Arenas (1), Norte 2 #169, 5-23-61
H. San Cristóbal (1), Norte 4 #243, 5-11-40
Palenque (these accommodations are located in the town)
H. Lacroix (1), Hidalgo #18, 5-00-14
H. Vaca Vieja (2), 5 de Mayo #42, 5-03-77
H. Misol-Ha (2), Juárez #14, 5-00-92
Pátzcuaro
Posada la Basílica (3), Arciga #6, 2-11-08
H. Los Escudos (3), Portal Hidalgo #73, 2-12-90
H. Concordia (1), Portal Juárez #31, 2-00-03
H. Valmen (1), Lloreda #34, 2-11-61
Playa Azul
H. Delfín (2), V. Carranza, 6-00-07

H. María Isabel (2), Av. Madero, 6-00-30
Playa del Carmen
H. Delfín (2), Av. 5 and Calle 6, N/A
Posada Lili (1), Av. Principal, N/A
Posada Barrancas
Mansión Tarahumara (4), resv: Mansión Tarahumara, Box
1416, Revolución 100, Chihuahua, Chih, 31310, tel. 14/12-79-43
H. Posada Barrancas (4), resv: Hotel Santa Anita, Box 159, Los
Mochis, Sin. 81200, tel. 681/2-00-46
Progresso
H. Miramar (1), Calle 77 #124, 5-05-62
H. Playa Linda (1), Calle 69, N/A
Puebla
Hostal de Halconeros (1), Reforma #141, 42-74-56
H. Teresita (1), Av. 3 Poniente #309, 41-70-72
H. Colonial (3), Calle 4 Sur #105, 46-41-99
Querétaro
H. Hidalgo (2), Hidalgo #14, 2-00-81
H. Plaza (2), Juárez #23, 2-11-38
H. Mirabel (4), Constituyentes Orientes #2, 4-35-85
H. Impala (3), Corregidora Sur #188, 2-25-70
Reynosa
H. Nuevo León (1), Díaz #540 Norte, 2-13-10
H. Rey (2), Díaz #556 Norte, 2-29-80
Río Verde
H. Plaza (2), Plaza Constitución, 2-01-00
H. Santander (1), 5 de Mayo #16, 2-09-00
Saltillo
H. Saade (2), Aldama Poniente #397, 3-34-00
H. de Avila (1), Padre Flores #211, 3-72-72
Plaza Urdiñola (2), Victoria #207, 4-09-40
San Blas
Posada Casa Morales (2), Cuauhtémoc #197, 5-00-23
H. Flamingos (2), Juárez Poniente #105, N/A
H. Las Brisas (4), Cuauhtémoc #106, 5-01-12
San Luis Potosí
H. Anáhuac (1), Xochitl #140, 2-65-04
H. Progreso (2), Aldama #415, 2-03-66
H. de Gante (2), 5 de Mayo #140, 2-14-92
San Miguel de Allende
H. Parador de San Sebastian (1), Mesones #7, 2-07-07
H. Quinta Loreto (2), Calle de Loreto #15, 2-00-42

H. Central (2), Canal #19, 2-08-51
Tapachula
Hospedaje Colonial (1), Av. 4 Norte #31, 6-20-52
H. Fénix (2), Av. 4 Norte #19, 5-07-55
Teapa
H. Jardín (1), Plaza Independencia #123, N/A
Tehuacán
H. Iberia (2), Av. Independencia #217, 2-11-22
H. Monroy (2), Reforma Norte #217, 2-04-91
H. México (4), Reforma and Independencia, 2-00-19
Tepic
H. Sierra de Alicia (3), Av. México #180, 2-03-22
H. Imperial (1), Av. México #208, 2-01-09
Tula de Allende
H. Lisbeth (1), Ocampo #42, 2-00-45
Uruapan
H. Mirador (1), Ocampo #9, 2-04-73
Nuevo Hotel Alameda (3), 5 de Febrero #11, 3-41-00
H. Villa de Flores (2), Emilio Carranza #15, 2-16-50
Valladolid
H. Zaci (2), Calle 44 #191, 6-21-67
H. Moria de la Luz (3), on the main plaza, 6-20-70
H. Don Luis (2), Calle 39 #191, 6-20-24
Valle de Bravo
H. Los Arcos (3), Bocanegra #310, 2-00-42
H. Mary (2), on the main plaza, N/A
Veracruz
H. Imperial (2), Lerdo #153, 2-01-73
H. Santillana (2), Landero y Coss #209, 32-31-16
Gran Hotel Diligencias (3), Independencia #1129, 31-31-57
H. Rias (1), Morelos #359, 32-42-46
Villahermosa
H. San Miguel (1), Lerdo #315, 2-15-00
H. San Francisco (2), Madero #508, 2-31-98
H. Madan (3), Av. Pino Suárez #105, 2-16-50
Zacatecas
H. Río Grande (1), Calzada de la Paz #313, 2-53-49
H. Colón (2), López Velarde #502, 2-04-64
H. Condesa (2), Juárez #5, 2-11-60

Index